THEN THEY CAME FOR ME

"A superb account ... Insightful and brave."
Jane Corbin, journalist and reporter for *Panorama*

"*Then They Came for Me* is the story of those who fight to inform and enlighten their society. Fortunately, Iran is not only a country of Ahmadinejads and mullahs, the country is also blessed with plenty of Maziar Baharis."
Shirin Ebadi, Nobel Peace Prize Laureate and author of *Iran Awakening*

"A riveting, brutally honest account, *Then They Came for Me* is one of the most powerful prison memoirs I have ever read. This haunting and unforgettable book will make you angry at the prison that is today's Iran, and happy that a fine journalist like Maziar Bahari escaped to tell the truth about the regime."
David Ignatius, author of *Body of Lies*

"A fascinating walk through Iran's tumultuous recent history. Students of the region will welcome Mr Bahari's insightful contribution."
Joseph Wilson, former US Ambassador and author of *The Politics of Truth*

D1136195

ABOUT THE AUTHORS

Maziar Bahari is an award-winning journalist, documentary filmmaker, and human-rights activist. A correspondent for *Newsweek* from 1998 to 2010, he was born in Tehran, Iran, and immigrated to Canada in 1988 to pursue his studies in film and political science. Bahari's documentaries have been broadcast on stations around the world, including BBC 1, HBO, and the Discovery Channel. In 2009, he was named a finalist for Spain's Prince of Asturias Award for Concord, often described as Spain's Nobel Peace Prize; he was nominated by Desmond Tutu. He lives in London with his wife and daughter.

Aimee Molloy is the co-author of three previous books: *Jantsen's Gift* with Pam Cope; *This Moment on Earth* with Senator John Kerry and Teresa Heinz Kerry; and *For God and Country* with James Yee. She also served as an editor of Laurie Strongin's *Saving Henry*. She lives in Brooklyn, New York with her husband.

THEN THEY CAME FOR ME

A Story of Injustice and Survival in
Iran's Most Notorious Prison

Maziar Bahari

with Aimee Molloy

ONEWORLD

A Oneworld Book

First published in the United Kingdom and C   by Oneworld

T   ns 2013

Orig   dom House,
an imp   n of Random

The mo   r of this work
has b   Designs and

                                                     Library

ISBN 978-1-85168-954-5
Ebook ISBN 978-1-78074-083-6

Designed by Abby Kagan

Printed and bound by CPI Group (UK) Ltd, Croydon, CR0 4YY

Oneworld Publications
10 Bloomsbury Street, London, WC1B 3SR

To Moloojoon, Baba Akbar, Maryam,

Paola, and Marianna

They smell your breath

lest you have said: I love you,

They smell your heart:

   These are strange times, my dear....

They chop smiles off lips,

and songs off the mouth....

   These are strange times, my dear.

—AHMAD SHAMLU, 1979

CONTENTS

PROLOGUE

I could smell him before I saw him. His scent was a mixture of sweat and rosewater, and it reminded me of my youth.

When I was six years old, I would often accompany my aunts to a shrine in the holy city of Qom. It was customary to remove your shoes before entering the shrine, and the caretakers of the shrine would sprinkle rosewater everywhere, to mask the odor of perspiration and leather.

That morning in June 2009, when they came for me, I was in the delicate space between sleep and wakefulness, taking in his scent. I didn't realize that I was a man of forty-two in my bedroom in Tehran; I thought, instead, that I was six years old again, and back in that shrine with my aunts.

"Mazi *jaan,* wake up," my mother said. "There are four gentlemen here. They say they are from the prosecutor's office. They want to take you away." I opened my eyes. It was a few minutes before eight, and my mother was standing beside my bed—her small eighty-three-year-old frame protecting me from the four men behind her.

I sleep without clothes, and in my half-awake state, my first thought wasn't that I was in danger, but that I was naked in a shrine. I felt ashamed and reached down to make sure the sheets were covering my body.

Mr. Rosewater was standing directly behind my mother. I

would later come to learn a lot about him.

He was thirty-one years old and had earned a master's degree in political science from Tehran University. While at university, he had joined the Revolutionary Guards, a vast and increasingly powerful fundamentalist military conglomerate formed in the wake of the 1979 Iranian revolution. I would come to know that his punches were the hardest when he felt stupid. But when he appeared in my bedroom early that morning, the only things I understood about him were that he was in charge, and that he had a very large head. It was alarmingly big, like the rest of his body. He was at least six foot two and fat, with thick glasses. Later, his glasses would confuse me. I had associated glasses with academics, intellectuals. Not torturers.

I wrapped the sheet tightly around my body and sat up. "Put some clothes on," Rosewater said, motioning to the three men behind him to leave the room so that I could get dressed. I found comfort in this: whatever their reason was for barging into my house, he was still respectful, still behaving with a modicum of courtesy.

They kept the door slightly ajar, and I walked to my closet. Things were beginning to come into clearer focus, but his rosewater scent lingered and my thoughts, still confused, remained back in the past, at the shrine. What does one wear in a shrine? What's the best way to present oneself? I had just finished putting on a blue collared shirt and a pair of jeans when the men pushed their way back into my room: Rosewater and another man, who wore a shiny silver sports jacket and a cap.

They circled the room, surveying everything. I had been spending most of my time over the last two years with my fiancée, Paola, in London. We had got engaged six months earlier, and had been preparing for the birth of our child in four months' time, and I had never really settled in at my mother's house. I could sense their frustration as they took stock of the mess in my small room. Heaps of books sat on the floor beside stacks of videotapes and DVDs and an untidy pile of laundry. I had not organized my desk for months, and it was covered with old newspapers and notebooks. All journalists working in Iran have to be accredited by Ershad—the name is shorthand for the Ministry of Culture and Islamic Guidance—and I had given my mother's address as my place of work. They'd thought they were going to find an office at my mother's house. Instead, they were picking through piles of underwear.

"If you want, I can organize things and you can come back tomorrow," I said with an apologetic smile.

"Zerto pert nakon," Rosewater said sharply. "Stop talking shit. Sit down and shut up. One more word, and I'll beat you so badly, I'll make your mother mourn for you." He scratched his side under his jacket, revealing the gun strapped to his body. I sat down, feeling my body grow heavy with fear. I, like most Iranians, knew of far too many people—writers, artists, activists—who had been woken up like this, then taken somewhere and murdered. I thought of my father and my sister, each arrested and imprisoned by previous regimes; I thought of my mother, who had been forced to live through all this twice before. I could hear my mother's voice in the kitchen, and my fear was joined by an overwhelming sense of guilt. How could my mother go through this again? Why hadn't I been more careful? Why hadn't I left Iran sooner?

"Would you like some tea?" I heard her ask one of the men in the kitchen.

"No, thank you."

"Why not? It seems that you are going to be here for a while. You should have some tea," she said.

"No, really. I don't want to impose."

I heard my mother laugh. "You arrived at my house at eight A.M. You are going through my son's personal belongings. I am going to have to put everything back in order after you leave.

What do you mean you do not want to impose?"

The man ignored the question. "Madam, please put on your scarf," he said.

Though I could not see my mother's face, I could imagine the condescending look she was giving him at that moment.

My mother's unveiled hair was illegal under Islamic law. I knew that her halfhearted obeying of the Revolutionary Guards' order was her attempt at defiance. She was telling them that while they might be able to control her body, they could never control her mind. The Guards rightly thought of my mother and me as parts of the "other Iran," those citizens who did not want to be the subjects of an Islamic ruler and would have preferred to determine our own destinies.

"I am eighty-three years old. Why should I put on my scarf?"

My mother's name is Molook. Growing up, we called her Molook *joon,* which in Persian means "dear Molook." Because my older brother, Babak, couldn't pronounce the *k,* he called her Moloojoon. The name stuck, and it was this name I used as I called out to her, doing my best to keep my voice from trembling: "Please, Moloojoon. Don't argue with them."

I heard her quick steps, and a few moments later she walked past my room, a blue floral scarf covering just half of her hair.

"Fine," I heard her say with polite disdain.

My room had a large bookshelf full of Western novels and music, with volumes signed by prominent Iranian reformists on one side and HBO DVD box sets and copies of *The Economist, The New Yorker,* and *Newsweek* stacked sloppily on the other. It was surely foreign territory to Rosewater. He continued to thumb through my papers and books, despite the look of obvious bewilderment on his face.

I sat on the bed watching him until, a while later, he told me I could go to the kitchen and eat breakfast while they continued to search my room. In the kitchen, my mother poured me a cup of tea and placed a few dates on a small china saucer. She then took a seat across from me at the breakfast table and silently pushed the dates toward me. "*Bokhor*," she said with a smile— "Have some"—hoping, I knew, to assure me that I would find the strength to survive this ordeal, whatever was to come.

I was humbled by her courage, though it didn't surprise me. My mother's strength has been a source of inspiration throughout my life. But I felt guilty as I thought about how painful it would be for her to watch yet another member of her family being carted off to prison for defying an Iranian regime.

*   *   *

It had been December 1954 when they came for my father. At the time, Iran was ruled by the shah, Mohammad Reza Pahlavi, a pro-Western autocrat. Of course, my mother didn't like to speak of the experience—of what it was like for her on that cold winter night when the shah's secret police and soldiers of the Royal Iranian Army raided their house. She was twenty-nine and my father twenty-seven, and they had been married for just two years. They lived in my mother's family home in the Sangalaj neighborhood of south Tehran with their first child, my older brother, Babak, who was then only ten months old, and two of my aunts. I was told that while my father's future interrogator, a thuggish man named Rezvani, insulted my father in front of his wife, child, and sisters-in-law, the soldiers ransacked the house, taking whatever they wanted for themselves. "They even went through your father's clothes," my mother remembered with her unfaltering sense of humor. "I caught one of them stealing some of his underwear."

For many years, my father had been a member of the Tudeh Party, the communist party of Iran. The party had been banned a few years earlier, after one of its members had been accused of an assassination attempt against the shah. But my father had continued his party work, organizing strikes and demonstrations against the government on behalf of the Union of Metal

Workers of Iran, and finding hideouts for persecuted party leaders. After being held for many months, during which he endured solitary confinement and torture, he was charged with belonging to a treasonous organization and sentenced to fifteen years in prison.

Each week of my father's incarceration, my mother carried my brother, Babak, to one of two prisons, Ghezel Qal'eh or Qasr, and waited outside for hours to find out if she would be allowed inside to visit her husband. Very often, she and the family members of other political prisoners were turned away. Meanwhile, as she raised Babak on her own and worked as a primary school teacher, she fought tirelessly for his release, using every connection she could. Eventually, it worked. My father's sentence was reduced from fifteen years to two. The man who came home to her was even stronger than the one who had left.

Although my father had been tortured so badly by the prison guards that he had lost all of his teeth and his toenails were deformed, the many months he spent in solitary confinement had made him only more resilient and determined. The shah's torturers crushed the Tudeh Party, but not my father. After his release, he was just as large a figure to his friends and relatives as he'd been before. As far as I could tell, he enjoyed this role. He was an impressive man, with large, beautiful eyes and full lips. He had dropped out of school, but he knew hundreds of classic Persian poems by heart and spoke like a university-educated orator. He had tried to shape himself after the heroes of Soviet socialist realist novels: enigmatic proletarian revolutionaries who could have been successful in any profession, but instead chose to dedicate their lives to the ideals of the communist revolution. Helping the helpless and fighting for a better future for Iran had become part of my father's identity.

As my father matured, he realized that revolutions and violence couldn't heal Iran's historical maladies. Despite the torture he had suffered at the hands of the regime, after he was released from prison, in February 1957, he joined the government of the shah and tried to change the system from within. Through a combination of hard work, charm, and intelligence, he became a high-ranking manager in the Ministry of Industries and Mines and, eventually, the CEO of the government's biggest construction company. As the CEO, my father made the welfare of the workers and their families his top priority. He helped them with housing, health insurance, and pensions. He proudly said that as a CEO, he was achieving what he'd never accomplished as a union activist.

Despite his hatred of the shah's dictatorship, my father, and many other young Iranians of his generation, supported the monarch's efforts to modernize the country. During the two decades that my father worked for the government, new industries were developed, many Iranian students were educated in the West, and Iranian arts and culture were heavily influenced by Europe and America. The shah's Western allies, especially the United States, backed this rush to modernity, as well as the tyrannical rule that came with it. In many ways, the shah was the perfect partner for the West. He supplied Western nations with cheap crude oil and bought their most expensive high-tech military equipment for his ever-expanding army. The shah also allowed the United States to spy on Iran's northern neighbor, the Soviet Union.

Many traditional and religious Iranians were alienated by this process of rash modernization. Even as a child, I could see that many of my relatives who lived in the poorer, more religious parts of the country held a grudge against my family because of my father's position in the shah's regime. They hated the fact that we lived in a big house and had a color television (a big deal in 1970s Iran), and they disapproved of our choices: my sister and mother refused to pray or wear the veil, and my father and his friends went through a few bottles of imported

Scotch during their weekly poker games.

Even though the shah's intelligence agents suppressed his critics, the gap between the religious masses and the shah's pro-Western dictatorship gradually widened, and eventually this triggered an anti-Western, fundamentalist movement led by a high-ranking Shia cleric, Ayatollah Ruhollah Khomeini. Between 1965 and 1978, Khomeini lived in exile in neighboring Iraq, and from there, he communicated with his followers through photocopied leaflets and audiocassettes, manipulating people's grievances against the shah and his relationship with the United States—claiming, in particular, that the shah and the States were working together to eradicate people's religious beliefs. Khomeini promised to bring justice, independence, and prosperity to Iran. As more Iranians supported Khomeini, the shah became more desperate and insecure. In January 1978, the shah's army opened fire on a gathering of Khomeini adherents, which succeeded only in bringing about greater public support for the Islamic movement. After a year of demonstrations and violent protests, the shah was overthrown, and on February 11, 1979, the Islamic Republic of Iran was established. Khomeini returned to Iran and was named the supreme leader—the spiritual leader of the country and the man with the final say in all affairs of the state.

It was not only religious Iranians who had supported Khomeini. Many secular Iranians who believed in the separation of mosque and state had also been in favor of Khomeini's revolution. They simply had had enough of the shah's despotism and kowtowing to the West, and they craved the democratic government and freedom of expression Khomeini promised. Even my father, who had come to hate the idea of a violent revolution and believed that the shah's regime could be reformed from within, was happy about the shah's downfall and the abolishment of American military and intelligence bases in Iran. "I'm not sure what will happen next," my father used to say with tears in his eyes. "But I can never forgive the shah and his American patrons for killing dozens of my friends."

My father and many other Iranians who'd supported Khomeini's revolution without knowing what would happen next paid a heavy price. Within a short time after coming to power, Khomeini set out to establish a fundamentalist government more repressive than the shah's. The Islamic government began its systemic repression by summarily trying and executing many leaders of the shah's army on the rooftop of Khomeini's residence. Some days, while the revolutionaries were inside, having lunch or dinner with Khomeini, dozens of the shah's security and military personnel would be murdered on the roof. Deciding that a new military organization was necessary to defend the newly established Islamic government against its enemies, Khomeini established the Revolutionary Guards. With their help, he began to crush opposition groups one by one—members of the shah's former regime, ethnic minorities, and political dissidents. Many of the very people who'd helped bring Khomeini to power perished during his purges.

The revolution's violent aftermath disrupted many lives and deeply affected my family; it utterly destroyed others. My father was immediately fired from his job and replaced by a young revolutionary with very little experience. Unable to find a job for years, he eventually had to retire and live on a small pension. That humiliation and shock affected my father far more than the torture he had had to endure in prison. He became a bitter and broken man, exasperated and easily agitated. He started to hate Khomeini and everything he stood for.

*   *   *

The second member of my family to be imprisoned was my sister, Maryam. In April 1983, when Maryam was twenty-six and

I sixteen, my parents received a phone call saying that Maryam had been arrested in the southern city of Ahvaz. Maryam had supported the Islamic Revolution from the beginning. She'd believed in Khomeini's promise that the end of the shah's reign would usher in an era of greater democratic values and freedoms. Maryam would quickly discover how wrong she had been.

It never surprised me that Maryam so vigorously supported the revolution. Like our father, she put everything she had into her beliefs. She was passionate about people, and wanted to help them. She was also very passionate about the arts. She took ballet lessons and loved to draw and paint. Maryam and I were two different people: she was compassionate and expressive, whereas I have always been reserved. Still, she was my best friend.

Even though Maryam was ten years older than I, we had an uncanny understanding of each other. We were so close that we could communicate with just a look, a sigh, or by a certain movement of our hands. Her taste in music, films, and books influenced me greatly, and our shared love for the arts brought us closer together. Maryam loved Al Pacino, and I have seen every film of his, beginning with *Dog Day Afternoon,* which I saw when I was eight. She loved Stravinsky's music and ballets, and throughout my life, I have tried to see every performance of *The Firebird* and *The Rite of Spring* I could get to.

In 1979, at the age of twenty-three, Maryam followed in my father's footsteps and became a member of the Tudeh Party, which, despite the regime change and Khomeini's promise of tolerance, was still illegal. Two years later, she fell in love with Mohammad Sanadzadeh, an engineer who had recently graduated from Tehran University. They married in 1981 and moved to the city of Ahvaz, in the southern province of Khuzestan, where Mohammad had grown up. Soon after, their son, Khaled, was born. A year earlier, the Iran-Iraq War had begun, after

Saddam Hussein's army attacked Khuzestan. Iraq's border dispute with Iran had started in the shah's time, but in 1975, the shah had forced the Iraqi government to accept an accord, which had brought the dispute to an end. After the revolution, with the Iranian army having, in effect, been destroyed by the Islamic government, Saddam Hussein decided that he could use this opportunity to occupy parts of Iran and settle the border disputes. But within a short time, ordinary Iranians, the remaining members of the army, and the Revolutionary Guards repelled the Iraqi army; they took back most of the Iranian territory by early 1982.

When Maryam and Mohammad moved to Ahvaz, many cities in the region had been ravaged by Saddam's army. Many lives had been ruined, and thousands of people had lost their homes. Maryam and Mohammad had chosen Ahvaz so they could help the refugees of the war. They also worked hard—she as a teacher and he as an engineer—in order to provide for their son, Khaled. Maryam decided to teach in one of the poorest areas in southern Iran, the city of Shadgan; it took her three hours every day to travel there and back by bus. Maryam never complained about the wretched conditions in which she had to live and work. She was proud of what she did, and thought it was her duty to help the people.

In Ahvaz, Maryam and Mohammad both joined the local Tudeh Party cells. They were low-ranking members, responsible only for attending meetings, distributing literature, and helping the refugees. At the time, the Tudeh Party still supported Khomeini, and some of its members even helped the Revolutionary Guards suppress other political groups that were against Khomeini, in the hope of preventing the return of a pro-Western government.

But in early 1983, Khomeini began to arrest and jail Tudeh Party members. Soon the tortured party leaders, some of whom had spent more than twenty years in the shah's prisons and all of whom had supported the revolution, were paraded on state television, confessing to spying for the Soviet Union and acting against the Islamic government.

Mohammad was picked up by the Revolutionary Guards in the spring of 1983, in the second wave of arrests. A week later, they came for Maryam. She was sentenced to fifteen years in prison (which was eventually reduced to six), in a sham trial before a judge and no jury. She wasn't allowed a lawyer, and when she tried to object to the charges against her, the judge refused to let her speak. Though a six-year sentence was wholly unjust, at the time, my family and I were relieved that her life had been spared. The leaders of the Islamic regime were executing many political prisoners, and my parents knew many people whose children had been killed, including one young man who'd been put to death simply for writing to a friend that he feared the regime was on its way to becoming a fascist government.

With both of his parents incarcerated, Khaled came to live with my mother, my father, and me in Tehran. He was a cute, curly-haired toddler with a lot of energy and big, curious eyes. I was sixteen at the time. Part of me was excited—I had suddenly gained a younger brother. But on the first day he was with us, as my mother led Khaled by the hand through our house, it broke my heart to see how, from one room to the next, Khaled looked in each closet and under every bed for his mummy and daddy. He was not yet two years old.

My mother took Khaled into our home with her usual silent courage. For the next six years, while Maryam served her sentence for the crime of *moharebeh,* acting against Allah, my mother raised Khaled. And just as she had done three decades earlier with her husband, every month she would board a bus with Khaled and travel seventeen hours to visit Maryam in Ahvaz.

Maryam was released in 1989, once the Islamic government had killed most Tudeh leaders and was satisfied that the party no longer posed a threat. What Maryam told us about the beatings and torture of prisoners horrified even my father. Many of the torturers of the Islamic regime had been prisoners under the shah and knew exactly what methods of interrogation and torture could break a person. "It will take Maryam years to get rid of the prison memories, the nightmares," my mother told me a week after Maryam was released. I am not sure that Maryam ever fully recovered.

*   *   *

I thought I had done everything I could to avoid this suffering, and yet now the authorities had come for me. Since I'd first begun reporting in Iran, in 1997, making independent documentaries and writing for *Newsweek* magazine, I had taken every precaution and even censored myself in an attempt to stay below the radar. I'd chosen not to write about such sensitive subjects as separatist movements or ethnic and religious minorities. I'd made every effort to be honest and impartial, but I'd never been too critical of the regime, and certainly never of Supreme Leader Ali Khamenei, who had taken over in 1989, after Ruhollah Khomeini died. I was very careful about whom I socialized with, dealing infrequently with foreigners—whom the government, as a rule, mistrusted. I had rarely dated in Iran to avoid provoking the country's moral police. I was acutely aware of the government's level of tolerance for things, and was careful not to cross any lines.

I detested revolutions; I believed, instead, in reconciliation and reform. I accepted the complex—or, perhaps, oppressive—steps I had to take to keep the government from becoming suspicious of me, because the most important thing to me was to be able to continue to do my work as a journalist. Having grown up under the despotic regime of the Islamic Republic—a regime under which information was controlled and severely limited—I understood that a lack of information and communication among a populace leads only to bigotry, violence, and bloodshed. Conspiracy theories about unknown "others"—the West, multinational companies, and secret organizations— being in charge of Iran's destiny had stunted my nation's sense of self-determination and, as a result, its will, leaving genera- tions of Iranians feeling hopeless and helpless. I felt it was my job to provide accurate, well-reported information and, in doing so, help the world to have a better understanding of Iran and in my own way build a gradual path toward a more demo- cratic future.

My loved ones—particularly my mother, my sister, and my fiancée, Paola—had worried for years that I would be the next person in my family to be arrested, but I'd repeatedly assured them that I would not risk my life for any cause. That morning, however, as I sat silently at the breakfast table with my mother and watched Rosewater walk angrily out of my bedroom with a box of my notebooks in his arms, I saw that in the eyes of such men, despite all my caution, I was a danger to the author- itarian rulers of the country and, by extension, to the Islamic Republic itself. I knew then that as much as I had tried to avoid my father's and sister's fate, I was about to pay the same price, or perhaps a higher one.

Part I

THE TUNNEL
AT THE END
OF THE LIGHT

CHAPTER ONE

"Are you sure you're pregnant?" I had asked as I leaned down to kiss Paola's stomach. "Maybe it's something you ate."

Her voice sounded tired as she walked me to the door. "Just get back home as soon as you can," she said. She had had more than enough of my traveling. I had spent the last several weeks in Iran, reporting on the upcoming presidential elections for *Newsweek* and producing a film for the BBC, and now, after just a week in London, I was heading back again. Her patience for my silly jokes was running thin. We gave each other a long kiss good-bye, and when I finally pulled away from her, her eyes were full of tears.

In the taxi from our flat in north London to Heathrow Airport, I couldn't ignore the pangs of guilt I felt for leaving Paola alone again. I had promised her I'd be with her during her pregnancy, but in the five months since she'd found out she was carrying our first child, I'd already broken that promise twice. As much as I wanted to be with Paola in London, reading the pregnancy books piled near our bed, I knew that I had to get back to Iran to report on the historic elections just days away. I needed to witness for myself the choice my nation was about to make. There was so much at stake.

There were four candidates in total, but two of them—Mehdi Karroubi and Mohsen Rezaei—didn't stand a chance. The real battle was between the incumbent, Mahmoud Ahmadinejad, and his chief opponent, Mir Hossein Mousavi.

I believed that the reckless policies of President Ahmadinejad's government were ruining Iran. His economic mismanagement had caused high rates of inflation and unemployment, and his irresponsible rhetoric had created far too many enemies. But even more disturbing was that by the end of his first four-year term, and with the well-known support of Ayatollah Khamenei, the country was well on its way to becoming a dictatorship.

A former member of the Revolutionary Guards himself, Ahmadinejad had bestowed on the Guards a dangerous amount of power. When the organization was created, in 1979, the Guards was mostly a voluntary force with very few resources, led by guerrilla fighters who had been active against the shah. In the years immediately following the revolution, the Guards had effectively become the new government's trusted army and police force, tasked with crushing the groups they deemed anti-revolutionary. But in the thirty years since—and most notably under Ahmadinejad's presidency—the Guards' political power had grown to such a degree that it surpassed that of the Shia religious leaders who had been ruling Iran for years. In addition to operating ever more effectively as a military force, the Guards had also gained control of much of Iran's economy and, most alarmingly, had taken over the nation's nuclear program. In fact, by the time of the June 2009 presidential election, it appeared that Ahmadinejad and the Guards, with Khamenei's blessing, were trying to tighten their grip on the country and return Iran to the claustrophobic days of the 1980s, where any voice of dissent would be brutally suppressed.

According to the Iranian Constitution, the supreme leader makes the final decision about all affairs of the state. The president, as the head of the executive branch, is in charge of the day-to-day running of the country. Even though the president has to listen to the supreme leader's directives, a strong president—one who has the support of the public and knows how to manipulate the loopholes in the system—can attain a level of independence that allows him to challenge the supreme leader.

From 1989, when Ali Khamenei became the supreme leader, until Ahmadinejad's election in 2005, Khamenei had two strong presidents: Akbar Hashemi Rafsanjani and Mohammad Khatami. At times, they harshly, albeit privately, disagreed with him, so in order to keep the public's support, Khamenei tolerated these differences of opinion and did not speak out publicly against Rafsanjani or Khatami. The presence of these relatively independent presidents curtailed the supreme leader's power and kept Iran from becoming a totalitarian state, even though it always remained, in essence, a brutal authoritarian regime.

Now, with his handpicked president, Ahmadinejad, in place, Supreme Leader Khamenei could gain absolute power and snuff out anyone who sought to challenge him. While to many Iranians this was a terrifying prospect, to many of those who supported Ahmadinejad, there could be no higher goal. For they didn't think of Khamenei as merely the leader of the country; to them, he was Allah's representative on earth, a god-king who should have absolute control over the citizens' lives.

Though the supreme leader is supposed to remain impartial when it comes to elections, it was clear that Khamenei supported Ahmadinejad in his quest to amass power. A month before the elections, in a speech in the province of Kurdistan, Khamenei had criticized "those who exaggerate problems in Iran" and asked Iranians to vote for "the candidate who lives more modestly, is not corrupt, and understands people's pain." Khamenei did not mention any names, but there was no doubt that he was urging people to support Ahmadinejad.

With the help of Khamenei and the Guards, Ahmadinejad had taken every measure to secure his reelection. With the rising price of oil, which accounts for 80 percent of Iran's revenue, the government had billions of dollars to spend. Ahmadinejad had been unabashedly using quite a bit of this money to hand out unguaranteed loans for anything that could secure him a vote: mortgages, college educations, even weddings. The amount and the number of loans granted had been steadily rising in the months before the election, as Ahmadinejad traveled around the country and reminded the anxious crowds that only he would continue to support the poor like this. Should anyone else come to power, he claimed, loans would be cut and the poor would suffer. Ahmadinejad was, in effect, trying to buy his reelection.

In many ways, Mousavi was Ahmadinejad's opposite. He had served as the prime minister of Iran from 1982 until 1989, though the office was never clearly defined by Iran's Constitution and was abolished after Khomeini's death, in 1989. Mousavi was now one of the leaders of Iran's reformist movement, part of a generation of ex-revolutionaries who wanted to bring an end to the extremist policies and rhetoric of the recent past and move Iran more progressively toward greater respect for freedom of expression and human rights and rapprochement with the rest of the world. Mousavi believed in a more open and democratic interpretation of Islam than Khamenei and Ahmadinejad, and was campaigning on the promise to bring more accountability and transparency to the Islamic Republic. Those who supported him hoped that under his leadership, there would be less government and religious interference in the personal lives of Iran's citizens, giving them more freedom in matters ranging from the way they dressed to how they conducted business. What this meant, it was quietly understood, was that Mousavi would do what he could to curtail the power of the supreme leader.

Of course, among the many unknowns in the upcoming election was the question of how, exactly, Mousavi would accomplish this goal. He could not talk in specifics. The election supervisory councils, whose members were selected by Khamenei, could easily disqualify Mousavi if he ever criticized the supreme leader openly. In Iran, only candidates who are approved by the supreme leader and his selected officials can qualify to run for office. In fact, Mousavi was the reformists' main candidate only by default; all the other candidates had either been disqualified by the supervisory councils or had chosen not to register because they knew they would be disqualified.

Iran's labyrinthine system of government puzzles foreigners and Iranians alike. The complex structure is derived from the fact that "Islamic Republic" itself is a contradiction in terms. On the one hand, the government follows democratic procedures, such as elections and referendums, through which people choose their president, members of parliament, and other government officials. On the other hand, according to the Iranian Constitution, the supreme leader has the final say in all affairs of state, affording him absolute power. But there are cracks in the system, and through these cracks light sometimes shines.

According to the Constitution, the supreme leader can overrule parliamentary bills and even force a president to step down. In practice, however, he rarely goes directly against the will of elected officials because he also needs some degree of support from them, and the people who have voted for them, to maintain his political, religious, and popular legitimacy. There have been times when the supreme leader did not exert enough control over the selection of candidates and certain reformist politicians entered parliament and even became president. In May 1997, Mohammad Khatami was elected president despite the fact that Khamenei openly supported the other, more conservative candidate. Almost three years later, in February 2000, reformist politicians took over the parliament. By the end of Khatami's presidency, in 2005, the supreme leader and his conservative supporters had learned a lesson.

They set up a stricter qualification process for parliamentary and presidential candidates; in 2009, out of 476 men and women who registered, only four men qualified as presidential candidates. All the qualified candidates had been high-ranking members of the regime since the 1979 revolution.

Now the vote would take place in just three days, and as my plane began its descent into Tehran, I tried to push away the guilt I felt for leaving Paola again and remember that I was in a unique position to help others understand the complex nature of my government. I relished the opportunity to report on the upcoming elections. It seemed that the nation, and much of the world, was waiting to find out the results, as was I. I had always argued for nonviolence and peaceful change of government. I believed that many people in the Iranian government understood that suppressing people inside the country and alienating the rest of the world would result in a disaster that would not only hurt the people but also weaken the government's ability to lead the country. I hoped that Khamenei and his cohorts could understand that young Iranians were becoming increasingly educated and were changing every day, and that the government had to change as well. The alternative to a peaceful change was chaos and violence, more international condemnation and economic sanctions. More suffering for my people.

I had promised Paola that I would make up for my absence. "You mustn't worry, I'll be back a week after the election," I'd told her the night before as we sat at the dinner table, enjoying our first candlelit meal together in months. "We will get married in July. And I'll be with you every day until you give birth, and for at least three months after that. I won't go to Iran or any other place in the world, no matter how big the story." As we cleared the dishes and she helped me pack, I felt excited about everything that awaited me: more time with Paola, the birth of our child, and, with the election of a new progressive leader, a new hope for my country.

* * *

As soon as I arrived in Imam Khomeini International Airport, just after four A.M., I knew that I'd made the right decision. The airport felt electric. Crowds of foreign journalists packed the customs area, lugging large camera cases and equipment behind them. Typically, the Iranian government restricted the number of visas it issued to foreign reporters, but with the upcoming election, it had issued hundreds, hoping to show the world Islamic democracy in action.

It was still dark outside when I left the airport, and the June air was thick and steamy. Among the cars waiting to pick up passengers, I spotted Mr. Roosta, a driver for a cab company I frequently used when I was in Iran. Mr. Roosta ran toward me and took my suitcase. There was a big smile on his face, partly hidden by his thick white mustache.

"*Salaam, Aghayeh Bahari,*" he said. "Hello, Mr. Bahari. How about that Mousavi? It seems that we are winning!"

I was surprised to hear him say this. When I had spoken to Mr. Roosta a couple of weeks earlier, he had told me that he didn't intend to vote. I had urged him to reconsider his position. "Can you stand four more years of this idiot Ahmadinejad?" I'd asked him.

"I can't even stand one more day of him," Mr. Roosta had replied. Then he'd looked at me with a knowing smile. "My dear Mr. Bahari, our votes will never count. *Khodeshoon*"—"they"—"will choose who will rule over us."

This is not uncommon thinking among Iranians. For twenty-five hundred years Iran was ruled by tyrannical and often corrupt men, and in the two centuries prior to the Islamic Revolution, Russia, Great Britain, and America interfered freely in Iran's internal affairs. With this long history of foreign invasions and successive dictatorships, many Iranians believe that the shape of events in Iran is decided by this shadowy "they"—an imaginary conglomerate composed of Western nations, multinational companies, and corrupt Iranian politicians.

I had never liked the expression *khodeshoon*. My father had always believed that blaming your problems on "them" was a cowardly way of escaping responsibilities. "It's *maa,* us," he used to say. "We fuck up and blame it on them. It's as simple as that." My father always added a bit of spice to his language to make his points.

I told Mr. Roosta that I really didn't know who "they" were but, regardless, we had to use the only weapon at our disposal to get rid of them: our vote. Mousavi's election, I argued, would send a positive message about Iran to the rest of the world, which was at best agitated and at worst provoked by Ahmadinejad's irresponsible comments and policies. While nobody could describe Mousavi as a Jeffersonian democrat, at least he wasn't denying the Holocaust, insulting world leaders, and threatening countries with destruction, as Ahmadinejad did on a consistent basis. If nothing else, he would be a solid step in the right direction.

Now, just two weeks after this discussion, I was happy to see that Mr. Roosta had changed his mind and was planning to vote. He'd even taped a large picture of Mousavi on the back window of his cab.

"Have you put Mousavi's picture on the rear window so you can't look back in anger anymore?" I joked.

"In this country, Mr. Bahari, it helps not being able to look back," Mr. Roosta said. "And with this heat, it also helps that he doesn't let the sunlight through."

Exhausted from the flight, I settled into the seat for the hour-long drive to my mother's apartment in central Tehran, where I stayed whenever I was in Iran. The billboards along the Persian Gulf Highway—some advertising luxury items like BMW cars and Tag Heuer watches, others bearing the faces of Ruhollah Khomeini and Ali Khamenei—were familiar and did not reveal much about the state of the country as it neared the elections. But more than half an hour later, when we finally reached Navab Street, I felt as if we had entered a whole new Tehran. The walls around the city were covered with posters and banners for the candidates—far more than had been there when I'd left Iran just a week earlier. Plastered with their vibrant red, white, and green posters, the colors of the Iranian flag, the city walls looked like an Iranian version of a Jasper Johns collage. I noticed a few posters in support of the two fringe candidates, Mehdi Karroubi, the former speaker of parliament, and Mohsen Rezaei, a former Revolutionary Guards commander, but the main fight for space on the walls was between Ahmadinejad and Mousavi.

In some of his campaign posters, Ahmadinejad wore his trademark beige jacket and duplicitous smile. The three intertwined circles—the symbol of nuclear energy—were noticeable in many posters. Ahmadinejad had made Iran's controversial nuclear program a matter of national pride, presenting himself as the candidate who would best champion Iran's right to become a nuclear power. In some posters, he stared sternly at the camera against a background of floating atoms.

While Ahmadinejad looked aggressive in his posters, Mousavi appeared subdued and modest. An architect and abstract painter, with a graying beard, a big nose, and thick glasses, Mousavi seemed uncomfortable as a politician. Now in his late sixties, he resembled a retired professor who just wanted to get on with life. But he was the man with whom our hopes lay. Hope against all hope.

*   *   *

The sun had fully risen by the time I arrived at my mother's house, just before six A.M. I hoped to not wake my mother, but she was already up and waiting for me. "Mazi *jaan*," she said, hugging me—"dear Mazi." Recently, her hugs had become longer and tighter.

"How are you, Moloojoon?" I asked, handing her two big tins of her favorite chocolates, which I'd bought for her at Heathrow Airport. She didn't answer. Instead she walked into the kitchen and put a plate of *sangak* flat bread and feta cheese on the table.

"Have you had breakfast?" she asked. I knew she was avoiding my question. She sat down and drank her tea, with sour cherry jam, in silence. She looked tired, and even older than her eighty-three years. I could see the sadness in her eyes.

In July 2005, my father had died after suffering a stroke. Almost two years later, in June 2007, my brother, Babak, who was fourteen years older than I, died of a heart attack at the age of fifty-four. And then my sister, Maryam, who was the closest person to my mother and me, lost a short battle with leukemia in February 2009. My mother and I were all that was left now, and that had brought us much closer to each other.

"So, how are you, Moloojoon?" I repeated.

She just shook her head and said, "How can I be, Mazi *jaan*? How do you want me to be?"

I had no answer. I knew that the burden of her grief was so heavy, she was reluctant to share it with me. With her silence, she thought she could protect me.

Sitting in the kitchen, I began to find the silence unbearable, but I didn't know how to break it. I didn't want to upset her. I stood and took a bottle of smuggled Johnnie Walker whiskey from a kitchen cabinet and poured a little into my tea, hoping this would help me sleep.

"Would you like to have *baghali ghatogh* and fish for lunch?" my mother asked, changing the subject, as she unwrapped a chocolate. *Baghali ghatogh* is a dish from the north of Iran, where my mother is from. It is made with broad beans, a variety of herbs, and eggs. My brother used to refer to *baghali ghatogh* as "Moloojoon's specialty," and we all loved it more than any other dish she made.

"You need to have your lunch before going out to report on this *ashghal*," she said, referring to Ahmadinejad. *Ashghal*, the Persian word for "rubbish," is the strongest insult in my mother's lexicon.

Good, I thought. My mother, like a typical Iranian, was dealing with her grief through a combination of cuisine and humor. I knew then that there was no point in pressing her to speak about her grief, and turned instead to her other favorite topic: politics.

My mother met my father through the Tudeh Party, when she was a twenty-five-year-old chemistry student at Tehran University. The party had assigned my father to indoctrinate students at the university about the proletarian struggle. Like many educated young people of her generation, my mother believed that communism was the answer to Iran's underdevelopment. She had read the books of Soviet writers like Maxim Gorky and Mikhail Sholokhov, and had developed a romantic understanding of socialism. To my mother, my father—with his broad shoulders and large, dark eyes—was not only a handsome, articulate party cadre, he was like a character out of a novel.

In 1953, when the shah's government started to crack down on communists, my mother paid a heavy price. She was dismissed from the university and was suspended from her job as a primary school teacher for one year. Since then, Moloojoon, like my father, had been disenchanted with the idea of revolution, but she had never lost her interest in politics. The first words she taught me to read were not the ones other children learned—"table" or "bird"—but Yassir Arafat and Golda Meir, the names of the Palestinian and Israeli leaders. During my preschool years, Moloojoon's attempts to teach me to read involved not flipping through children's books but perusing the political commentary section of newspapers. She was a good teacher. By the time I started school, I knew how to spell words like "surplus value" and "interventionism," even though I had no idea what they meant.

"I've made a decision," my mother told me as I sipped my tea and whiskey. "Not voting means a vote for Ahmadinejad. I'm going to vote for Mousavi."

This was surprising. Like Mr. Roosta, my mother had long felt disappointed by Iranian leaders, and it had been a long time since she had voted.

"What made you decide to vote this time?" I asked her.

"The debate, especially the way Ahmadinejad personally attacked Mousavi," she said.

A few days earlier, on June 3, Ahmadinejad and Mousavi had taken part in a televised debate. They had attacked each other vehemently, stirring up tensions among the voters. Mousavi told Ahmadinejad that his government had undermined the dignity of the nation. "It has inflicted heavy damages on us and created tension with other countries. It has left us with not a single friend in the region," he said. In response, Ahmadinejad snickered and accused Mousavi of being part of a corrupt group of Islamic Republic elites who had been illegally benefiting from their positions in government since the beginning of the revolution.

Ahmadinejad then showed a copy of the doctoral degree issued to Mousavi's wife, Zahra Rahnavard, and argued that the degree had been obtained illegally. "This is lawlessness. My government is based on laws and regulation," Ahmadinejad said, staring at an exasperated Mousavi.

Family is a sacred institution in Iran. While I had thought Ahmadinejad would be universally criticized for his rude comments—this was the first time a candidate had ever attacked another candidate's wife publicly—his supporters commended his directness, calling the allegations a necessary step to reveal the real identities of the reformists. The debate polarized Iranian society more than at any other time I could remember.

"The debate showed the true nature of Mousavi and Ahmadinejad," my mother said. "Mousavi was calm and polite and talked about substantial issues. Ahmadinejad has no manners. He was as vulgar as ever. *Ashghal!* After that debate, I decided to vote for Mousavi."

"You've made a wise decision, Moloojoon," I told her, before kissing her cheek and going to my room to sleep.

*   *   *

When I woke up two hours later, I couldn't wait to get out on the streets of Tehran. I called my friend Mazdak, a photographer and an avid fan of Mousavi's, who was always the first person I got in touch with when I arrived in Tehran. He told me that the night before, hundreds of thousands of Mousavi supporters had formed a twelve-mile-long chain on Vali Asr Avenue, the longest street in Tehran. The line had been referred to as the "green line," as Mousavi had adopted green as the official color of his campaign. Green has long been associated with Islam; it signifies that Islam is a religion of peace. Mousavi's supporters wore green T-shirts and wristbands and carried green banners and flags. "We will build a green Iran" was their slogan, meaning a country at peace with itself and the rest of the world.

Mazdak had taken part in the "green line," and his voice was still hoarse from screaming. "It was like being in a World

Cup final, Maziar, but more exciting," he said. "Mousavi was our Pelé."

Mazdak would be taking photographs of a group of Mousavi supporters in Robat Karim, a working-class neighborhood about twenty miles south of Tehran, that day, and I told him I'd meet him later. But first I had to decide how to get there.

Given Iran's suffering economy and high rate of unemployment, many Iranians—even those who are highly educated—earn a living by using their motorcycles as unofficial taxis, and the streets surrounding Vali Asr Square were crowded with men standing near their motorcycles, hoping for a fare. I told the driver I chose, a young man named Davood, that I wanted to go to Robat Karim. I also wanted to make a few stops along the way, at various campaign offices and coffee shops where I knew people would be gathered to have political discussions, and where I could easily conduct interviews. Luckily, Davood was interested in politics and was eager to help me out. He was less keen on respecting the traffic laws. Just seconds into our trip, he pulled his bike out of the traffic and onto the pavement, where he weaved through the pedestrians.

"Shame on me, shame on me," he said loudly when people yelled at him. "These young people today, they have no manners!" he offered sarcastically, then turned to me and winked. When we couldn't drive on the pavement, Davood masterfully navigated through the slightest gap between cars and sometimes, to my horror, trucks.

The effect of years of chaos and insecurity, war and revolution, can easily be seen in the way Iranians drive: these generally courteous people turn into monsters behind the wheel. They rarely allow another car the right of way and honk their horns as soon as a pedestrian steps into the street. Road rage—even using machetes against other drivers—is not unheard of in Iran. As a friend of mine once put it, "The disgraceful way we drive is like crapping on more than twenty-five hundred years of Persian history, arts, and culture."

As he drove, Davood told me that he had been kicked out of university in his native city of Tabriz. "I installed satellite dishes in people's houses to make money," he said. Owning a satellite dish is a crime in the Islamic Republic, but many people hide dishes on their balconies and rooftops. Davood was arrested and fined the equivalent of £2,000. The police also notified the university, and he was expelled. Even so, he considered himself lucky. Those who install satellite equipment can be sentenced to many years in prison.

Since then, Davood had been trying to earn a living with his motorcycle in Tehran, but he was having a hard time making ends meet. That did not, however, stop him from looking stylish. His shoulder-length hair was wet with gel, and his goatee was immaculately trimmed. He had undone the top three buttons of his white shirt. If he were a bit slimmer, he could have passed for an Iranian Ethan Hawke.

I told Davood to take his time when we reached Vanak Square, which was still covered with green leaflets and banners from the night before. Street sweepers in orange overalls were trying to clean up the mess, and at every intersection, Mousavi campaign volunteers—mostly men and women in their twenties—were distributing more leaflets. As we passed, I took one from the hand of a young woman. *Khodafez, Dictator,* it said over a picture of Ahmadinejad. Good-bye, Dictator.

"Are you glad to be back home?" Davood shouted over the noise of the crowds and traffic. Knowing he could charge me twice the normal rate if he found out that I lived abroad, I had told him that I had been visiting Europe on business for a few weeks.

"Yes," I said, "very much." The truth was, I had never been so thrilled about being in Tehran. I'd first moved away in 1986, just a few months after finishing secondary school, and since then, I had never wanted to live permanently in the country of my birth. When I left, Iran was six years into the war with Iraq, and all men were required to serve in the military. I didn't believe in the war, and knew I had to get out of the country. With the help of a smuggler, I snuck into neighboring Pakistan and made my way to Canada, where I studied film and journalism and, while retaining my Iranian citizenship, eventually became a Canadian citizen as well.

Once I'd begun my career as a reporter, I had been spending more and more time in Tehran and had grown to love working there more than anywhere else in the world, but I still felt that the city was not a place where I'd ever choose to settle down. Successive Iranian governments had destroyed many beautiful traditional houses with Persian gardens and had built gaudy, quasi-modern high-rises in their place. The mountains that surround the city trap the smog, and with a population of twelve million people and thousands of cars and motorcycles crowding the streets, Tehran is among the most polluted cities in the world. On the back of Davood's motorcycle, I could feel the heat of carbon monoxide on my face and taste the diesel fumes on my lips. But as we whizzed between the cars, while young men and women wearing green danced on the pavement and in the middle of the streets, I didn't wish to be anywhere else in the world.

The last time I had witnessed such exhilaration in the city was February 11, 1979, the day of the victory of the Islamic Revolution, when the shah, Mohammad Reza Pahlavi, was removed from power. I was twelve years old and had gone to a demonstration at Tehran University with Maryam. My sister belonged to a generation of young Iranians who grew up learning about such progressive ideas as democracy and human rights, concepts the shah pretended to adhere to, though in truth he believed democracy would only hinder Iran's move toward industrial progress and could be allowed only once Iran prospered economically.

During the revolution, Maryam was studying Persian literature at Tehran University and was among the first students who
staged strikes and took part in the demonstrations against the
shah. Even though our parents did not agree with the idea of
revolution itself, deep inside they despised the shah for what he
had done to them and their comrades. Therefore, even though
they were worried about Maryam's safety, they quietly encouraged her to take part in the demonstrations and didn't mind my
accompanying her.

That day, as we had walked among the crowds of thousands
that had gathered, Maryam began to grow worried. She feared
that the demonstrations were going to get violent and said she
thought we should go back home. I knew that she wanted to
stay and take part, so I asked her to give me money for a taxi
and stay behind without me. Of course, I had no intention of
going straight home. I used the money to buy a hot dog—food
my mother forbade us to eat—and walked home slowly as I
ate it.

The whole city felt as if it were on fire. I saw young men in
different neighborhoods attack police stations and take the
guns they found there. As I got closer to our house, six blocks
north of the former U.S. embassy compound, some teenagers
were firing celebratory bullets into the air. I asked our neighbor's son, Gholam Ali, to pass me a pistol. He put me on his
shoulders and I shot into the air as well, feeling as powerful as
an adult. The shah's thirty-seven-year dictatorship had finally
come to an end. "Tyranny is over," we chanted. "Death to the
shah! Long live Khomeini!"

A few years later, as soon as Khomeini fully secured his grip
on power, he ordered the imprisonment and execution of many
of the same young men and women who had risked their lives to
bring him to power. Their crimes—often punishable by death—

included everything from possessing an "anti-revolutionary" leaflet to plotting against the "holy" government of the Islamic Republic. Gholam Ali, on whose shoulders I'd ridden in 1979, assassinated a government sympathizer in our neighborhood in 1983. He was caught and executed a few days later.

As important as the 1979 Islamic Revolution was in the history of Iran, I knew that the 2009 presidential election could be an even more historic occasion. A few decades ago, this fight would have occurred with guns and Molotov cocktails. This time around, young people were battling it out with posters, pamphlets, and discussions. They were tired of thirty years of the stringent rules of the Islamic Republic, and surely they were angry, but in their joyful faces, and in the air of the city, I also felt a certain sense of patience and a desire for peace. Unlike their fathers' generation, these young Iranians valued life above violence. They supported Mousavi, but were not ready to die or kill for him. Through the Internet and satellite television, they had learned about the rest of the world. These young Iranians around me wanted simply to express themselves, to exercise their democratic rights, and to live a normal life like other young people around the world.

Davood stopped his bike near where a large group of young men and women were listening to loud music from a stereo on the pavement. The music was a medley of Beyoncé, Madonna, the Iranian pop singers Googoosh and Mansour, and the national anthem, "O Iran, O Bejeweled Land." On any other day, these kids could have been arrested for the crime of disturbing the public morality. But this morning, as hundreds of foreign journalists walked the city covering the preelection campaign, the Iranian government was letting them be. The regime needed to show the world its capacity for tolerance and, even more importantly, needed the young Iranians' votes in order to preserve its legitimacy.

As we approached the fashionable Sorkheh Bazaar shop-

ping center, I asked Davood to pull over. This center was one
of the locations where Tehran's *bache marouf*—the "it" girls
and boys—hung out. In November 2008, the Public Morality
Office of the Tehran police had issued an order to all boutiques
in Tehran banning the selling of "provocative, decadent Western clothes" such as miniskirts, tank tops, stiletto shoes,
low-cut dresses, and shorts. But these items could still quite
easily be purchased in the Sorkheh Bazaar. Laws in Iran are not
made to be followed; they are made to be broken, albeit as sur-
reptitiously as possible.

I got off Davood's bike and walked around the bazaar. The
shops had not changed much since I was a teenager. I approached a crowd of young men and women. The guys had
strange, spiky hairdos and were wearing Tommy Hilfiger and
Diesel shirts. The girls were in faux Versace and Gucci head
scarves. Their toenails were painted green and blue, and they all
wore green wristbands.

I introduced myself and told them I was writing for an American magazine, assuring them that their statements wouldn't appear in any Iranian media; many people in Iran fear what the
government may do to them if they express their opinions freely.

I said that I used to hang out here when I was a teenager.
"They used to call us punks," I told them. "What do they call
you these days?"

"Devil worshippers!" a young man named Farzad told me.

"You look more like a member of Backstreet Boys than
Judas Priest," I said jokingly.

"Ahmadinejad and his people don't need any basis to call
you names," Farzad said.

"They just know we look different, so they call us devil
worshippers," added a young woman named Tina, her messy,
highlighted blond hair spilling out from underneath her faux
designer scarf.

None of them thought that Ahmadinejad was the right rep-

resentative for an educated nation like Iran, with a sophisti-
cated ancient civilization at its roots. "How can this monkey be
our president?" asked Tina. She pointed to the people nearby.
"Look around you. Do you find anyone as ugly as Ahmadinejad? But the fact that he's ugly wouldn't matter, if only he were
polite." She then made a face as if she had bitten into a hard
lemon. She wore a manteau, a tunic that many Iranian women
prefer to the chador, a cloak that covers the whole body. Manteaus are more practical than chadors; while they still conceal
the shape of a woman's body from the gaze of strangers, they are
less constricting, allowing greater ease of movement. Like most
fashionable Iranian women, Tina had shortened her manteau—
which was hot pink—and had stretched it tightly across her
body, enhancing her curves.

The Islamic government's intrusion into every aspect of people's lives over the last three decades had made apolitical young
men and women into political activists. In many countries, even
authoritarian ones, young people can parade their vanities on
the streets and express their youthful rebellion through fashion,
dance, music, and other arts. But in Iran, all of these things are
under severe government control. The police can arrest anyone
they say looks un-Islamic. A woman who wears too much
makeup or shows too much of her hair under her scarf or too
much of her body—even an ankle or an elbow—can be punished with hefty fines, lashings, and months of imprisonment.
The same rules are applied in dealing with boys with curious
haircuts or tight T-shirts.

Members of the morality police stroll the streets looking for
people to harass and arrest for these indiscretions. Police officers
are assigned to these units only after they demonstrate a certain
level of religiosity and ideological devotion to the system, and
once chosen, they must go through an indoctrination process
about Islamic values and the West's subversive campaign to corrupt Iran's Muslim youth. Even though the morality police are

asked by their superiors to avoid physical confrontation, they are ordered to force into submission those who argue with them.

To me, Farzad, Tina, and their friends were not silent victims of the Islamic government's close-mindedness; they were loud rebels. They risked severe punishment for living the way they wanted to. "You remember Shamlu's poem?" Farzad asked me. He then recited the Iranian poet Ahmad Shamlu's lines about the erratic behavior of the Islamic government in the years following the revolution.

"They smell your breath
lest you have said: I love you,
They smell your heart:
     These are strange times, my dear. . . .
They chop smiles off lips,
and songs off the mouth. . . .
     These are strange times, my dear."

Everyone in the group became silent as Farzad repeated the poem's refrain. "Our parents may have allowed the government thugs to smell their breath," Farzad said defiantly. "But our generation fights back."

Before I left the Sorkheh Bazaar, Tina tried to make sure that I would present them correctly in my article.

"Please don't write that we don't believe in religion because of the way we're dressed," she implored me. "We don't want to turn Iran into a decadent place like Las Vegas. We love our religion, but we want to have some freedom."

* * *

As I thought about the stories the young men and women had told me about trying to lead normal lives under the watchful eyes of the government, I remembered how it had felt to be young and oppressed in Iran. The long hair and tight jeans I'd worn as a teenager came at a price. My friends and I often had to run away from the members of the local *komiteh,* or "committee." These committees, which enforced moral values around the country, were separate entities from the Revolutionary Guards, but many of their members were Guards members as well.

I was arrested by committee officers once and, as my punishment, forced to sit down on the pavement and have my head shaved. The man who sheared off my hair told me that he hated the European and American tourists who had traveled to Iran in the shah's time wearing tight jeans or miniskirts. He called all tourists and Western-looking Iranians hippies. "If it were up to me, I would behead all you hippie shah supporters," he said as he wielded the old-fashioned, broken barber clippers. There was no point arguing with him or telling him that my father had spent many years in the shah's prisons. Indoctrinated as he was, he saw any kid wearing tight jeans with long hair as a remnant of the shah's decadence.

Back home, my father announced that he liked my new haircut. "It suits you better," he said. "I never liked your long hair." It was only when I told him about the circumstances behind my haircut that he launched into a barrage of insults against the Islamic Republic and how it was trying to shove its ideology down people's throats. My parents never cared much for my sartorial and musical choices, but they never criticized me. They saw the fact that I wore tight jeans with white socks and Adidas sneakers and listened to Yaz and Depeche Mode as simply my generation's expression of dissent. And even though they had long since given up on the usefulness of revolutions, my parents appreciated dissent much more than any other parents I knew. Whereas many of my friends were asked by their parents to do whatever they could to avoid incensing the authorities, my father valued my attempts to live outside the government-enforced norms. As some of our relatives used to say, only half-jokingly: trouble was in my family's blood, and each member of the Bahari family would get into trouble sooner or later.

* * *

It was not only the fashionable middle class, like the kids I met in the Sorkheh Bazaar, who supported Mousavi. In dozens of interviews I conducted at different local campaign offices in south Tehran and its poorer suburbs that day, I found that many lower-income people also supported Mousavi for the same reasons the middle class did. Rampant corruption in Ahmadinejad's government and Iran's status as an international pariah—that many nations distrusted and feared Iran—were the two main complaints Mousavi supporters had against Ahmadinejad. Both issues touched upon the basic concept of a citizen's right to determine his or her destiny. Three days before electing their next president, many Iranians thought that it was finally time they had a right as a nation to decide their own future.

Davood explained to me that many supporters of Mousavi were disillusioned former revolutionaries. Over a lunch of *dizi,* a traditional Iranian dish made with lamb, potatoes, and chickpeas, Davood told me that his father had been a staunch revolutionary and had fought for five years in the war with Iraq. His devotion to his country had left him with an artificial eye and leg. But while he was still a loyal citizen, Davood's father had no respect for the current Islamic regime. He despised the officials in the Ahmadinejad government and saw them for what they were: corrupt, power-hungry hypocrites.

"Because my father is a decent man, he lives on a pension of two million rials [about £150] per month," Davood said. "But my father's cousin is as dirty as a dog. He's a billionaire." His father's cousin, a real estate developer in Tabriz, had worked closely with the government of the shah before the revolution.

"Ever since then, he's made his money by bribing successive Islamic government officials," Davood noted, a look of disgust clouding his face.

Despite Davood's disdain for traffic laws, it took us almost six hours to cross the city, and it was nearly four P.M. when we finally reached Robat Karim, one of the poorest suburbs of Tehran. I spotted Mazdak taking photos of a group of young Mousavi supporters distributing leaflets. Like many good photojournalists, Mazdak is usually calm to the point of invisibility. But that day, the fifty-year-old professional bubbled with the excitement of a teenager. He eagerly embraced Davood and me and introduced us to some local Mousavi campaigners. Mazdak couldn't stop talking about his experience of the green line demonstration the night before, where he and his wife had stood alongside their twenty-two-year-old son and eighteen-year-old daughter.

"It was like going to a political picnic! I've never seen anything like it, Maziar," he said, grabbing both of my arms. "Everyone was marching peacefully. There were some clashes with Ahmadinejad supporters here and there but nothing serious." Like a delirious drunk looking for someone, anyone, to talk to, Mazdak couldn't stop telling me about what was happening around him. "Something has changed in this country, Maziar. People have become political and won't take this government's shit anymore. Ahmadinejad's people know their days are numbered, and they have accepted the idea of defeat," he burbled excitedly.

Ahmadinejad was essentially using an already existing system to get reelected, a system that had made millions of Iranians dependent on the government. I spent an hour or so with Mazdak, walking among the gathering crowds. Most of the Mousavi supporters on the streets were young, educated people repulsed by how Ahmadinejad was manipulating their neighbors and families. Most of the Robat Karim residents were migrants from villages whose livelihoods depended on government handouts, and the slightest change in the government could significantly affect their income.

Areas like Robat Karim are called *hashieh,* or the margins, and the migrants themselves are commonly known as *hashieh neshin,* the margin dwellers. Each major city in Iran has a large *hashieh.* Most candidates ignore *hashieh* residents, but Ahmadinejad aggressively campaigned in these areas, warning that Mousavi was out to cut government subsidies. Since the start of the Iran-Iraq War, in 1980, the Islamic government had been selling many basic items, including rice, sugar, flour, and gasoline, to citizens at subsidized prices. This service costs the government billions of dollars every year. Though on its face the policy is intended to help the poor, consecutive governments in Iran had used it to buy people's loyalty. But no Iranian official had ever used the system as aggressively as Ahmadinejad was doing.

Additionally, since the beginning of the revolution, the regime had also placed almost one million families—or about five million people—under the protection of the Imam Khomeini Relief Foundation. Through this charity, families receive around the equivalent of £30 per month. Targeting people's economic fears and simultaneously offering short-term solutions, Ahmadinejad's teams throughout the country had been stirring up fears that, if elected, Mousavi was going to make poor Iranians even poorer.

Rasool, a young engineering student I met in the crowd, told me that Robat Karim was sharply divided between the educated and the uneducated. "The educated vote for Mousavi and the uneducated vote for Ahmadinejad. When you're poor and ignorant, you can be easily manipulated."

For an engineering student, Rasool had an impressive knowledge of social problems in Iran. "According to the government's own statistics, out of seventy million Iranians, ten million live in absolute poverty," he said. "We have almost two and a half million drug addicts. Percentage-wise, that's more than any other country in the world, and there are five million officially unemployed young men and women. This government doesn't want people to know about what's going on in the country. It wants to keep the people uninformed."

I wondered where Rasool had got his information. He took me to the rooftop of a three-story building and showed me satellite dishes sprouting like mushrooms from many roofs in Robat Karim. "There are an increasing number of satellite television and Internet users in the area," he said. "They are the only way we can have correct and uncensored information in Iran." Many sites, including *The New York Times*' and CNN's, are filtered in Iran, but Rasool's family and friends—like so many Iranians—had found ways to buy satellite antennas on the black market and used filter busters to access the forbidden Internet sites. In the period before the election, BBC Persian television, broadcasting out of London, and Voice of America, from Washington, D.C., had become the main sources of information for many Iranians. "Most people with the Internet and satellite can learn about the lies of the government and they'll vote for Mousavi," Rasool told me. "But the ignorant will vote for Ahmadinejad."

*   *   *

Back on the street, the enthusiasm of the Mousavi supporters was intoxicating. I was so excited about the desire for change in Robat Karim that it was hard for me to pull myself away from the area. But I knew I had to visit Ahmadinejad's campaign headquarters on the southern part of Vali Asr Avenue to gain a better understanding of the situation. Davood reluctantly agreed to take me there. It was after seven P.M. when we arrived. The sun had already set, but it was still hot.

There is a clear class divide in Tehran. The rich live in the northern part of the city, in tall high-rises on wide streets. In the southern part of Tehran, the streets are crowded and narrower, the houses significantly more modest. The building that held Ahmadinejad's campaign headquarters could have belonged to any factory worker or junior government employee. I had been here on reporting trips twice before, but the house was so nondescript that I had a difficult time finding it.

There were dozens of shoes piled one on top of another in the entrance of the headquarters. In accordance with Islamic practices, I removed my shoes, then went inside to look for Alireza Asadi, a student leader with the campaign whom I had met a month earlier at a rally. Inside, the office was even more modest than its façade.

The Ahmadinejad posters on the walls of the headquarters, proclaiming his humility and religious devotion, made me sick. Groups of young Ahmadinejad supporters were poring over maps and lists. Alireza took Davood and me to a corner, where we couldn't hear what was being discussed.

Alireza was an engineering student and a classmate of Ahmadinejad's younger son, whose name is also Alireza. They were both part of the Islamic society of their university as well as members of the Basij, the volunteer arm of the Revolutionary Guards, which has a unit at every government office and school in Iran. The Basij's mission is said to be defending the ideals of the revolution. This vaguely worded mission allows the Guards commanders to use the paramilitary group in any way they desire. That had included ransacking student dormitories, attacking opposition newspapers, and even staging assassination attempts against reformist politicians.

At the rally, when I had asked Alireza why he'd joined the

Basij, he'd looked at me as if the answer were obvious.

"There's nothing I'm more proud of than being Basiji," he told me proudly. "The Basij is the backbone of this country."

One of the things that fascinated me most about Alireza was that he was so unlike the stereotypical Ahmadinejad supporter, who is typically poor, uneducated, and close-minded. The son of two physicians, Alireza had spent the early part of his life in England. But the devout Muslim family had decided to return to Iran when Alireza's sister hit adolescence, finding British society inappropriate for bringing up a good Muslim teenage girl. "Most British girls are corrupt, as you know," Alireza told me once, unaware that Paola, my fiancée, was British. "As soon as they can, they start whoring around," he added with a cheeky smile.

Even though he'd left England for Iran at the age of eight, Alireza talked about British society with the authority of a sociology professor at the London School of Economics, and as we sat across from each other on the faded orange wall-to-wall carpet of the campaign headquarters, he spoke with the same conviction about why Iranians should reelect Ahmadinejad. To him, it was very simple. According to the Iranian Constitution, he pointed out, the president has very limited power. The main power lies in the hands of the supreme leader, who has the final say in all major decisions in the country. Many who support the supreme leader don't think of him merely as the political leader of the country, but also as the highest Shia religious leader, who can control all aspects of their lives.

Shiism, or Shia Islam, is the second-largest denomination in the religion. The majority of Muslims are Sunnis. Shias are the majority in only four countries in the world: Iran, Iraq, Bahrain, and Lebanon.

The division between Muslims started after the death of the Prophet Mohammad in A.D. 632, due to political differences. The Sunnis believed that one of the close allies of the Prophet was his rightful successor. The Shias believed that Ali, the Prophet Mohammad's cousin and son-in-law, was the Prophet's rightful successor.

Ali is the first imam, or saint, of Shias. Sunnis call all their local religious leaders imams.

Most Shias believe in the sanctity of twelve imams: Ali and his eleven direct descendants. The twelve imams are regarded by Shias as "the infallible," those who never committed a sin. During their lifetime, the Shia imams interpreted the teachings of the Koran for their followers and were responsible for the welfare of their followers.

Shias regard the twelfth and last imam, Imam Mahdi, as their Messiah. According to Shia history, Imam Mahdi went into hiding in the eighth century to escape persecution and will return to establish a peaceful and just Islamic society.

During Imam Mahdi's absence, Shias have a duty to follow a religious leader, called a *marja,* who interprets the teachings of the Koran for them.

Marjas are chosen from the ranks of grand ayatollahs, high-ranking religious scholars, and each Shia Muslim is free to choose the *marja* of his or her choice.

Most Shias in the world believe that the role of the *marjas* is limited to teaching about Islam and taking care of the weak and the needy. But in the 1960s, Khomeini took the concept of the *marja* a step further and divined his *velayat-e faqih* theory, about the leadership of the supreme jurisprudent. According to Khomeini, a supreme jurisprudent should not only teach his followers about Islam but should rule an Islamic government with absolute authority, ensuring that all affairs of the country are conducted in accordance with Islamic teachings. Given that this leader will be in charge of all the systems of checks and balances in the country, it is not difficult to see why Iran became a dictatorship soon after Ruhollah Khomeini came to power in 1979.

Most Shia clerics in Iran and around the world never accepted Khomeini's theory and believe in a separation of mosque and state. But by stirring Iranians' nationalist sentiments, Khomeini gained popular support and led the Islamic Revolution, which established the first *velayat-e faqih* government and installed Khomeini himself as the first supreme leader.

After Khomeini's death in 1989, Ali Khamenei succeeded him as the *valie faqih,* the supreme jurisprudent, or supreme leader. His followers simply call him by his unofficial title: Agha, the master.

That is what Alireza, the young Ahmadinejad supporter, liked to call him.

"We are not a nation, we are the *umma,*" Alireza told me, using the Arabic term for the Islamic community. "As the *umma,* we have to obey the commands of Agha. The most important characteristic of Ahmadinejad is that he is devoted to Agha," Alireza said. "Ahmadinejad is a man who has dedicated his life to Agha and the return of the imam."

I could see that Davood was getting uncomfortable as Alireza told us that our votes were not worth anything and that our destiny could be determined only by Agha. When it was time for us to leave, Davood avoided having to kiss Alireza, as would have been appropriate, and did not even shake his hand. "We'll invite you to our celebration ceremony," Alireza said before kissing me on both cheeks.

"Mr. Maziar, I'm going to start the motorcycle," Davood said, practically running toward the door.

Davood was waiting for me outside of Ahmadinejad's campaign office. "You are a very patient man, Mr. Maziar," Davood told me as we drove north. "I could've killed that guy."

"He has a right to his opinion," I said. "Anyway, Khamenei is the one who should be upset now. Just look at all these people. Do you think Ahmadinejad has any chance to win?" It was evening, and hundreds of young men and women in bright green shirts and scarves still lined the streets, singing patriotic songs.

In the evening, more people gathered in the streets. I didn't want to go home. I asked Davood to take me to his neighborhood, a working-class area called Poonak in west Tehran. There, the street was blocked off and hundreds of young people were holding a party. I called Paola from my mobile phone and told her that as much as I missed her, I was very happy to be in Tehran at this moment.

I knew Paola understood my exhilaration. When we'd met, at a lecture about the Middle East conflict in a London journalists' club in March 2007, I was on my way to Iraq to produce two documentaries about the ethnic conflict in that country for Channel 4 and the BBC. At the time, a number of journalists had been kidnapped or murdered and it was a dangerous assignment. But Paola knew that I would be careful and shared my excitement about the trip.

Now, pumped up by the excitement and emotion of that moment in Poonak, I told Paola, "I feel like I'm witnessing history. I can't wait to show you everything I've been recording here." I had been out for sixteen hours by then, but I didn't notice my exhaustion. Like many Iranians, I, too, was intoxicated by the prospect of change; I, too, lent my voice to the chant heard throughout Poonak that night: "Ahmadinejad, bye-bye! Dictator, bye-bye!"

Davood finally drove me home at around two A.M., and as I prepared for sleep, I knew that whatever the outcome of the election—a Mousavi victory, an Ahmadinejad resurgence, a second round of voting—something had changed in Iran over the course of this campaign. Iranians from unexpected quarters had started to express themselves, and the leaders of the Islamic Republic now faced the uncomfortable reality that the people were demanding to be listened to.

As I tried to sleep, I envisioned an Iran free of men who think that to be true Muslims they need a master controlling every aspect of their lives. I knew that Mousavi was not a leader who would bring about a profound change to the country, but getting rid of Ahmadinejad, the man who had disgraced the country and imperiled its well-being for four years, was a start.

CHAPTER TWO

I came out of the shower the next day to the sound of my mother panicking in the kitchen. "Mazi, Mazi!" she cried out. I ran out of the bathroom to see what the problem was and found her staring open-mouthed out the window. Outside, Davood sat idly on his motorbike, waiting for me. I had asked him to pick me up at ten A.M., and he was right on time.

"Everyone knows that motorcycle drivers are just mad," my mother said. "The only people crazier than them are their passengers." Even though I had taken almost twenty trips to Iraq to report on the war, I don't think I'd ever seen her as worried for me as she was at that moment.

Losing her husband, elder son, and daughter in such a short period meant that my mother worried about me more than ever. As I got ready to go, Moloojoon followed me around the apartment, reminding me about the fatal accidents caused by motorcycles.

I kissed her good-bye. "Don't worry," I said. "He's just giving me a short ride to a friend's office." I knew she knew that I was lying, but we had an understanding. She trusted my judgment.

I said hello to Davood and jumped onto the motorbike behind him. He had apparently done some research overnight.

"I Googled you," he said. "Aren't you afraid of making all

these films and writing all these reports about this government?"

"Not really. I try to be careful and not to step on their tails," I answered, using a Persian expression, as Davood headed the wrong way down a one-way street. "I'm frankly more worried that your driving will get me into trouble."

Davood didn't laugh. "I noticed a couple of people waiting for us in a Peugeot when we went to see your friend in Robat Karim yesterday," he said. "There was another car parked toward the end of your street today. They followed us, but I think we lost them. I wasn't sure at first, so I didn't mention it."

I thought he was just being paranoid. "Right, Davood. As if you need a reason to drive like this," I said.

"Don't worry, Mr. Maziar. I'll take care of you," he assured me.

Davood and I spent the morning visiting a few more Mousavi and Ahmadinejad campaign offices around the city, and when we were done, at around three o'clock in the afternoon, I paid him for the whole day and told him he could go home. As much as I liked and trusted Davood, I couldn't take him to my next appointment.

I was going to see Amir, a friend of mine who'd previously worked for the Ministry of Interior, which is in charge of elections in Iran. Now in his early sixties, Amir had joined Khomeini's movement in 1963, when he was just sixteen years old. Over the course of the last fifty years, he had come to know some of the highest-ranking members of the Iranian government, and he understood the inner workings of the system as well as anyone in the country. The information Amir gave me over the years had hardly included state secrets, but despite the amazing morass of the Islamic system, he had a great ability to connect the dots and somehow make sense of the nonsensical behaviors of the regime.

In addition to being one of my most trusted sources, Amir was also, despite our age difference, one of my best friends. His brother had worked for my father's company in the shah's time and had spoken often of my father. "My brother used to say that Mr. Bahari was the best boss he had ever had," Amir said. "I had an immense respect for your father. He was not religious in a traditional sense, but his honesty and his big heart made him one of the most religious people I know."

To me, Amir represented moderation, and the idea that there were decent people in the system, people who were working to change it peacefully from within, gave me hope. Amir abhorred Ahmadinejad, whom he regarded as a misfit, a low-ranking former local governor and Revolutionary Guard who had somehow managed to become the president. But Amir ultimately blamed Khamenei for Ahmadinejad's rise to power. "It's amazing how people can be deceived by flattery," Amir had said to me not long after Ahmadinejad was first elected. "The relationship between Mr. Khamenei and this man is like a landowner and a serf."

Amir had held an important position during the presidency of Ahmadinejad's predecessor, Mohammad Khatami, a pro-reform president who believed in a more open and democratic interpretation of Islam. In 2005, when Ahmadinejad was elected president, he forced the resignation of many high-ranking government officials. Amir left the Ministry of Interior, but he had retained very good contacts inside Ahmadinejad's government.

Two weeks earlier, Amir had shown me a secret poll conducted by the Ministry of Intelligence—the country's equivalent of MI5 and MI6 in one—in the capitals of all of Iran's thirty-one provinces. The poll demonstrated that Mousavi was well ahead of Ahmadinejad and predicted that Mousavi would win the election with sixteen to eighteen million votes to Ahmadinejad's six to eight million. Surveys are not usually accurate or reliable in Iran. People don't trust the pollsters, and many Iranians are afraid that by expressing their opinion they can get into trouble. But because Ahmadinejad's own intelligence officials had con-

ducted the poll, I found it to be trustworthy and had written an
article about it for *Newsweek*.

Amir's office was large and mostly unfurnished and, like the
offices of most Iranian reformists, it had a temporary feel about
it, as if he was prepared to leave at a moment's notice. His desk-
top was empty, except for one yellow file and a few photographs, and the only decoration on the walls was a large framed
poster of the Sheikh Lotfollah Mosque, a marvel of Persian ar-
chitecture in the city of Isfahan. The dust on the frame showed
that it had been there for a long time, and that it had been ne-
glected. When I walked in that morning, I smelled the sweet
scent of *gaz*, which may be one of the most delicious confec-
tions in the world (and one of the main causes of cavities in
Iran). One of Amir's relatives owned a pastry shop in Isfahan,
and every now and then he sent Amir some *gaz*, which always
put him in a good mood. But that day, the *gaz* didn't seem to be
having the desired effect. Amir was worried and agitated. He
rested his head on his left hand and scratched his chin nervously
as he talked to me.

I barely had time to get out my notebook and pen before he
launched into an explanation of what he expected would happen with the election: if there was no vote rigging, Mousavi
would win the majority of votes, and the election. But, he explained, that was a very big if.

Amir noted that Ahmadinejad seemed to have been preparing himself for this election—and the potential for defeat—for
a long time, mostly by appointing the right people to key political positions, especially in the Ministry of Interior. For Ahmadinejad, the right people usually meant members of a new,
more inexperienced, and therefore more malleable generation
of the Revolutionary Guards, men who had not fought in the
Iran-Iraq War. "Men who have experienced war will never support this idiot's bellicose rhetoric," Amir said. "War heroes hate
war and know it can only cause mayhem and destruction. It is

this new adventurous and corrupt generation of the Guards who act as the foot soldiers of Mr. Khamenei and support Ahmadinejad's extremism."

The Revolutionary Guards had been continually expanding its power, and redefining itself, since the organization's inception in 1979 as a military force. After Saddam Hussein's army invaded Iran in September 1980, many young men joined the Revolutionary Guards, wanting to defend their country. During the war, the Guards' power expanded into other areas. While the official Iranian army mostly carried out its military duties, the Guards started import-export companies and built industries. After the November 1979 takeover of the American embassy in Tehran, the United States and its allies imposed economic and military sanctions against Iran. The Guards obtained illegal arms from the international arms black market and developed its own engineering organization to rebuild the infrastructure destroyed by the Iraqis. Its leaders started a new front in the regime's war against the West and Israel, by training Hezbollah militia in Lebanon. Under Ruhollah Khomeini, the Guards practically had free rein. By the time the cease-fire between Iran and Iraq was signed in 1988, the Guards had become one of the mightiest institutions in Iran.

Its influence expanded further after Khomeini's death in 1989, when Ali Khamenei replaced him as the supreme leader of Iran and Akbar Hashemi Rafsanjani became president. Rafsanjani believed that Iran had to be economically developed and Iranians prosperous before human rights and freedom of expression could be introduced into Iranian life. In the postwar chaos, many Guards members took advantage of this opportunity. Pushing the competition out through threats, intimidation, and brute force, the Guards' main engineering company, Khatam ol Anbia (the Last Prophet), became Iran's main industrial contractor, receiving many lucrative contracts in the infrastructure, oil, and petrochemical sectors.

After the war, many members of the Guards resigned and started their own import-export companies with branches outside of Iran. They used their connections inside the government to monopolize parts of the market. The corruption of former guardsmen became legendary as they threatened their competitors, avoided customs, and evaded duty taxes.

As the supreme leader, Khamenei chooses and dismisses each and every commander of the Guards. By selecting only people who are extremely loyal to him as commanders of the Guards, Khamenei tried to turn the Guards into his own private army. Yet many commanders resisted becoming slaves of Khamenei's, and while they largely remained loyal to him, they also maintained a good relationship with other prominent members of the regime, such as Rafsanjani and Mohammad Khatami.

This caused a split within the Guards. After many reformists within the regime supported the student riot in 1999, Khamenei ordered the creation of a series of ideological courses, which they called Basirat, or Wisdom, for a selected group of younger members of the Guards. Basirat was more than an indoctrination process; it was also a filtering process for creating the Revolutionary Guards' intelligence unit, which eventually became the country's main intelligence-gathering and security organization.

According to my friend Amir, the Guards' intelligence unit had been instrumental in rigging the 2005 election, when Ahmadinejad became president. It was during the four years of Ahmadinejad's presidency that the Guards had taken over many important economic centers of power in Iran, including the oil industry and the nuclear program. The Guards became Iran's biggest industrialists, owning many front companies under different pretenses and names in Iran and abroad. There had been several reports of current and former members of the Guards setting up companies in Iran, Dubai, and Canada—which, on the surface, had no connection with the Guards—for the purpose of laundering money for the Guards. In order to continue its monopoly over Iran's economy, the Guards needed a friendly government in power. Amir said that Guards leaders were preparing to use every resource at their disposal to get Ahmadinejad reelected.

If elected, Mousavi would not be able to stop the Guards, but a transparent government, which he was promising to create, would no doubt interfere with the Guards' control of Iran's politics and economy.

Amir told me that after the 2005 election, one of the commanders of the Guards had asked that Amir and all his close associates be removed from the Ministry of Interior. "He knew that my team would never accept tampering with people's votes," Amir said. "So they fired all of us."

The current Minister of Interior, Sadegh Mahsouli, took the cake when it came to corruption. A Guards commander in the 1980s, he had forced many people to sell their houses to him at a fraction of what they were worth. He and his Guards buddies then demolished those houses and built high-rises on the properties. Mahsouli had also taken millions of dollars in bribes from Kurdish and Shia Iraqi refugees who were forced, by Saddam Hussein's government, to move to Iran in 1991, during the First Gulf War.

In March 2008, when Mahsouli was appointed minister, I decided to write an article about him, but after a few interviews, Amir warned me that I should be very careful about publishing my findings. "The Guards have become like a mafia," he said at the time, looking me in the eye. "They have taken over the country and can easily eliminate you if they wish."

I remembered Amir's warning from more than a year ago as I watched him now, holding his chin with one hand and tapping nervously on his desk with the other. The sun was shining through the blinds, creating ominous lines on Amir's face; he looked as if he were behind bars. "With Mahsouli in charge of

the elections, I'm beginning to fear that Ahmadinejad has almost guaranteed his reelection," Amir said. "They have done
their best to manipulate the public before the elections, and
now they're frightened that their plans may not work. Mahsouli is exploring different ways to rig the votes."

Although Amir opposed everything Khamenei stood for, he
had several photos of himself and Khamenei on his desk at
home. In one of the photographs, Amir was sitting next to
Khamenei as he lay in a hospital bed.

Once, Amir saw me looking at the pictures.

"I've known Mr. Khamenei for more than forty years," he
said, taking the first photograph in his hand and cleaning the
wooden frame with his index finger. "After the assassination
attempt against him in June 1981, his right hand was paralyzed
and he almost lost his life. Mr. Khamenei was like a brother to
me then, and I visited him all the time in the hospital. You know,
Maziar, he is a cultured man. He's been reading a novel every
week since I've known him. He's a poet and likes traditional
Iranian music. I don't think he was so interested in power when
he was made supreme leader in 1989." Amir paused and picked
up another photo. In it, Khamenei, Amir, and a group of other
Islamic Republic officials were sitting on their knees in a circle
around Ruhollah Khomeini. It didn't look like a government
meeting; it was more like a saint giving an audience to the faithful. "Leadership of the Islamic Republic was a cloak that fit
Imam Khomeini," Amir noted. "It looks too big on Mr. Khamenei. But power is even more addictive than heroin, and Mr.
Khamenei is hooked on it now."

Back in the office, Amir's mobile phone rang. He had to join
Mousavi and a group of his advisers for evening prayers. "Amir
jaan," I said as I stood to leave. "You're telling me Mousavi will
win for sure but they are going to change the results?"

Amir held my hand in his. "The only chance of having a fair
election is if Mr. Khamenei prevents the Ahmadinejad gang and

the Guards' intelligence unit from rigging the votes. All we can do is pray that the supreme leader will make a wise decision."

On my way home that evening, as I passed by murals of Khamenei on walls throughout the city, Amir's words stayed with me. I hoped that Khamenei would consider saving his legitimacy not by helping Ahmadinejad steal the election but by listening to his people. Of course, I highly doubted he would do that. As Amir had said, Khamenei was intoxicated by his power and wanted to expand it by having an obsequious subordinate he could control. And that man was Mahmoud Ahmadinejad.

As I passed yet another group of young men and women dressed in green and holding Mousavi signs, I knew that the people of Iran, silent for so long, had finally found their voice. The question now was: Would Ali Khamenei choose to listen?

CHAPTER THREE

In Iran, the weekend is celebrated on Thursday and Friday, and Friday is called Jom'eh, which means "gathering." On this day, Muslims are supposed to pray together. Many do but many others, if they can afford it, spend the weekend on the shores of the Caspian Sea, about three hundred miles north of Tehran. Others go hiking in the Elburz Mountains, in north Tehran. This is how I spent many of my weekends in Iran, and it was the only way I wanted to spend June 11, the day before the election.

I left my mother's house at four A.M. with a plan to hike into the mountains for as long as I could and then descend by cable car. Every reporter prays for a chance to come across a life-changing story. Reporting the election was mine. I wanted to hike long enough to clear my head and put some distance between myself and politics, in the hope of keeping some perspective.

* * *

The music and fresh mountain air calmed me down. "My baby's going to be born in four months' time," I hummed to myself as I hiked. "In four months' time I will be a father." The idea energized me, and as the sun rose over Tehran, I walked briskly.

By ten A.M., I was hot and winded. I sat down to eat the dates I had packed. All of Tehran was spread out before me. As usual, a dark cloud of smog hung over the city. I poured a little of the tea I had brought and slowly ate my dates. The exhaustion of the last few days had settled in my body, but even so, I believed myself poised on the edge of so much possibility: a better future for my family; for my career; and, I prayed, for my country. I felt invigorated and happy.

After I packed my things and began the walk to the cable car, a sad, old voice, as thick as the smog covering the city, began to croon in my ears. It was Leonard Cohen, singing "Everybody Knows":

Everybody knows that the dice are loaded
Everybody rolls with their fingers crossed
Everybody knows that the war is over
Everybody knows the good guys lost
Everybody knows the fight was fixed

Cohen's words have an unrivaled ability to put a tunnel at the end of the light. While listening to Cohen, I remembered Amir's words. The possibility of Khamenei making a wise decision was quite remote. After all, despots are hardly known for their inclination toward fairness.

When I returned, my mobile phone rang. It was Amir. "Where've you been?" He sounded nervous. "I've been trying to call you all day. Come to my office as quickly as you can."

An hour or so later, when I walked into his office, he immediately put his index finger to his lips, then asked me to sit down. "How is your mother, Maziar?" he asked, taking my mobile phone. He turned it off and removed the battery. It was believed that Iranian security could eavesdrop on your conversations through your phone, even if the power was turned off.

"She's well, thank you," I said, feeling ill at ease as Amir handed me a piece of paper. "I'm so happy to hear that," he said.

The paper was an open letter from Mousavi to Khamenei that would be made public in a few hours. Never before had a presidential candidate written such an irreverent letter to the supreme leader. In it, Mousavi expressed concern that members of the supervisory councils and election observers were acting in favor of Ahmadinejad and that Ministry of Interior officials were creating obstacles for Mousavi's representatives who were supposed to supervise the preparation of ballot boxes and the counting procedures.

Mousavi also complained about the interference of the Revolutionary Guards and the Basij in the electoral process. He said that Ahmadinejad was illegally using government money and government offices for campaign purposes. In his letter, Mousavi also warned the supreme leader that some groups were trying to tamper with people's votes. None of these accusations were new—at least not to the voters—but it was important that a candidate had taken a bold step and was voicing the people's concerns.

"Please be sure to tell your mother that I was asking about her," Amir said, sliding another piece of paper slowly across the desk.

The page contained a phone number and a message: "Call me on this number from a public telephone tomorrow. Don't give it out to anyone. I think we're being watched."

CHAPTER FOUR

All day on Friday, I thought about Amir's warning, but I didn't know what to do. I was sure that the Guards and Ministry of Intelligence agents were watching some reporters, but there was no way for me to know if I was one of them. My father had always said that in a dictatorship, the fear that the rulers want to instill in the people is more important than what they can actually do. "They can't assign a secret agent for every citizen," my father used to say. "But they try their best to make you believe that you're being watched all the time."

I was mindful of Amir's warning but decided to carry on reporting. The day of the election was cooler than normal. Rather than the typical ninety-degree June weather, the temperature hovered in the high seventies. I was happy for the relief from the heat. My body ached from the previous day's hike, and I couldn't bear the idea of spending hours on the back of Davood's motorcycle. I called Mr. Roosta instead. Ershad, the Ministry of Culture, had asked the foreign press to report from one specific polling station, but I had never thought of myself as part of the foreign press. I was an Iranian, so I planned to visit as many polling stations as I could. At ten A.M., as I waited for Mr. Roosta's cab to arrive, I called Amir on the number he had given me. I didn't recognize the voice of the man who answered.

"He's not here."

"Could you tell me at what time he'll be there?" I asked.

"And you are?"

"A friend of his."

"Mr.—?"

I hung up.

I became worried about Amir. I knew that he had been threatened several times by the Guards and that its leaders were trying to find any excuse to put him behind bars. I climbed into Mr. Roosta's car and decided to call Amir later; I had work to do. My first visit was to polling stations in the Qeytariyeh area, in north Tehran, where Mousavi's campaign headquarters was located. Hundreds of people waited in line outside of every venue. I found the same thing at the polling stations in Robat Karim and other southern suburbs. In some places, people had to wait more than two hours for their turn to vote. Many of the people I spoke with were voting for the first time in their lives. They were excited and impatient and passed the time in heated political discussions.

Visitors to Iran are often surprised to find that, unlike in most Middle Eastern dictatorships, there are not that many uniformed policemen or army officers in Iranian cities. That is true until you take out your video camera or try to interview people—then you are surrounded within a few minutes by undercover and uniformed police.

I managed to interview just two or three people at each of the first five polling stations before I was asked to leave by security agents in civilian clothes. They never introduced themselves, but I later learned that they reported to the Ministry of Intelligence. I'd expected that it would be like this throughout the day, so I wasn't surprised when a uniformed policeman hastily dismounting a motorcycle stopped me as I left a polling station on Gisha Street, in west Tehran, where I'd just cast my vote for Mousavi.

Apparently, an undercover agent at the station had called the police.

"Where are you from?" he asked.

From the single-striped badge on his dark green jacket, which he had awkwardly tucked into his trousers, I gathered that he was a second lieutenant in the Tehran police force. Unlike the Revolutionary Guards and the Basij, the police are less indoctrinated, and concerned mostly with matters of general security.

The second lieutenant's thin mustache and stubble were covered with sweat, as if he had rushed to the station in a hurry. I showed him my press card and said I was a reporter and cameraman for *Newsweek* magazine and its website. He called his superior officer on his two-way radio receiver. "Sir, there's a man who interviews people for New Zealand."

"*Newsweek*," I corrected him.

"Shut up!" he yelled, pushing me around and telling me to face the wall. "He is *interviewing* people!" He said the word "interviewing" as if it were a capital crime. "Should I arrest him?"

This was not the first time I had been stopped by a policeman. Usually when it happened, they would call someone from Ershad and I would be let go within minutes or, much more rarely, a few hours. As any journalist in Iran can attest to, 80 percent of your time is spent dealing with officials, and only 20 percent working. I had long ago accepted this reality, so I faced the wall obediently and waited for the verdict.

"I don't know, sir," I heard him say. "He looks Iranian, but he says from New Zealand." He came closer to me. "Hey, you! Do you speak Farsi?"

"Yes, sir. I do," I replied politely. "I'm an Iranian citizen. I just voted."

"Come here, Mr. Colonel wants to talk to you," he said curtly.

"Hello, sir. This is Maziar Bahari from *Newsweek*," I began. "My accreditation was issued by Ershad. I came here to conduct interviews about the election, but I was asked to leave. I was doing exactly that when the officer stopped me."

Mr. Colonel explained that because of security threats, police officers were being more vigilant that day. The colonel then apologized for the inconvenience and asked me to pass the walkie-talkie to the policeman.

"Yes, sir! Should I arrest him, sir?" the second lieutenant asked eagerly. He looked uncomfortable with his boss's reply and turned his back to me. "Yes, sir!" He put the walkie-talkie on his belt, next to his gun, and asked me, "Do you know Mr. Colonel? He sounded angry with me." Then he looked at me apologetically. "I just follow orders. They called and said that you were doing interviews. Sorry to bother you."

"No problem, sir. You're just doing your job," I said. "At least it's a nice cool day for the election. So who will you be voting for?"

He gave me a surprised look. "Now you're interviewing me?!"

"No. I'm just asking. Have you voted already?"

"I think Ahmadinejad."

"You think? You have to vote today. You must've made your mind up already."

"Yeah, I've already voted for Ahmadinejad. They say the other guys are going to stop the subsidies and are going to fire a lot of policemen."

"Who says that?"

"Aghidati-Siasi," he said, referring to the ideological and political bureau. Every base of every branch of the Iranian armed forces, which includes the national army, navy, and air force, the Revolutionary Guards, and the police, has an Aghidati-Siasi office. The office is in charge of religious indoctrination of the armed forces personnel. The supreme leader chooses the director of Aghidati-Siasi, who is expected to act as the leader's eyes and ears in the military. Aghidati-Siasi branch officers are usually junior clerics who give the armed forces officers religious training and make sure that everyone prays and fasts. Aghidati-Siasi also works closely with army intelligence units to spot "undesirable elements" in the military.

"We had a few sessions with Aghidati-Siasi—they talked about different candidates and they told us that Mr. Ahmadinejad is the best candidate." He looked worriedly at my voice recorder and walked toward his motorcycle. "I hope you don't get me into trouble, sir. I can lose my job for talking to you."

After I got into Mr. Roosta's car, I tried Amir again. He answered the phone, but didn't want to stay on too long.

"Don't call me again," he said. "Just come here, to the temporary office, as quickly as you can." The day before he had sounded nervous; now he sounded scared.

The office was in Zaferanieh, an exclusive area in north Tehran. Before reaching the office, I called Alireza at Ahmadinejad's headquarters to see how he was feeling.

"Mr. Ahmadinejad's votes are above twenty million," Alireza told me. "We expect it to go as high as twenty-five million. I'll call you later."

I hung up with a lump of cold fear in the pit of my stomach. There are no exit polls in Iran. At about five P.M., more than four hours remained before the polling stations closed. It didn't make sense that Alireza would know the number so early. Once again I thought of Leonard Cohen's words.

Everybody knows that the boat is leaking
Everybody knows that the captain lied
Everybody got this broken feeling
Like their father or their dog just died

For the first time I began to think that perhaps I should re-sign myself to a different outcome than the one I had been hop-ing for. Perhaps Mousavi was fighting a losing battle. At the temporary office, I rang the buzzer Amir had told me about on the phone: the third one from the top, with the logo of a con-struction company. Someone in a state of fear answered the video intercom.

"Who are you?" he asked, in a direct—and wholly un-Iranian—manner.

"I want to talk to Mr. Amir," I answered.

"Who are you?"

"Maziar Bahari."

"Wait," he directed me. It was a few seconds before he re-turned. "Come in," he instructed. "Wait in the lobby."

The building was a gaudy modern structure with brown marble and golden railings. There was a large brown leather sofa in the lobby. Before I could sit down, the elevator's doors opened. From inside, Amir waved hurriedly for me to join him.

"Did anyone follow you here?" he said, wiping the sweat from his forehead with his white handkerchief.

"I don't think so."

Amir had not pushed the button for any floor. "Okay. Get back in the car and ask your driver to circle the area and come back after ten minutes. I will look from the window to see if anybody's following you."

"What's happening?" I asked as calmly as I could.

"It's a coup d'état, a military takeover by the Revolutionary Guards," Amir said. "Now go."

Amir's words worried me, but more than anything, I was worried about the future of the country. The consequences of the Guards taking over the government were so horrifying that I didn't even want to think about it. I didn't want to envision the claustrophobic society that would create, or the possibility of a military confrontation with another country if the Guards came to power.

I had to invent an excuse to get Mr. Roosta to drive us around the block a few times without arousing his suspicions. As he rolled down the window to ask what was wrong, I told him that I had decided to buy some pastries for my friends. In the car, I kept my eyes trained on the side mirror to see if anyone was following us. There was no one. I had never seen Amir so afraid. What did he mean by a coup d'état? I wondered. Had the reformists seen the results and did they want to take preemptive action and accuse Ahmadinejad supporters of vote rigging? Had Ahmadinejad and the Guards managed to pull off a scam that meant that he had got himself elected four hours before the polls closed?

I could barely concentrate on what I was ordering from the pastry shop. I called a friend of mine. He told me that the Fars News Agency, which was run by the Revolutionary Guards, had just announced—at five-thirty, three and a half hours before the polling stations closed—that Ahmadinejad had won the election with more than twenty million votes.

When we pulled back in front of Amir's building, fifteen minutes later, he was walking out the door with another Mousavi adviser I knew.

I jumped out of the car. "Have you heard about the Fars News report?"

"Yes, we have," the other man said. "That's why we're leaving."

The man got inside his car and started the engine. Amir told me in a hurry, "I'll call you later tonight, Maziar. They have staged a coup. Votes are rigged, ballot boxes are missing around the country, and Ministry of Interior computers have been hacked. We don't know what exactly has happened. But one thing we know is that there's been a coup. We have to go now.

You have to go now. I don't think you were followed. But we have to move. They may raid this office at any time."

Amir got into the car, then rolled down the window. "Mousavi will have a press conference tonight," he said. "Someone will call you in an hour or so." With that, the car sped down the street.

I tried to push aside my feelings about what Amir was saying—my fears about what might be happening in my nation—and do my job.

Like many other journalists, I had planned to spend part of the night, after the polls closed, at the Ministry of Interior, where the votes were being counted. But at eight P.M., when I arrived at the ministry headquarters in Jihad Square, the streets around it were blocked by hundreds of policemen and officers from the anti-riot unit, fully armed with pistols and high-voltage clubs. I got out of Mr. Roosta's car and approached a policeman at a checkpoint in the square. After I showed him my press card, the policeman politely asked me to wait and went to speak to his superior. He came back and apologized, explaining that no journalists from the foreign press were allowed inside.

Unusually for June in Tehran, it suddenly started to rain. The rain made the anti-riot policeman's knee and elbow pads look shiny. I tried to insist that I be allowed in, and had begun explaining that I had reported on elections in Iran in the past and was always allowed into the ministry, when an anti-riot commander approached us. His face was hidden behind a plastic shield, shiny from the rain. He pushed me toward Mr. Roosta's car, then beat its hood with his club.

"*Berin gomshin!*" he yelled at me and Mr. Roosta. "Get lost!" He pointed the club at me. "If you stay one more minute *koonet mizaram, madar jendeh,*" he threatened. "I'll fuck you up the arse, you motherfucker." Angry and upset, and soaking wet from the rain, I got back in the car and told Mr. Roosta to take me to my mother's house. Later, I would be very grateful that I had not pressed the issue. I learned that many protestors were arrested and kept in the basement of the Ministry of Interior that night. They were beaten and raped with clubs by the same anti-riot police who had threatened to sodomize me.

When I arrived at my mother's house, she was sitting quietly in front of the television with her cousin Jafar. They were eating sunflower seeds, and the plate in front of them was stacked with shells.

"Is he going to win again?" my mother asked me sadly, without taking her eyes off the television.

"It seems so," I answered.

Jafar, who was in his seventies and was usually very mild-mannered, shook his head, a look of disgust on his face. "Khamenei would never have allowed Mousavi to get elected," he said. "He doesn't want a president. He wants a servant like Ahmadinejad. Mousavi would be his own man and would stand up to Khamenei. They only allowed Mousavi to run to stir people's emotions and make them show up at the polls so they can say they are a popular regime."

As the presenters on the state television shamelessly praised Khamenei and what they called Iran's "Islamic democracy," a small panel at the top right corner of the screen showed the number of votes for each candidate. Ahmadinejad's numbers were rising dramatically. Mousavi and the other two candidates, Karroubi and Rezaei, were not even shown to be winning in their own places of birth. If these results were true, they were an unprecedented development in Iranian politics.

I couldn't bear to watch. I lay down on my bed and called Paola. I needed to hear her voice and talk about my homecoming, to tell her how much I'd been dreaming about lying beside her and kissing her pregnant belly. But Paola, too, wanted to talk only about the election.

"Is it true?" she asked. "Did he really win?"

"Sadly, yes," I answered. As I tried to tell her about the

events of the day, I was overwhelmed by a feeling of utter exhaustion, and only then did I realize that I had barely slept since landing in Tehran three days earlier. Trying to relive the experience was too much for me. I said good-bye to Paola and called a taxi to take me to Mousavi's press conference.

The press conference was held in an anonymous building off Africa Street. In his public appearances, Mousavi usually seemed far more like a subdued artist than a charismatic politician. But that night, he was a changed man. He acted defiant and confident. The support he had been receiving from millions of Iranians had made him animated and inspiring. As he stood before a room full of almost fifty journalists and cameramen, he explained that he didn't regard the official result as an end to his campaign. "Any result other than one indicating my victory will be wrong and manipulated," Mousavi proclaimed. The reporters in the room, mostly Iranians working for the foreign media, looked at one another with surprise. Even though we were trying our best to remain professional, I know that, like me, most others in the room were rooting for Mousavi.

I had rarely felt more patriotic, or more depressed, than I did that night. I was worried about the future of Iran and angry at the thugs who were going to rule it for, at least, the next four years. It was as if bandits had kidnapped one of my loved ones. But the thought of Mousavi fighting for his votes thrilled me. Maybe he could stop the pro-Ahmadinejad thugs from carrying out their military takeover by mobilizing the people.

* * *

That night, when I got back from the press conference, I turned off my mobile phone and unplugged the landline in my room. I knew I would be receiving dozens of calls, and all I wanted to do was sleep. At nine the next morning, I found that I had thirteen missed calls and four messages from Mousavi's office. His people were eager to get coverage from foreign media, since Iranian state television was not giving them any airtime.

"Mr. Mousavi and his wife, Mrs. Rahnavard, are allowing interviews today, in the *Etela'at* building at two P.M.," one message said. *Etela'at* is a state-controlled newspaper, but its editor was friendly to Mousavi.

In the living room, my mother was reading *Beyhaqi's History*, a book about Iran in the Middle Ages that told the story of Hasanak the Vizier, a competent minister to a king in the eleventh century who was hanged in favor of a useless but ingratiating successor.

"*Rooz az no. Roozi az no,*" she said. "Same kind of day. Same kind of action. This country has been plagued by these *ashghal*, rubbish, rulers for centuries." She looked tired. She laid the book on her lap. "I knew I shouldn't have voted. At least then I could have kept my integrity intact. This way I feel used. It seems like I have voted for this *ashghal* system."

My mother's gloominess set the mood for the rest of my day. Economic hardship, decades of political turbulence, and polluted air have made Iranians a borderline depressed nation. In fact, in the 1990s an adviser to the mayor of Tehran suggested that they add Prozac to Tehran's water to revitalize the citizens. But on the day after Ahmadinejad's reelection, no amount of antidepressants could have helped many Tehranis. The misery in the air was almost unbearable.

From my contacts, I learned that the supreme leader, Khamenei, had called Mousavi on the afternoon of the election and told him that he understood that Ahmadinejad had won. Khamenei asked Mousavi to accept the defeat gracefully, and even promised him a major position in the new administration. Mousavi told Khamenei bluntly that it was too early to decide. "The people have to make a decision. Not you," Mousavi said. He hung up on Khamenei and refused to meet him that day.

A few hours later, Khamenei sent a message to the people of Iran congratulating them on their historic achievement. He called Ahmadinejad's reelection "a divine sign" in support of the Islamic Republic.

Afterward, the Revolutionary Guards received an order directly from Khamenei's office to take preemptive measures to stop the reformists from stirring the public to protest against the election result. Since most Mousavi supporters were communicating primarily through text messaging, the government stopped the service. Mousavi's offices were ransacked that night, and their computers and files confiscated. Prior to the election, the Tehran police had announced that they were preparing themselves for an operation called Eghtedar, the Might. It was nominally meant to guarantee the security of the election but it was, under Khamenei's direction, becoming a means of managing the threat of unrest.

Under the supervision of Khamenei's intelligence adviser, a man named Asghar Hejazi, and Khamenei's second-eldest son, Mojtaba Khamenei, the Guards had compiled a list of reformist activists to be arrested. "Mojtaba Khamenei is worried about who will eventually succeed his father as the supreme leader. So, he is trying his best to prevent someone he cannot control coming to power," a source in the Intelligence Ministry told me at the time. I later learned from intelligence officials that the Guards—in effect Khamenei's private army and answerable to no one but him—had taken over all intelligence and security operations in the country a few weeks before the election. In other words, the Guards were in control of the country.

That day, as I went around Tehran trying to visit my sources, the streets were full of guardsmen, uniformed police officers, and plainclothes security agents carrying walkie-talkies. Basij forces were also on many street corners, watching people's every movement. If a coup d'état means a military takeover, then indeed a coup had been executed by the Revolutionary Guards.

I had my video camera in my rucksack, but with the number of police officers on the streets, I knew it would not be possible to film. I decided, instead, to take shared cabs around the city and talk to the people in the cab with me. I asked each person in the cab about their thoughts and feelings regarding the election, but most people were not interested in talking. Only Ahmadinejad supporters spoke freely—and they were few and far between that day. So I dropped the cab strategy and began eavesdropping on conversations in buses and on the streets. Some young people were discussing the number of votes Ahmadinejad had won in different provinces, expressing their disbelief that he had gained such a majority over Mousavi. Over and over again, I heard many people lament the fact that their vote had been stolen.

When I arrived at the *Etela'at* offices, I saw many friends and colleagues who worked for foreign media waiting outside the building, along with a growing crowd of Mousavi supporters. Mousavi had released a statement on his website saying that he didn't accept the election results. Now it seemed that his supporters wanted to hear it directly from him and show their loyalty. Hundreds of people were being held back by police officers, who had cordoned off the entrance to the building. They were politely asking those of us who showed our press credentials to go home, explaining that there was no press conference and that Mousavi was not inside. We didn't believe the police, and most of us waited in the building's parking lot to see him arrive. As we waited, more people approached the building. The policemen—who seemed uncomfortable with the task of controlling the crowd—became even more nervous. I could hear their commander calling for extra forces. He approached us and asked us to leave the area, this time not so politely.

"All journalists are spies," the commander said. "If you don't move from here in the next five minutes, we'll put all of

you in the truck and take you to Evin." The mere mention of
Evin, the most notorious prison in Iran, where many political
prisoners were held, sent chills down our spines, and we left
immediately.

A couple of blocks away, I called Davood to see if he was
free to drive me around the city. I had received a few calls from
friends, telling me about clashes they were witnessing between
young people and the Basij and the Guards, and I wanted to
investigate this myself. But Davood did not answer his phone.

I decided instead to take a taxi to Mousavi's headquarters in
Vali Asr Square. Clearly, I was not the only person who'd had
this idea. Outside of the headquarters, hundreds of people were
gathered, and here, too, they were being held back by the
anti-riot police and the Guards, who were blocking the pavement leading to the headquarters and turning away anyone
who approached. I pushed my way through the crowd toward
an officer and shouted to him that I needed to get to a shop on
the other side. He shouted back at me to move on, but just as I
began to pull away, a plainclothes officer came from behind me
and kicked me hard in the back. He then pushed me toward the
line of anti-riot police. I fell onto one of the officers, who in-
stantly kicked me and struck my arm with his club.

"*Gomsho, madar ghahbeh,*" he yelled. "Get lost, motherfucker."

Stunned by the pain in my back and arm, I was somehow
able to keep my wits about me. I was not a reporter anymore; I
was part of the people. Holding my throbbing arm, I glanced
quickly around me. The policemen were holding high-voltage
clubs rather than their traditional batons. I knew then that they
had foreseen that there would be chaos following the election,
and had come prepared. My thoughts turned to the video camera in my bag. If they were to find it, they would arrest me on
the spot. I walked away swiftly with my head down, weaving

through the crowd as if I were just an ordinary pedestrian caught in the chaos.

I later learned that the police had been given clear orders to disperse all gatherings close to Mousavi's office or the Ministry of Interior building, a ten-minute walk away. They didn't want people sharing information or potentially plotting some sort of retaliation, and so they reacted violently as soon as they saw more than two people talking. As I quickened my pace, I glanced back at the crowd to see a number of policemen striking people's legs and backs with their clubs.

I was watching this atrocious spectacle from the far side of the street when suddenly an anti-riot policeman charged toward me and the other bystanders. "What are you looking at, *ha-roomzadeha,* you bastards?" the officer barked, as he and others thrust their plastic shields into the crowd and lashed out with their clubs. I wanted to get a better look at the officers, but their faces were blurred behind their thick plastic anti-riot panels. I stood for a moment in stunned disbelief before I was quickly jolted back to reality with a shove from the crowd. A wave of people began to run away from Mousavi's headquarters. I ran too, swept along in the crowd, and as we bolted, people shouted out to one another about where to go. Shops and offices along the street opened their doors to passing men and women searching for a place to hide. I suppose that we had all suspected that the police would stop some demonstrators, but no one had anticipated this level of violence.

As I ran, I saw two mothers who were trapped by the crowd and desperately holding on to their children. No matter which way they turned, there was a wall of people, and the police were approaching fast. The mothers cried out to the crowd for help. An old man with a Muslim prayer cap and white stubble on his face was standing at the door of a nearby building. On hearing the cries, he pushed his way through the crowd and reached out to both women. He took them by their arms and began pulling them toward his building. One of the mothers, with a chubby face and the big dark eyes of a Persian miniature, nodded her head again and again in a gesture of thanks to the old man as she ushered first all the children and then the other mother into the building before quickly stepping in herself. The old man shut the door just as the anti-riot policemen lunged toward them. With the door slammed in their faces, the policemen retaliated by kicking the metal and slamming it with their clubs. The man refused to open the door. The rest of the crowd, which had until that moment remained passive toward the police, grew suddenly wild with indignation.

"Velesh kon, velesh kon!" they chanted. "Leave him alone!" They began to throw anything they could get their hands on at the officers. Stones and tree branches were hurled, and the officers, realizing that they were outnumbered, ran away. The crowd cheered, but only momentarily. Almost immediately, out of nowhere, dozens of policemen on black motorbikes roared to the scene from the north side of the street. When the motorcycles stopped, no one knew what the officers were going to do. Suddenly five or six officers got off their bikes, took out bulky black guns, and simultaneously fired tear gas into the crowd. Some tear-gas canisters exploded in the air and some released the chemicals as they hit the ground. It took most people a few moments to understand what had hit them. Everyone rushed to escape, but there was no way out.

As we were trapped from the north and the south, we tried to find another way out. Luckily, I had gone to school in the area and knew the streets quite well. On one occasion back then my friends and I fought with, and had to escape from, a group of Basijis in the very same streets. As the Guards charged toward the crowd from the south and the policemen from the north, I darted down a side street I had taken shelter in twenty-five years earlier, and I kept running until I was out of breath.

I stopped near a medic who was tending to a sixteen-year-old boy. His brother kept on calling his name: "Reza, Reza *joon.*" Reza was semiconscious, and his blue short-sleeved shirt was drenched in blood. His brother, Maysam, was standing nearby, throwing the books he had been holding in the direction of the riot police.

"Khaar kos deh ha, madar jendeh ha!" he yelled, his voice brimming with anger. "Sisterfuckers, motherfuckers!" These are the worst insults in Iran, but enraged by the sight of his brother covered with blood, Maysam didn't seem to care.

I ran up to Maysam and asked what had happened. He told me that he and Reza were coming back from language school when the riot police attacked them without provocation, striking them with clubs. When Reza fell on the ground, a plainclothes intelligence officer kicked him in the head. The medic, an older man with stubble on his chin, looked pained as he tended to Reza's wounds. I asked the medic if he needed any help. When he glanced up at me, I saw that he was on the verge of tears.

"I didn't know this is what they wanted to do. I didn't know," he said. When I asked him what he meant, he told me that he worked for Iran's Red Crescent organization—the Muslim version of the Red Cross. He and his colleagues had each been called at home the night before and had been told to be ready for a showdown.

I said good-bye and kept walking until I found a man on a motorcycle who agreed to take me to my mother's house. As we bounced over the rocky streets, I felt a sharp pain in my back, and noticed that my right arm where I'd been hit with the club had gone numb.

*   *   *

As soon as I got home, I swallowed a few painkillers, hoping that my arm was not fractured. The government had issued a ban on reporting about any postelection demonstrations, and I knew that many reporters would be afraid to disobey the ban. But I felt differently. Given my knowledge of Iran, my contacts in the government, and my sources in the foreign media, I was in a unique position to report on the disputed election and the chaos that followed.

I wanted to talk to Paola, but I was afraid to call her; I didn't want her to hear the pain or fear in my voice. I was also anxious about what I knew I was going to have to tell her eventually: that I wouldn't be coming home in a few days, as we had planned. If things were going to get violent, I had to stay and report on them. Unlike many stories I had covered in the past, I cared very deeply, on a personal level, about this one. A voice inside me, maybe my father's or Maryam's, was urging me to stay and witness what would be the result of the turmoil that had taken over our country.

I was relieved to find my mother asleep in her bedroom. I had Reza's blood on my shirt, and I didn't want her to see it. I quietly closed the door, washed my shirt, and turned the television on. Khamenei's picture filled the screen. A narrator was reading his letter to Ahmadinejad on the occasion of his victory. "Enemies may want to spoil the sweetness of this event with some kind of ill-intentioned provocations," the voice said over different close-ups of Khamenei's solemn face.

I hit Mute and watched in silence as images of the triumphant Ahmadinejad and self-satisfied Khamenei saturated the airwaves. I brought my laptop to the living room and began a story for *Newsweek*. "If an electoral fraud, tantamount to a coup, has indeed happened, most people believe that it was staged with Khamenei's blessing," I wrote.

That evening, the Ministry of Interior released the final count: Ahmadinejad had received 24,592,793 votes, and Mousavi 13,338,121. The votes for the other two candidates were negligible. If these numbers were taken as accurate, only two conclusions could be drawn: either all the surveys by different government agencies in the run-up to the election had been wrong, or Iranians as a people are so unpredictable that no survey or poll can predict their voting patterns. Alternatively, and this was my feeling given my conversations with Amir and what I'd witnessed on the street that day, something else was at play: under Khamenei's command, the Guards had helped officials at the Ministry of Interior rig the votes and reelect Ahmadinejad. Ahmadinejad was the only candidate who guaranteed that the interests of the supreme leader and the Guards were protected. I suspected that Khamenei had supported rigging the election so flagrantly to prove that he was the one in charge and no one could do anything about it. The sporadic clashes around the country over the next two days suggested that I was not alone in thinking that.

*   *   *

The next day, Sunday, June 14, Ahmadinejad held a press conference in the office of the president, on Pasteur Street in south Tehran. In the large white room with its decorative varnished wood panels, I sat among the dozens of Iranian and foreign journalists, taking notes and concentrating on remaining professional, even as I felt the anger inside me growing. The newly reelected president spent the first part of the press conference boasting about his win. When reporters asked about allegations of vote rigging, he barely batted an eye: Mousavi supporters "are like a football team that has lost a game but keeps on insisting that it has won," he said. He flashed a malicious smile and added, "You've lost. Why don't you accept it?"

Ahmadinejad's handlers carefully chose the reporters who were allowed to ask questions. Except for a few journalists, most of them wasted time by lobbing the same questions about the future of Iran's nuclear program. Ahmadinejad had been asked that question several times in the past and had a perfectly

formulated answer: Iran wants nuclear energy for peaceful purposes and because it is our inalienable right. I was so angry with
the many journalists who didn't dare confront him about what
was on all our minds: the election result and the postelection
protests. Finally, the interpreter asked Max Rodenbeck of *The
Economist* to come forward.

"Mr. President, you accused the foreign press of a slander-
ous campaign against Iran, and, in fact, we see with our eyes
and we hear with our ears—and I think there are hundreds of
us here now—and what we have seen is an election whose results millions of Iranians do not believe in. Why hasn't the full
count of the election been revealed? Do you think that this
could damage the legitimacy of your own government, of the
Islamic Republic, as well as the prestige of the supreme leader?"

I later learned that Max was chosen because Ahmadinejad's
people thought that a reporter from *The Economist* would ask
a question about the economy. The president stared at Max for
a long time before answering. "Where did you hear that the
people do not accept the vote count? Have you been in touch
with forty million people? You see the few people you like to
see. That is your mistake. You give these reports to your peoples
and your governments, and you are misleading them, too."

He then invited Max, as well as the rest of the reporters in
the room, to join him at a rally afterward. There were hundreds
of thousands of Ahmadinejad supporters in Vali Asr Square
when the other journalists and I arrived there about an hour
later. Many of them carried pictures of Ruhollah Khomeini and
Ali Khamenei. A few people carried pictures of Mousavi with a
large X painted over his face.

Ahmadinejad took the stage like a rock star. Surrounded by
his bodyguards, he congratulated the people for electing him
and spoke of his honest campaign. As his supporters started to
tear the pictures of Mousavi and the other candidates from the

walls around the square, Ahmadinejad claimed that unlike his competitors, who were the representatives of the wealthy and powerful, he was the president of poor and ordinary Iranians.

He repeated his football analogy and said that the supporters of the losing team were trying to change the results. "But it doesn't matter what a bunch of *khas o khashak*"—dust and dirt—"are doing," he said. "The pure tides of this nation will eventually get rid of them."

Ahmadinejad's speech added insult to the Mousavi supporters' injury. People could accept a defeat, but not humiliation. Everywhere, afterward, people talked about Ahmadinejad's use of the phrase *khas o khashak*. Mousavi had asked his followers to avoid any confrontation with the security forces and to reject the use of violence, and up to this point, most people had restrained their anger. But that was changing fast. Calling millions of citizens "dust and dirt" was the last straw.

Young people all around Tehran started to clash with the police and the Basij. The police exhibited no restraint in attacking protestors and passersby alike. As the people became more frustrated, the police and the Guards became more organized. The anti-riot units had orders to leave no space for Mousavi supporters to move in the city. They took over the pavement and beat up anyone who didn't get out of their way.

I went around the city by motorcycle and taxi, and when there was no way to get through the traffic, I walked. The city was quickly sinking into bedlam. Gangs of anti-riot police on motorcycles roamed the streets, menacing drivers and stopping traffic seemingly at random. A driver on Beheshti Avenue honked his horn in protest when policemen on motorcycles blocked his way. Within an instant, three or four cops got off their bikes and smashed the car's windows with their clubs. They seemed to have a personal grudge against side mirrors and didn't stop hitting the car until both mirrors fell to the ground. The driver put

his hands on his head and ducked down, but one of the policemen dragged him out of the car and to the pavement, where
another officer started slapping him.

"What are you looking at?" a policeman asked me as he
pushed my face away with his hand. I didn't see his face; all I
could see were his black leather gloves with the tips of the fingers cut off and a shiny fortified plastic elbow cap strapped on
top of his black uniform. "Nothing, nothing," I said, striding
away as fast as I could.

As I walked wearily along Vali Asr Avenue that evening, I
saw four or five officers beating an old woman with a club because she'd protested that they were blocking the entrance to
her house. The woman collapsed with the first blow. Her black
head scarf fell to her shoulders. As I saw the club hitting the
woman's backside, I felt her pain in my body as well. It was the
same kind of electric instrument I'd been hit with the day before. Watching this scene but unable to act, I felt like a coward.
I had my video camera in my rucksack, but I was afraid to take
it out. I was afraid to help the woman because I didn't want to
risk arrest and imprisonment. I felt as if my feet were pinned to
the ground. I wanted to beat the attackers off, but there were
too many of them for me to be able to help her. As I was debat-
ing what to do, the beating ended. As soon as the Guards moved
away, I and a couple of other men helped her into her house.

"Khamenei will pay for this. He will pay for this," she said,
crying gently.

Feeling utterly helpless, I went back home. At nine P.M., I sat
down weakly in front of the television. Ahmadinejad's victory
speech and Khamenei's message congratulating him were playing on a repeating loop. The extent to which this government
was willing to publicly humiliate its people was revolting.

Before long, my phone rang. It was Davood. He said that he
and his buddies had been drinking since the election results. "I
feel much better now. We spent the evening fighting the local

Basij members," he told me. "We staged our own revolution here last night." He agreed to pick me up around eleven P.M. and take me to his neighborhood.

That night, the streets in Poonak were covered with rubbish and the plastic rubbish bins were on fire. "Welcome to Palestine," Davood said. I watched a group of young people attack a local Basij base—an anonymous-looking office building—with sticks and stones. *"Basiji bia biroon,"* they yelled to the Basij members, daring them to come out.

Davood introduced me to his friends in the crowd. They told me that the night before, ten people wearing green had smashed the windows of neighborhood shops. "They had covered their faces so no one would recognize them," one young man said. "They wanted to blame it on the greens, but when we searched them, three of them had Basij cards on them."

As I listened to these stories and watched Davood and his friends throw rocks and pieces of a destroyed railing at the base, I was speechless. How had we got here? These were the same kids who had demonstrated peacefully in the days leading up to the election, who had gone to vote peacefully on Friday. Now, all their dreams were shattered.

Davood told me that they were not sure whether anyone was in the building but they were happy to throw stones at it anyway, just to let off steam. Davood could see that I was uncomfortable. He put his head close to mine and screamed over the noise: "What do you want me to do, Mr. Maziar? They've kicked me out of school. I'm unemployed. What can I do?" When he pulled back, he had tears in his eyes. I had no answer for him. "I'm going to buy a gun tomorrow," he told me. "We'll show them what we're capable of."

During the annual hajj, Muslims' pilgrimage to Mecca, pilgrims throw stones at a pillar that represents Satan. Like those pilgrims, the young people in Poonak were throwing stones at the Basij, who, for them, symbolized the evil in the country. I began to wonder when this kind of symbolic attack would turn into real attacks against Basij members, not only with tree branches and stones but with guns and Molotov cocktails.

When I got home, I tried to find out what was going on in different parts of the country by contacting some of my friends on Facebook. Despite the government's effort to block Facebook, many Iranians used Freegate, a filter buster developed by Chinese dissidents to circumvent government censors; they used Facebook and Twitter to communicate with the outside world and with one another. In fact, Iran had the largest community of bloggers outside of the United States and China. There were more blogs in Persian than in any other language except English. The Iranian government's long-standing monopoly on information was being challenged not only on the streets but also in cyberspace.

By this time, Facebook was the most reliable source of information. There were reports of sporadic demonstrations all around the country, but it seemed that the police had succeeded in intimidating ordinary people in most cities and preventing them from taking to the streets. The police warnings had no effect on university students, however. Students in many dormitories around the country staged pro-Mousavi demonstrations and clashed with the police. In some instances, the police ransacked the dormitories and arrested a number of students. From different postings on Facebook, I learned that the worst atrocities that night were committed in the men's dormitory of Tehran University. Police had apparently been called by campus security after a group of students were heard chanting anti-Ahmadinejad slogans. After the police and Basij units entered the dormitory, security closed the gates so that no one could get out. Every student from the dorm—whether he had taken part in the demonstrations or not—was dragged out of his room. Outside the dorm, the anti-riot police piled them together and beat them with clubs. Many were kicked until they became unconscious. In some cases, the anti-riot police sodomized the students with clubs. At least seven students were killed.

That night, I heard the sound of chaos in my dreams; but before I woke up, it was Amir's voice that echoed around me: "All we can do is pray that the supreme leader will make a wise decision." Power blinds, and I feared that Khamenei's blindness could only mean disaster for my country and my people.

CHAPTER FIVE

I woke up the next morning to a disturbing email from a friend of Amir's:

"He has been arrested. Call me."

On the phone, the friend told me that Amir had been arrested that morning, along with dozens of pro-Mousavi politicians, including former ministers and vice presidents. The news of the arrests had gone viral.

"Should I be worried about myself?" I asked.

"Not now. Just be careful," he answered.

That morning, I tried to reach my friends and sources within the government. Nobody was answering the phone. Everyone had suddenly gone silent.

I had asked Davood to pick me up at nine A.M. to take me to a few appointments and then the demonstration planned for four P.M. on Revolution Avenue. Reacting to Ahmadinejad's speech after his victory, when he'd called his opponents a bunch of dust and dirt, Mousavi supporters had named their protest the Dust and Dirt demonstration. Word of the gathering had got around through Internet sites and was reported on satellite television. But Davood was uncharacteristically late, and not answering his phone. He called me at nine-thirty.

"Where the hell are you?" I asked angrily.

"Come to the corner of Motahari and Vali Asr," he said.

"What do you mean?"

"Mr. Maziar, just come to the corner. I will wait for you there."

The instructions were so strange that I began to grow worried. I remembered Davood telling me about the men in Peugeots he had seen waiting on my mother's street. Her apartment was on a dead end, so there was not much traffic. I could easily spot strangers if they were waiting for me outside. I went to the rooftop before leaving the house and looked down. There were three Peugeots parked along the street, but that was not particularly unusual—even though Peugeots are the government's cars of choice, ordinary people drive them as well. A few people came out of an office down the block. Nothing looked suspicious. I was late for my appointments and angry with Davood. I walked ten minutes to the corner he'd indicated and spotted him sitting on his bike.

"What's going on?" I asked.

"There were a couple of people waiting at the end of your street, Mr. Maziar."

"Yes, because there are offices on our street."

"But these two looked really suspicious. I just know they were from the intelligence service."

I was getting fed up with Davood's erratic behavior. As I climbed onto the bike behind him and he began to drive, I noticed that he smelled of sweat and alcohol and that his hair was messy.

"Have you been drinking?" I asked him.

"Just a little bit, Mr. Maziar," Davood said remorsefully. "I can't sleep at night. We had another fight with the Basijis after you left."

"Bezan kenar," I ordered him. "Stop here."

He pulled over. "Sorry, Davood, I can't let you drive if you drink like this. Go get some rest today, and if you're clean and sober tomorrow morning, call me." I took another motorcycle to see some friends and contacts, then went back to my mother's house.

There, my mother had just finished preparing fish and *torshi tareh,* a light vegetarian stew with rice. She had a mysterious ability to know what food I was in the mood for. When I needed energy, she would prepare *fesenjoon,* a chicken or duck stew with walnuts and pomegranate sauce, or *morgheh torsh,* a chicken dish with unripe grapes and split peas. On a day like this, when I was in a hurry and had to have a light meal, she would prepare *torshi tareh* or *mirza ghasemi,* scrambled eggs with tomatoes and eggplant.

As we ate, she told me that at the local market that morning, she'd heard that many people had decided to take part in the Dust and Dirt demonstration. "People are planning to come to the streets to take back their votes. I wish I could join them. If I were even ten years younger, I would," she said, as I savored every spoonful of my *torshi tareh.* "But I'm worried that, with my back pain, I won't be able to escape if the Guards attack the protestors." My mother was speaking from experience. She had taken part in many demonstrations in her youth and knew how suddenly and unexpectedly violence could break out.

"Do you think these *ashghals* will just sit on their hands and tolerate people protesting against them?" my mother asked as I made Turkish coffee for her and myself.

Years of seeing her country brutalized by one government after another had taught my mother to expect the worst. She was not expecting Khamenei and his regime to act rationally. "When it comes to the tyrannical leaders of this country, none of them has been able to see beyond the tip of his nose. They just want to rule and pillage the country for as long as they can without thinking about the consequences for the people or themselves."

"Yes, you may be right, but what about legitimacy?" I asked.

"Don't you think Khamenei wants to stay in power as a legitimate leader?"

My mother—perhaps surprised by my naïveté—turned away and drew my attention to the news program on the television. Throughout the day, the state radio and television stations had been warning potential demonstrators that the Ministry of Interior had not issued a permit for any demonstrations. They emphasized that the security forces would punish the demonstrators as harshly as possible in accordance with the law.

"Legitimacy?!" my mother exclaimed with disdain. "Do you think they even care what people think?" She turned off the television, threw the remote to a corner of a couch, and joined me in clearing the table. "Just be careful when you go out."

*   *   *

I was very curious to see how many people were going to turn up at the Dust and Dirt demonstration, and how the government would respond. My guess was that, at best, a few thousand Mousavi supporters would take to the streets, the security forces would beat them up, and most people would go home. Mousavi would eventually accept defeat and return to his government job as the director of the Academy of Arts.

I couldn't have been more wrong.

I arrived at the demonstration at about four-thirty. The scene reminded me of the demonstrations against the shah I'd witnessed in November 1978, when I was eleven. Today, there were at least two million people, most of them in their teens and twenties, preparing to march along the same route from Revolution Square to Freedom Square. I struck up a conversation with Ahmad, a fifty-four-year-old academic. "We walk along this route because it has taken us a long time to reach freedom since the revolution," Ahmad said. He had taken part in the 1978 march as well. "I see many similarities between what hap-

pened then and now. In both cases, we had a clear mandate.
Then we wanted to overthrow the shah. Today we want this
little man"—Ahmadinejad—"who has stolen our votes to re-
sign and accept the people's votes."

There were so many bystanders, it was almost impossible
to move through the crowd. Knowing that they were being
watched by people around the world, many of the demonstrators carried banners in both Persian and English. *"Khas o khashak toei, doshmaneh Iran toei!"* they had written. "You are
dust and dirt, you are the enemy of Iran." And: "Where is my
vote?"

I was amazed, as we began to march, by the silence of the
demonstrators. There was no chanting, no angry words—just
a peaceful ribbon of green flags, bandannas, wristbands, and
scarves moving from Revolution Square toward Freedom
Square with an air of quiet and calm. As we marched, the sea
of green grew larger and stronger, and the security forces lining
the street looked on with surprise at the mounting number of
people. As usual, I had a video camera with me, an old Sony
PD 100 I had not used for many years. I hesitated to take it
out. I didn't want it to be confiscated, and I certainly didn't
want to be arrested. As I watched the crowd of thousands filling Revolution and Freedom Avenues, though, I felt energized.
Worriedly, I pulled the video camera from my bag and held it
in the air, doing my best to get shots of the crowd. I spotted
many familiar faces: colleagues, friends, and acquaintances
who had come to the demonstration alone or with their families. In defiance of the government's decree that journalists
should not report on the demonstrations, there were also a fair
number of Iranian and foreign journalists in the crowd. I also
saw many of the young filmmakers with whom I had worked
over the past few years.

Despite the growing numbers and the strength of the demonstration, the protestors tried to avoid any confrontation with

the security forces. They smiled at the police officers and waved flowers at the police helicopters that hovered over the crowd. From the looks on the faces of some officers we passed along the way, it was obvious that many would have loved to join us.

Even with the sporadic violent clashes of the day before, many people still hoped for peace. Many protestors, especially the young men and women who had endured years of having their hair shorn by the Basij or who had been beaten for not appearing Islamic enough, would have loved to have thrown stones and taken over the Basij buildings. But they contained themselves. Many people believed that a compromise was still possible. They wanted the government to either re-count the votes or hold another election. The general feeling among people was that if the government listened to their voices, they would be willing to exonerate it for many of its injustices in the past and start anew.

The Basijis, on the other hand—normally so rash and confrontational—were clearly intimidated by the sheer size of the crowd. Whenever the protestors passed by the Basij compounds on Freedom Avenue, I spotted Basij members peering at the crowd through the curtains. Despite the demonstrators' determination to keep the peace, you could feel the tension in the air.

Whenever the demonstrators passed by murals or posters of the supreme leader, they raised their green symbols or their fists to prove to him that they were a force to be reckoned with. A middle-aged man near me summarized it best when he told his young daughter, "If Khamenei had a brain in his skull, he would think about his own survival and listen to the people."

When I filmed the march from an overpass on Freedom Avenue, I could see that the horizon had become green. All afternoon, I'd felt buoyed by the peaceful nature of the demonstration, but soon after I arrived in Freedom Square, I noticed smoke billowing into the sky a few blocks north. Then I heard the sound of gunfire. Having worked as a war reporter, I immediately wanted to run toward the shots. Hundreds of others had the same idea.

I filmed as I moved through the crowd, holding the camera above my head. Several youths were attacking a two-story building in a narrow street a block north of Freedom Square. It was a residential street, and the buildings that lined it all looked the same. When I got closer, I realized that they were attacking a Basij base.

Basijis in anti-riot gear fired tear gas at the crowd, and I saw Basij members on the rooftop of the base firing warning shots into the air. They were trapped in the building, surrounded by youths who were pelting them with Molotov cocktails. I later learned from several intelligence officials that an opposition group, the MKO, had most likely organized the attack on the Basij. The MKO (Mujahideen Khalq Organization) is a cultlike Marxist-Islamist group that has been based in Iraq for the past three decades; its goal is to get rid of the Iranian regime. Its sympathizers had acted as agents provocateurs among the protestors, inciting violence; they continued to do so throughout the day. I kept filming as the MKO members and young people instigated by the MKO eventually brought down the fence around the Basij base. Before long, the Basijis stopped firing warning shots and began shooting indiscriminately into the crowd of protestors. The two Basijis on the roof did not seem to care if the people they were shooting at were attackers or passersby. Many peaceful demonstrators in the crowd panicked and started to throw stones at the compound.

The Basij responded by shooting at the young men who'd jumped over the fallen fence and were running toward the building. One man in his early twenties was shot as he tried to leap over the fence. The sharp ends of the collapsed fence looked like the tridents used by gladiators in ancient Rome. The boy's slim body dropped onto the fence as soon as the bullet entered his body. He went into cardiac arrest and slowly rolled over onto the ground. I recorded the young man's climb and fall. Horrified to have filmed a man's death, I couldn't move until the Basijis started to spray bullets in my direction. Then I went behind a wall and held the camera outside, looking at the scene through the monitor. Another young man was shot in the head while trying to kick down the door of the base. People raised his body and took it toward the main street. *"Mikosham an keh baradaram kosht,"* they chanted, their voices filled with rage. "I kill those who killed my brother."

Some young men in the crowd stopped attacking the base and carried the boy's body to the hospital at the end of the street, a block away from where the peaceful main demonstration was still under way. But they understood that their efforts were futile. He was already dead. As I filmed the men carrying the body with my video camera raised in the air, I felt paralyzed, utterly helpless. My country was on fire, and all I could do was film.

As the Basij started to spread bullets into the crowd, as people scrambled to take cover, as bloodied people ran out of the street, and as MKO supporters started to chant, "Death to the Islamic Republic," I continued to film.

"Hush. Be quiet! Change the slogan! *Allahu akbar!* God is great!" screamed a couple of older men trying to get the crowd out of the street. "We haven't come here to say, 'Death to the Islamic Republic.'"

"We're here to support Mousavi," said another woman. "Not fight!"

A small group of young men approached a few of the older men who were trying to calm people down. *"Khafeh shin madar saga!"* one said, throwing punches at an older man. "Shut up, you sons of bitches!" The crowd erupted into a brawl.

"Death to Khamenei!" cried a teenager as he joined the others hitting the older men. I turned my camera toward him.

"Nagir! Nagir! Don't film!" He grabbed at my video cam-

era, but I shoved it under my arm and quickly sidestepped away from him. With my back against the wall of a building, I slid my body away from the crowd. An older couple blocked others from getting at me, helping me escape.

"Get out as soon as you can," an old woman told me.

When I broke free from the crowd, I ran as fast and as far as I could and hailed the first motorcycle I saw. I wanted to edit the footage immediately, to show the world what was happening in Tehran. I knew that I had the only professionally filmed footage of the Basij shooting.

I told the motorcycle driver to take me to the Laleh Hotel, in the city center, where I knew Lindsey Hilsum, a reporter for Channel 4 News, was staying. Within a few hours, my film, which was credited to an anonymous source, was broadcast on Channel 4 News, and then on most of the important news programs in the world.

Later that night, one of my sources in the Ministry of Intelligence told me that in the end, seven people were killed during the demonstration in front of the Basij base.

"Do you think it's safe for me to write about the attack on the Basij?" I asked him.

"Everyone knows that you filmed the attack," he said. "The Basijis were filming you filming it."

Nervous that the Basij had its eye on me, I decided that the best course of action would be to mention publicly that I had filmed the Basij attack. Up to that date, my footage was the most incriminating documentation of Basij violence against Iranian citizens. I knew that the authorities would not be happy with my footage and that they would question me about how I'd managed to record it. I didn't want it to look surreptitious and wanted to be able to answer that I'd simply filmed what had happened in front of me, the way I had always done in the past.

Later that night, I wrote an article for the *Newsweek* website expressing my fears and hopes for the future. "Mousavi's supporters are planning to stage another peaceful protest tomorrow," I wrote. "Tonight, it is difficult to predict what that will bring, or what the end result of the cycle of demonstrations will be."

* * *

Amir was released the next day and called me soon after. When I went to see him, he told me that he'd been among a group of pro-Mousavi politicians who had been rounded up and taken to Evin Prison for two days. "We were warned that if we don't calm the situation, we will be responsible for whatever might happen to us," said Amir. According to him, Mousavi was quite upset about the attack but he was not going to let the terrorists hijack the green movement—which was how the support for Mousavi was becoming known. Mousavi had decided to tell his supporters to take to the streets one more time and avoid any confrontation with the police and the Guards that could provoke further violence.

When I told Amir what I had witnessed the day before, he made a confession that surprised me.

"Maziar *jaan*," he said with melancholy in his voice, "I never told you this, but I always had my doubts about Mousavi's abilities as a leader. But today . . . he is a changed man. I was with him an hour ago, and I could see that he has finally realized what an important role he can play in the history of this country. He has finally become what people wanted him to be: a strong leader with a clear vision about what he wants to achieve."

After the demonstrations had begun, Amir said, Khamenei's secretary, Vahid, had contacted Mousavi to organize a meeting between the two men.

"Let's re-count the votes; then we'll talk," Mousavi had responded. He'd told Vahid to tell his master not to call him again, unless he had something new to say.

*　*　*

The peaceful demonstrations continued for three days without further intervention by terrorist groups. During those days I was very proud of my people. Iranians were going to achieve something rare in a Muslim country. Hitherto, mass movements in Muslim countries had been either in support of fundamentalist groups or in favor of Western models of democracy. But the people of Iran were choosing a third way. The goal of the green movement was to establish an indigenous Iranian democracy, one that at its helm could have religious men, such as Mousavi, but would still respect human rights, freedom of expression, and women's rights.

Millions of people took to the streets over those three days. As the crowds grew in confidence and size, the regime became more and more paranoid. When I tried to call a friend four days after the election to find out more about Mousavi's plans, mobile and Internet communications had been cut. The government had shut down wireless communications between two and nine P.M., from an hour before until an hour after the demonstrations, to stop people from telling one another where the protests would be or any news about them. By doing so, the government was disrupting its own activities as well and was losing millions of dollars every hour. But it was a price Khamenei was willing to pay to cut down the size of the demonstrations.

On the morning of Tuesday, June 16, I received a fax from Ershad, the Ministry of Culture; it had been sent to all Iranian and foreign reporters. Ershad asked all of us to stop reporting on the demonstrations and warned that continuing to do so would result in punishment. The fax didn't specify the kind of punishment, but we all guessed that it could be annulment of our press cards or temporary detention. I immediately went to a friend's office to make backups of my tapes.

A few minutes after I started to digitize the tapes, an Ershad official I was friendly with called and asked me to visit him. At our meeting, he told me that I should be careful about what I was reporting. Apparently, the day after the election, the Revolutionary Guards had summoned Ershad officials and told them "to put a leash on foreign media" or they would be fired from their jobs and arrested. Knowing that I was the one who'd filmed it, the Ershad official told me that the Guards had complained about the footage of the attack against the Basij base. A chill went down my spine. As my friend spoke, he paced restlessly around his office. I'd never seen him so worried.

In order to calm him, I read him a few passages from my latest *Newsweek* article, "Who's Behind Tehran's Violence?," which had been posted on the magazine's website the night before. In the article I blamed terrorist groups for using people's peaceful demonstrations to incite violence. I'd quoted one of the demonstrators as saying, "I think some small terrorist groups and criminal gangs are taking advantage of the situation. Thirty years after the revolution and twenty years after the war, the majority of Iranians despise violence and terror. My worry is that if the government doesn't allow reforms to take place, we will fall into a terrorism abyss like the years after the revolution."

My friend played with his green worry beads as I translated the article for him. I told him that I had nothing to hide and that I had even mentioned that I'd filmed the attack in the article. I assured him that by this time in my career, I'd grown accustomed to criticism from all sides. Usually, the Islamic government and different opposition groups criticized my films and articles for remaining neutral; they would prefer that I take sides.

My friend stared at a heap of foreign magazines and news-papers. "Maziar *jaan,* we all know that you are fair in your re-porting," he told me. "That is why the extremists don't like you."

*   *   *

Listen!
The shadows are stepping by . . .
We must flee.

These lines from the poem "The Wind Will Carry Us," by the modern Persian poet Forough Farrokhzad, ran through my mind again and again as I lay in bed that night. Since my fa-ther's death, I had been using his study as my bedroom, and I could hear his voice each time I entered his room. I was sur-rounded by my father's books and his souvenirs from countries around the world. But that night it wasn't my father's voice I was hearing. It was my sister's, Maryam's.

Don't you see?
Our roof is shaking in fear of collapse,
and over this roof, an immense dark cloud,
like a dull, grieving crowd,
is expecting the moment of cry.

On Thursday, I woke at four A.M. and decided to go back to the mountains, to clear my head. Before I left, I sent an email to Maryam's son, Khaled, who had been living in Australia since 2008, to tell him about the news I had received from Ershad and the Revolutionary Guards' displeasure with the footage I had shot. A few years ago, I had given Khaled a list of friends to contact in case anything happened to me, thinking it best to take some precautions, and I wanted to update it.

When I arrived at the base of the mountain, I called Paola in

London. She was surprised by my poetic mood when I recited the original Persian and then the English translation of the rest of Forough's lines to her.

Listen!
The shadows are stepping by . . .
We must flee.

Paola knew the poem because we had watched an Iranian film inspired by Forough's words. "This is beautiful, Mazi, but . . ." She paused. "It's ominous. Have you booked your ticket to London?"

"Not yet. I'll do it when we hang up." But on some level, I knew I had to stay on and bear witness to history.

You,
O green like the soul of the leaves,
Leave your lips to the stroke of mine,
And savor them like swell flavor of an old wine.

If we forget
The wind will take us away,
The wind will take us away.

*   *   *

Later, alone in the mountains, I found my thoughts turning again to Maryam. As I began the slow ascent, I remembered the last time we had hiked this path.

In 2007, not long after our brother, Babak, died, I'd taken Maryam to these mountains. She was not athletic and had had a hard time keeping up.

"I'm running out of breath, Mazi *joon*. I can't do this anymore," she'd said after just half an hour climbing the steep hills.

"Come on," I'd replied. "Just a few more minutes. Otherwise, you're not going to burn any fat." Now I regretted having said this.

I couldn't shake the idea that she was beside me. I was sixteen when Maryam was arrested, and for so many nights afterward, I'd lain alone in my room, cursing the people who had taken my sister away.

During the six years of her imprisonment, my parents worried every day about what might happen to her. Many of my father's prison buddies' children were also in the Islamic government's jails, and I often overheard the conversation among these old men, and their futile attempts to understand the vicious circle of history.

Maryam's husband, Mohammad, was released in 1988, and Maryam a year later. Both had suffered months of solitary confinement and endured many sessions of torture. Even though they did not support the regime, they remained patriotic and were committed to helping their country in any way they could. They even named their daughter Iran, a name modern parents rarely choose.

These thoughts of Maryam stayed with me, and it was only after I had taken the cable car down the mountain that I once again felt a part of what was happening in Tehran that day. I pulled out my phone, and saw that I had five missed calls from Mohammad.

"Khaled told me about what happened in Ershad yesterday," he said. "Can you get a ticket to leave for London tonight? It's not safe for you here."

I went home as quickly as I could, spurred on by the anxiousness in his voice. He knew far too well what the Iranian government was capable of. Mohammad had been like a brother to me since he and Maryam had married; in many ways, he was closer to me than my own brother, who had spent most of his adult life in the United States. Mohammad was just as worried about me as Maryam would have been.

Yet as much as I wanted to be back in London with Paola, as Mohammad had urged, I felt I couldn't leave. The biggest question had yet to be answered: What was Khamenei going to do? It had been announced that the supreme leader was going to lead the public prayers at Tehran University on Friday. Typically, Friday prayers are led by a rotating roster of imams from throughout Iran, chosen by the supreme leader. Their job is mostly to relay his message every week, and, except for a very few of them, they act as the leader's propaganda agents: speaking about the domestic and international issues of the day and advising people of the importance of following Khamenei's guidance. When Khamenei delivers the sermons himself, making a rare public appearance, it means there is something very important at stake.

Even though Khamenei had supported Ahmadinejad's re-election and had asked other candidates to refrain from opposing him, that didn't stop many people, myself included, from dreaming that Khamenei would find the courage to call for a recount.

I knew that Mohammad had a point, and that it was time for me to take the threats seriously. At the same time, I felt I could put these events in the proper context. I felt I had a responsibility to stay.

"Fine," Mohammad had said. "But don't sleep where they can find you."

That night I stayed at a friend's house.

CHAPTER SIX

The next day, Friday, June 19, turned out to be one of the most important days in Iran's modern history. I arrived at the Tehran University campus at ten-thirty A.M. for Friday prayers. The ceremony was scheduled to begin at one, but when I walked up to the campus gates, they were already closed. Officials from Beite Rahbari, the Leader's Office, as Khamenei's institution is called, were prohibiting reporters from entering. I was directed to a security office on the campus, where we would be allowed to view a televised version of the speech.

Khamenei's speech that day was the most important of his reign and would determine the path Iran was going to take: toward militarization and a more closed authoritarian state or toward a quasi-Islamic democracy. The fact that one man's words could determine the results of an election meant that Iran had already significantly moved toward a more totalitarian state. But that day, as I sat with a group of journalists, including my *Newsweek* colleague Babak Dehghanpisheh and Marie Colvin, from the *Sunday Times*, I knew we were all quietly hoping that Khamenei would make a wise decision—and the right one for the country.

How quickly we were proved wrong. Khamenei began his speech by blaming the Western media for instigating the unrest in Iran after the elections. He warned Mousavi and his supporters that if they continued their demonstrations, they would be responsible for the consequences of their actions. "If the political elite ignore the law, or cut off their noses to spite the face, whether they want or not, they will be responsible for the bloodshed, violence, and chaos that will follow," Khamenei said.

The room was utterly silent as we tried to absorb Khamenei's words. His threat that those who demonstrated would pay for their actions in essence granted the Guards great freedom to use violence. It felt as if a dark cloud had descended on the room. I was crestfallen, knowing that the result would not be overturned. I wanted to blame someone. But who? Khamenei? Or the people who called him their master?

I knew then that it was time to listen to the fears I'd been doing my best to ignore and make plans to leave Iran as soon as possible.

*   *   *

The next day, life in Tehran seemed to be returning to normal. Mobile phones were working again, people were going about their daily lives, shops were open, and the markets were busy. But as I strolled the city streets, preparing myself to return to London, I could sense an undercurrent of tension. It seemed as if people could speak to one another about nothing other than the election and, especially, about Khamenei's Friday sermon and what that meant for the demonstration planned for today. The fact that the demonstration was going to occur, despite Khamenei's warnings, made us feel as if the supreme leader had lost his legitimacy. He was just another tyrant, and at least some thirteen million Iranians, those who had voted for Mousavi, had said no to tyranny. I knew that later that day, I would witness many tragic scenes.

As I exited the house that morning, a local graphic designer I knew ran up to me and asked me to help him fill out his Canadian immigration form. Like many middle-class Iranians since the revolution, he had decided to leave the country. The insecurity of life in Iran was too much for him to bear. "This is not a place to live anymore," he said. "I've decided to sell my business and go to Canada." When I asked him what he was planning to do in Canada, he didn't have an answer. "I don't care about myself anymore. I'll go and clean the floors there. All I care about now is the future of my children."

As we talked on the pavement, I noticed that convoys of armored riot-control trucks with water cannons and crowd-control barriers were moving toward us, headed for the intersection of Revolution and Freedom Avenues, where the day's demonstration was scheduled to take place. The convoy of vehicles was followed by thousands of guardsmen and anti-riot police wearing black helmets and riding black motorcycles. Everyone on the pavement stopped and stared at this menacing scene.

"I hope they suffocate in those helmets," my friend said.

After lunch with my mother, I prepared to leave for the demonstration. I could see the worry in my mother's eyes, and knew that she didn't want me to go out. But we both understood that nothing could stop me from witnessing and reporting the events that could determine the future of the country. A few minutes before I left, Davood called me.

"I imagine you'll be going to the demonstration. Do you want a ride?"

I hadn't heard from Davood since reprimanding him a few days earlier. I asked him if he was sober, and he said that ever since I had got angry with him, he'd been channeling his anger at Ahmadinejad's reelection into playing football. "I'll bring my ball with me so you know that I'm not lying!" he said.

When I went out to meet Davood, he had, in fact, brought his football. "See, I'm an athlete. Not a drunk anymore," he announced proudly before hugging me. "I told myself hell's going to break loose today and I want to be with Mr. Maziar before he gets arrested."

"Well, thanks for your kindness," I said. "Now stop horsing around with that ball and get your arse on the motorcycle."

Davood gave me an army salute. "At your service, sir!"

Along Freedom and Revolution Avenues, we saw Basij members posted on every street corner. Many of them were government employees who didn't look that enthusiastic about their current posts. Most Basijis are essentially reservists; not much is asked of them, and they enjoy little perks for being in the force, such as extra rations for essential goods. The Basij members of every government office were told by the commander of the Basij that they had to guard a designated corner or they would be fired from their jobs. Revolution Square, the supposed center of the protest, was saturated with guardsmen and their water cannons. Still, their show of force was not keeping people away. Unlike on the previous days, demonstrators didn't assemble in the main streets; rather, they gathered in the side streets off Revolution and Freedom Avenues. The side streets became so full that people gradually started to walk around Revolution Square. As the crowd around the square grew from dozens to hundreds, the presence of so many citizens seemed to surprise the military forces. They had underestimated people's resolve to fight for their rights.

Even though the demonstrators were just walking around without chanting or carrying signs, the guardsmen looked intimidated and soon started to beat and arrest whoever had a green scarf or wristband. Soon after, the police started to fire tear-gas canisters into the crowds in the side streets, and motorcycle convoys of guardsmen dressed fully in black barged into the crowds, wielding black electric batons. People knew that if they stayed together in large groups, the guardsmen would not be able to arrest all of them. The guardsmen also stayed together, attacking and retreating as quickly as they could in order not to get overwhelmed by the crowd. I saw a boy caught on his own by guardsmen. They immediately ganged up on him, cuffed him, and took him away. There were hundreds of black prison trucks along the main roads.

Given the warnings I'd received from Ershad, I knew it was too risky to write anything about the demonstration or film it with my camera. However, I could always film with my mobile phone and send the images to media outlets, with instructions not to use my byline. I got off Davood's motorcycle near Freedom Avenue and started to record scenes of the police trying to disperse the crowd with tear gas, and people burning rubbish cans.

I stayed with a group of protestors, filming them chanting, "Death to Khamenei"—a crime that in theory can put someone on death row. A tear-gas container hit the ground right next to Davood and me. My eyes immediately began to burn with pain, and I shook my face, trying to wave air toward my eyes. I had learned, during the 1979 revolution, that rinsing your eyes with water makes the tear gas sting even more, but before I had a chance to tell this to Davood, he poured bottled water onto his eyes. He screamed in pain, and as I tried to calm him down, I knew that I had to drag him away from this scene immediately. Guardsmen were beginning to charge on the crowd, swinging their clubs.

I jumped on the front of Davood's motorcycle. I'd driven a motorcycle through the streets of Tehran many times when I was a kid, but it had been a long time ago. I drove away from the demonstration as fast as I could, until I reached Islamic Republic Avenue. Behind me, Davood was still wailing. I pulled up at the office of a friend. He agreed to send my footage to Channel 4 News as soon as he could.

After Davood's eyes felt better, we returned to the area near Freedom Avenue. There were no longer many protestors, just swarms of police officers. The protestors hadn't gone home, however—they had dispersed throughout the city. Groups of young people were hiding in side streets, looking for any op-

portunity to attack the military. Afraid of getting into one-on-one
fights with the youths, the guardsmen and the police stuck together, and attacked isolated protestors in groups.

When we turned from Freedom Street onto Imam's Legacy
Highway, neither of us was ready for what we saw. About thirty
guardsmen were being off-loaded from five armored vehicles.
They blocked the traffic and cornered a group of men and
women of different ages who were chanting "*Mijangim, mim-
irim, zellat nemipazirim*": We fight, we die, but we don't accept
humiliation. The guardsmen took out their electric batons and
started to beat the demonstrators viciously. I had never seen
anything even close to the anger the Guards displayed at that
moment. Everyone who was stuck in traffic at the intersection
was clearly disturbed by the violence. People started to voice
their objections quietly to one another; then they began to shout
in protest. They cursed the guardsmen and the government and
honked their horns. The guardsmen turned toward the stalled
traffic, and a few of them fired their guns in the air to disperse
the crowd. They yelled at the drivers to turn around, but police
officers had put up barriers blocking the surrounding streets.
There was nowhere to go.

Next to us, a man in a white hatchback honked his horn. In
the seat beside him, his wife gestured toward a guardsman
standing nearby.

"*Agha mariz darim,*" she told him. "We have a patient in
here, sir." I didn't get a chance to see if there was anyone in the
backseat before three guardsmen surrounded the car and began
to attack it with their clubs. Two of them beat on the hood of
the car while the other broke the windshield, then jumped onto
the hood and, through the broken windshield, kicked the man's
face with his military boot. He then cleared the shards from the
frame with his club and yanked the unconscious driver out
through the open frame. Still holding the man's hair in his hand,
the guardsman jumped off the hood. As he was dragging the

driver's bent and bloodied body out of the car, another guardsman jumped onto the hood and started to kick the man's wife
through the windshield.

"*Khafeh sho zanikeh!*" he yelled repeatedly. "Shut up, you
woman!"

When the traffic started to move again, we were forced to
drive away. Still the guardsman continued to kick the woman.
The last sentence I heard from him was "*Daseto bendaz!*" These
were the words that would stay with me for months afterward.
The guardsman was demanding that the woman put down her
hands—that she not touch him because it was un-Islamic for a
woman to touch a man who was not her husband, father, or
brother. As he beat this helpless, innocent woman, he was careful to adhere to the rules of his religion.

Witnessing the beating of the couple was the last straw. I felt
dizzy and couldn't even stand on my feet. I asked Davood to
take me home. The voice of the guardsman beating up the
woman, telling her, "Put down your hands," echoed in my
head. In the past few days I had learned that nothing can tire
you out more than helplessness. There was nothing I could have
done to help the woman getting beaten by the guardsman, but
I couldn't stop remembering her screams, and it drained the
energy from my body. I had to get rid of the voices.

At home, I turned on my computer and checked my emails,
only to find dozens of reports about a killing that had happened
earlier that day. An innocent bystander, a woman named Neda
Agha-Soltan, had been killed by a Basij member. It was not clear
whether Neda had been killed intentionally or if her death was
a tragic accident; Neda could have been any one of the thousands of Iranians who'd tried to peacefully express their anger
at Ahmadinejad's false reelection. Neda's innocent face bloodied by a thug became the iconic image of the brutal suppression
of the Iranian people by their own government.

Watching her dying in front of a video camera reminded me

of all the tragic scenes I had witnessed during the past few days. I couldn't take it anymore. I yelled, *"KHODAA, CHERAA?"* Why, God? I grabbed the bottle of Johnnie Walker and poured a glass for myself—then another glass and another one, until I was nearly drunk. I went to see my mother in her room, thinking she might be awake. Ever since Maryam's death, she'd had trouble sleeping. I found her crying in silence, hiding her face in her hands. I held her in my arms. I didn't want to calm her. I wanted to understand what we had been going through and why. But I didn't speak. I knew there was no answer. As my mother quietly hummed Maryam's name, I saw the images of all the women whose abuse I had witnessed that day. I held my mother tighter in my arms, her heart beating like a captured bird.

The tragedy that was engulfing our lives was unbearable. I kissed Moloojoon good night and sat in front of my laptop, looking at Facebook, hoping to distract myself, and saw that someone had posted a link from the *Time* magazine website, showing a series of photographs of pregnant women who'd painted their bellies. There was one with a teddy bear on it and another one with an underwater scene and an octopus. The photographs made me smile. I had to share them with Paola. I had to see her.

I called her to tell her that I'd made a decision: I'd come home in a day or two, be with her for a week, and then possibly return to Tehran for a few more days to follow the news. She didn't answer the phone. Instead of leaving a message, I emailed her the link to the photographs. "I'll see you very soon," I wrote.

The Johnnie Walker had gone to my head. I walked quietly to my room, lay down on my bed, and before I knew it, I was fast asleep.

Part II

NEITHER DEPARTED
NOR GONE

CHAPTER SEVEN

Sunday, June 21, 2009

Rosewater's knock came before eight the next morning.

When he and the three other men arrived, they told my mother that they had a letter for me. She went to open the door, and they pushed their way in.

As they stood over me while I lay in bed, trying to cover myself with the sheets, I felt confused but was somehow able to pull my thoughts together enough to ask them if they had an arrest warrant. Rosewater fished some papers from the jacket pocket of his cheap brown suit, which seemed to be a size too small for him. He kept his fat thumb covering the information on the bottom of the page, where the reason for the arrest was written, but I could see that the warrant was signed by Tehran's prosecutor general, Judge Saeed Mortazavi.

This was terrible news. Mortazavi was notorious for arresting people first and coming up with ridiculous, trumped-up charges afterward. Having single-handedly shut down more than sixty newspapers, Mortazavi was called the "executioner of the press" in Iran. He'd even once closed down a newspaper for promoting moral corruption after it had published a photograph of an old man dancing in a park. My father used to say that the most dangerous animal was the donkey, because of its stupidity and unpredictability. "The only thing more dangerous than a donkey is a donkey with a grudge against you," he'd add. "That makes him even more unpredictable. You never know when he's going to start kicking you." Mortazavi's unpredictability instilled fear in me. I always tried to keep away from him.

After they allowed me to dress, the men were back in my room: Rosewater and a man who was clean-shaven, which was surprising. Many Muslim scholars dictate that men shouldn't shave their beards, and most Iranian agents have beards, or at least stubble. I sat on the bed, watching them. I could sense their frustration as they took stock of everything. They went through the boxes of my books and films, thinking, I supposed, that I might have hidden something illegal in them. Maybe an AK-47 assault rifle, maybe eavesdropping equipment. Unfortunately for them, I had nothing incriminating in my mother's house. Rosewater pulled a DVD—Pier Paolo Pasolini's 1968 film *Teorema*—from the pile. On its cover was a profile of the actress Silvana Mangano, naked and covering her right breast with one hand.

"Is this porno?" Rosewater asked.

"No, it's an Italian art film."

"Confiscate it," he said to the clean-shaven man, who placed it in a separate pile on the floor. A lanky man with a long face and a beard made a list of everything in that pile.

"Why do you have so many films?" Rosewater asked, with what seemed like, for at least a moment, genuine curiosity.

"I've had a great interest in films since childhood," I answered. He gave me a harsh look and continued to search the closets. He didn't know it, but he was also looking through my father's belongings. One of the closets in the room was full of my father's files, books, and photographs. In the mid-1970s, my father had collapsed in Vienna, during a business trip, and been hospitalized for two weeks. He had kept all of his medical files, which were written in German. Rosewater was leafing through a box of them. He held up a letter dated 1976. "What is this?"

"I don't know."

"This is your room. How come you don't know what it is?"

"It is my late father's."

"God bless him," Rosewater and the clean-shaven man solemnly said at the same time. They put their heads down as if they were going to recite a *fatiha*, the Muslim prayer for the dead. When he looked up, he examined the paper again. "Tell me, what does it say?"

"I don't read German, so I don't know what it is."

"This is not German!" he said. "It is English! Take this," he instructed his partner. The search of my room continued like this for a long time.

"What is this?" He was holding a *Sopranos* box set. "Are these pornos?"

I remembered my father telling me about a prison guard he'd encountered who thought every foreign word with the "sh" sound meant hashish, including "Chicago" and "champagne." Maybe Rosewater believed anything that included the letters *p*, *o*, and *r* meant pornography.

"No, not porno," I said. "*Sopranos*—it's a television series about the Mafia."

The arrest crew seemed to be obsessed with pornography. They would ask me many times over the next three hours if I had porn. If nothing else, I thought, they were looking to charge me with possessing pornography, a crime for which you can serve a prison sentence or be flogged seventy-four times. I didn't have any pornography, but, I realized, I did have a few bottles of vodka in the refrigerator.

In 1983, not long after Maryam was arrested for her membership in the Tudeh Party, the Revolutionary Guards had raided our home and arrested my parents. The Guards had become suspicious of some friends of theirs who were members of the Tudeh Party, so they were arresting and questioning people close to them. I hid in my bedroom while they searched our house. When I finally found the courage to walk into the living room, I saw several bottles of my father's vodka lined up along one wall. They did not charge my father for political activities, but he was fined for having alcohol in the house.

Rosewater stepped out of the room for a few minutes. I was silently hoping they would not look in our refrigerator when the clean-shaven man interrupted my thoughts.

"Who is Soheila?" he asked me. He was holding a DVD marked "Soheila" that I had left in my DVD player. It was a recording of an eight-hour interview I had conducted with an Iranian madam. I said Soheila was a cousin of mine and it was the video of her wedding.

"So, it's a family video?" he asked. He put the DVD back where he'd found it and moved to another corner of the room.

"What are these?"

"Old French books." My father's uncle had studied in France in the 1930s, and I had been given a lot of his books.

"What about this?"

"Let me see," I said. He showed me a book called *Lancer du Javelot;* the cover showed an Olympic athlete throwing a javelin. I explained to him that it was a book about the sport.

"I don't think so," said Rosewater, coming back to the room. "Confiscate them!"

They were suspicious of anything they didn't know, and they didn't know much about most of the things they found in my room. Khamenei's paranoia, and his belief that everyone was conspiring against him, had permeated his system, including the men who were willing to risk their lives for him. I could see it in Rosewater's eyes. I'd always thought that there was nothing more frightening in someone in charge of your life than paranoia, and as I watched Rosewater clumsily rifle through my belongings, I understood that I could be one of the countless innocent people I'd known or heard about who'd suddenly disappeared, their bodies later found in a ditch. Drops of sweat slid down my sides.

I sat in silence watching him, and slowly realized that just as I was not prepared for him, he was not prepared for me, or for what he was finding here. This would become very symbolic of the whole ordeal I would go through. The Revolutionary Guards mainly arrested religious reformists—people who practiced Islam but also believed in democracy, and who challenged Khamenei's authoritarian interpretation of Islam. The Guards knew how to make sense of those people. But now, here I was, with my copy of the Koran next to a statue of Min, the Egyptian god of fertility, with his erect penis and flail, next to French books from the 1930s, a Vietnamese musical instrument, and box sets of an HBO series.

He found my passport and turned to a page stamped with a Cambodian visa. Paola and I had vacationed there a few months earlier. It was there that she'd found out she was pregnant.

"Where is this from? Is this Hebrew?"

"It's from Cambodia."

"Are you sure? I think it's Israeli."

"No, sir," I said, doing my best to sound as respectful as possible, hoping that this would help the whole ordeal end more quickly. "It says 'Cambodia' on it, so yes, I am sure."

He dropped the passport on the floor and took a step closer to me. "Don't answer me like that ever again. Just say yes or no."

"Well, I'm just telling you: it says 'Cambodia.'"

"Just say yes or no," he repeated angrily. I noticed the sweat on his forehead.

As much as I was trying to act as if I were not worried, inside, I was growing increasingly anxious. I wanted to have a conversation with these men: to tell them that whatever it was they were looking for, they had the wrong person. In my conversations with Iranian officials, I always tried to help them understand that the Iranian government was, in fact, lucky that I was working for the Western media. I knew my job. I knew my country. And I was a patriot. If they stopped me, I could be replaced by someone with an ax to grind against the regime. But as I watched Rosewater leafing angrily through my father's medical records, I knew there was no point in trying to reason with him. How can you reason with a man who sees the word "Cambodia" and thinks it's Hebrew?

"We should have brought a van," the clean-shaven man said. "We'll need to get all of this stuff back." He motioned to the growing pile beside him: all the things they were confiscating from me. DVDs. VHS tapes. Laptop computers. Several video and still cameras.

I had to go to the bathroom. When I asked Rosewater if I could have a moment to do this, he said yes. I locked the door behind me; immediately, someone began banging on it.

"Do not lock the door!" he yelled.

I opened the door. It was one of the men who had been waiting in the living room. "I have to use the bathroom," I said.

"I know. But keep it open."

"Can I close it a little?"

"Yes," he said, smiling at me. "But don't try to escape, because then I will have to come and chase you." The youngest member of the arrest team, he was tall and lanky and had a kind face. I thought of Kafka's character Josef K., from *The Trial*, getting arrested by men he thought were pulling a practical joke. I half-expected my interrogators to break down in childlike laughter, and explain the story behind this prank.

When I came out of the bathroom, my mother was speaking to Rosewater in the kitchen. He was sweating very heavily, the shirt under his arms dark with circles of sweat.

My mother had obviously noticed this as well. "Do you want a Kleenex?"

"No, no, no. Thank you very much."

My mother looked pointedly at his shirt and scoffed, "I think you should take it."

Rosewater suddenly seemed embarrassed. "Okay, thank you. I will take a Kleenex." He accepted the tissue from my mother and wiped the sweat from his forehead, but he kept his eyes trained on me. It was the look of a hunter, as if he wanted to kill me with a poison dart.

When they were finished, they told me I was to come with them.

"Where are you taking him?" my mother asked. She tried to hide the concern in her voice, but I heard it all too well.

"Don't worry," Rosewater said, smiling at her. "He is going to be our guest."

I hugged my mother and kissed both of her cheeks. I had no idea what they had in mind for me—they'd refused to tell my mother or me what I was being accused of. *It's fine,* I thought. *They need to make a big show of this. Intimidate me at my home, take me to their base. Question me for a few hours and let me go later today or, at worst, within a few days. Make an example of me for other reporters and filmmakers.* I was quite sure that while many political activists and reformists like Amir had been arrested, no journalists had been detained since the election, and certainly not anyone who worked for the foreign media.

"It's okay, Moloojoon," I gently told my mother. "This will be over soon. It's all a misunderstanding. I will be home soon."

As the men escorted me toward the door, I hoped I was telling her the truth. As soon as my mother closed the door behind us, they handcuffed me.

CHAPTER EIGHT

There were four Peugeots outside the house. Rosewater got into one, where a driver was waiting. I got into another with the man who'd written up the inventory and the young one who'd wanted to prevent my escape from the bathroom. The clean-shaven man got into the driver's seat. I noticed two women, fully clad in chadors, waiting outside one of the cars. One of them was carrying a machine gun. Because of the Revolutionary Guards' warning to Ershad a few days before my arrest, I had guessed that my captors were from that organization. When I saw the women, I became almost certain of it, as the Guards employs women to deal with the female family members of the people they come to arrest. My back stuck to the hot vinyl of the seat, and the handcuffs felt tight around my wrists. The man next to me, the young one with the kind face, noticed it and adjusted them. I looked out the window.

"What do you think you are looking at?! Don't look outside!" Rosewater's car had pulled up next to us, and he was yelling from the passenger seat, his large, dark face almost purple with anger. I turned my head away, wondering where one is supposed to look while inside a car, if not outside. I kept my eyes trained on my lap.

The car eventually turned north onto the Kurdistan Highway, and that was when I knew: they were taking me to Evin

Prison. Sitting at the bottom of the Elburz Mountains, in north Tehran, the prison was built in the late 1960s as a high-security detention center for political prisoners. It gained notoriety in the early 1970s when a number of members of Marxist and Islamist guerrilla groups were jailed, tortured, and executed there. Throughout the 1970s, there were rumors about the atrocities committed in Evin, and stories of Israeli and CIA officers helping Iranian agents interrogate and torture prisoners: pulling out their nails, administering electric shocks to their testicles, and raping the females.

Evin's notoriety as a prison grew after the 1979 revolution, when thousands of political prisoners were detained there and a new warden, Assadollah Lajevardi, was put in charge. Lajevardi embodied the Islamic regime in its nascent stage: he was ideological and brutal. As a political prisoner under the shah, he had himself experienced torture and imprisonment. He knew when torture worked and when it failed to break people. I had once interviewed a former Islamic guerrilla who later became a government minister. The problem with the shah's secret police, he'd said, was that they thought they could break a prisoner's will through physical pressure. But that often just hardened the victim's resolve. "What our brothers after the revolution have masterminded," he said with a grin, "is how to break a man's soul without using much violence against his body."

Evin is officially run by the judicial branch of the Islamic government. Separate wards in the complex are reserved for different intelligence and security branches: the police, the Ministry of Intelligence, the Revolutionary Guards. I wondered if I would be taken to the ward for prisoners of the Guards.

"Where are we going?" I asked the man with the kind smile.

"Why do you ask?"

"No reason—I just like to know where I'm going. Are we going to Evin?"

"We may be going to Evin, we may not be."

This was a typical response for an Iranian official: keep everything secret and make you insecure in every situation. A few minutes later, the driver looked into the rearview mirror and nodded to the man next to me. "Okay," my captor said, handing me a blindfold. "Take your glasses off and put your head down."

I did as I was told. I pulled the blindfold over my eyes and put my head in his bony lap. And with that, the sunshine disappeared.

*   *   *

After about ten minutes, I heard the man in the driver's seat speak to someone on his mobile phone, laughing.

"You need to get yourself a better mobile phone, so that my number appears. That way, you'll stop asking me who I am every time I call, Seyyed." *Seyyed* refers to descendants of the Prophet, but I would later realize that everyone who worked in Evin was called Seyyed, as a means of hiding their identity: Cook Seyyed, Fat Seyyed, Haircut Seyyed, and so on. I heard the sound of large gates creaking open, and the car moved forward again.

I was still wearing the blindfold when they led me out of the car. Someone guided me to a room and made me sit in a chair. I waited there for several minutes, until I was moved again to another room, where I was allowed to remove the blindfold. A man handed me a gray prison uniform and a pair of white plastic slippers.

"Put these on," another man directed me.

I stood alone in the room, wondering if I needed to remove my T-shirt and underwear. I decided to keep them on—my familiar Sunspel T-shirt and boxer shorts reminded me of my time with Paola in London, and I felt safer in them.

I was led to another room, where a man stood behind a camera set atop a tripod.

"Look at the camera."

The flash snapped, and the man's face remained etched in my eyes for a few moments. I remembered being very young and playing badminton with my sister outside. I'd look too long at the sun and then at Maryam, and then close my eyes. The silhouette of Maryam's face and her long, dark hair would appear behind my closed eyes, as if they had been branded there by a hot spit.

That photographer's face would be the last face I would see for many days.

One man put my blindfold back on, and I was handed to another prison guard, a man with an Azerbaijani accent. "Welcome to Abu Ghraib, Guantánamo, or whatever you Americans build."

"*Ghardash,*" I said, referring to him as "brother." "I am not an American. I am Iranian."

"Yes, but you are working for them, so you are one of them," he said, confident that he knew everything he needed to know about me.

I wondered what my father would say to this man. My father had been a master of communication, no matter the circumstance. I could hear him now: "Talk to him, Mazi *jaan*. You will be in his hands for the foreseeable future. Talk to him." I wanted to, but I didn't know what to say. Before I had a chance to think of something, I was led down a darkened corridor. The sound of a steel door closing behind me echoed in the hallway.

"Give me back the blindfold," the guard said to me. The door to my cell had two slots: a small square along the top and a wider one below. I handed the blindfold to him through the top slot.

Granted the privilege of sight once again, I looked around my cell. It was small: maybe twelve feet by five. There were two light fixtures attached to the ceiling, only one of which was working, and a small window on one wall, near the ceiling. The only things in the room were a copy of the Koran and a blanket. No toilet and no bed. I sat down on the floor and took everything in. At Concordia University, in Montreal, where I'd received my degree in communications and film, I had taken a course in communication analysis. One of our assignments was to analyze different spaces: to get a feel for the emotions they conjured. This one was impenetrable. The walls, which were covered in sheets of faux marble, felt as if they were made of cement blocks. Everything was dusty. The dirty carpet on which I sat was made of three different patches of green, laid together clumsily. The cell very much reminded me of how the Iranian government tries to portray itself: strong, enclosed, dominating.

I noticed something written on the wall of the cell. My captors had kept my eyeglasses, so I had to stand up and walk close to read it. There were three sentences, two in Persian and one in Arabic.

My God, I repent.
My God, have mercy on me.
Please, God, help me.

I sat back down on the floor, closed my eyes, and whispered these words to myself. I was petrified.

* * *

I must have fallen asleep, and when I woke up, noticing the spiderwebs on the ceiling, I thought of Zahra Kazemi, an Iranian-Canadian photographer. Zahra, who was known to her friends as Ziba, was an ambitious, dedicated journalist. One day, she called me to discuss story ideas and the difficulties of reporting in Iran. I advised her to be careful while working in Iran, no matter what the story: you never knew what would upset the authorities.

A few days after our conversation, Ziba was arrested while

taking pictures of families of prisoners waiting outside Evin. From what I heard later, the head of Evin security, a man named Elias, came out and tried to take her camera. When she refused to hand it over, he punched her in the head. Elias was wearing an Aqiq Yamani stone ring on his finger, a type of ring the Prophet Mohammad advised Muslims to wear to protect themselves from potential dangers. The force of the ring against Ziba's head fractured her skull. She fell to the ground and her head hit the pavement. According to the person who told me the story, Elias did not intend to kill her. But after they dragged her into the prison, they did not get her medical attention, and she soon died of internal bleeding.

Judge Mortazavi—the man who had signed my arrest warrant—declared that Ziba was a spy and that her death was the result of a stroke. Mortazavi was later accused of being personally responsible for Ziba's death by repeatedly kicking her in the head inside the prison when she objected to her arrest. Her body was buried under tight security. Elias was never tried and, as far as everyone knew, he still worked in Evin. To this day, no one has been held responsible for the murder.

I paced the length and width of my cell thinking about Ziba's tragic death, knowing that the man in charge of her case could be the one handling my case. I continued to pace: Six steps long. Two and a half steps wide. Six steps forward. Six steps back. Six steps forward. Six steps back. I started to count. I had almost got to one thousand when the top slot on the door opened. A man reached in, holding the blindfold.

"Put this on," he said. "Your specialist wants to see you now."

*   *   *

Strangely, my main worry at that moment was the thought of getting an eye infection. *What if others have worn this blindfold?* I thought as I fingered the threadbare black velvet. I wanted to wash it, but there wasn't a sink in my room.

"What are you waiting for?" the guard asked impatiently. I could see part of his face through the slot. His eyes were a deep blue. "Put it on."

I slipped it over my head.

"No, no. It's upside down. Put it on the other way." I began to pull it off. "Do not look at me! Turn around and face the wall. Face the wall! Don't you know how to put on a blindfold?"

"No, I don't," I said. "I don't have a lot of experience with them. This is my first time in prison."

That wasn't entirely true. In 1984, when I was seventeen, I was arrested and imprisoned for the crime of disturbing the public morality. My girlfriend, Anita, and I were in a café, drinking tea together. It is, of course, illegal in the Islamic Republic for a man to be alone with a *namahram* woman—a woman other than his wife, mother, or sister. The police who stormed the café that day let Anita go after some questioning, but I was taken to Qasr Prison. Being taken to the same prison where my father had been held for three years, three decades earlier, was exciting. I wanted to tell my own stories to my family and my friends. Soon after I arrived at Qasr, I was put in line to be interviewed by a social worker. There were two men in front of me. One of them had robbed a bank, and the other had raped a pregnant woman.

"And what did you do?" they asked me.

"I had tea with my girlfriend."

For four nights, I was kept in a communal cell with about forty other men: purse snatchers, drug smugglers, and—I remember this clearly—eight men accused of committing sodomy on a single young boy, whom they called "the peach." After my father used all the connections he had in the judiciary, the judge eventually gave me a suspended sentence of seventy-four lashes and let me go. My mother was waiting for me at the front door when I returned home, fresh lines of worry around her eyes.

"Seventy-four suspended lashes for having tea with your friend!" she said, with as much hatred as I'd ever heard in her voice. "What do they expect young people to do? Pray and say 'Death to America' all day?" She looked at my father. "Mazi should really leave this country next year."

By then, the Iran-Iraq War was in its fourth year. All secondary school leavers had to serve in the military, unless they performed very well on the universities' national entrance examination and had a letter of recommendation from their school's headmaster approving their "moral qualification." Given the fact that I had been expelled from eight secondary schools because of misconduct, I knew that I would never be admitted into any university, and my plan, from a young age, had always been to leave Iran as soon as I finished secondary school. My father had been reluctant to allow me to go—wanting me to remain with my family in Tehran—but soon after I was released from Qasr, everyone agreed that keeping me safe was all that mattered.

I left about fourteen months later, going first to Pakistan, then to Canada, to attend university in Montreal.

"This is good," my mother whispered into my hair as we hugged good-bye at the front door the morning I left for Pakistan. "It will be good for you to spend a little time outside of Iran. And then you can come back." She kissed my cheek and waved to me as I got inside a cab. I knew she would cry, but she hid her tears until I was gone.

* * *

As I pulled the blindfold back over my eyes, I hoped that this brief, odd experience of prison would be as short and uneventful as my first. Surely the meeting with my "specialist" would give me the opportunity to understand the accusations against me, and to explain my innocence. The blue-eyed guard led me through a courtyard, and I caught a glimpse of red paving tiles through a crease in the blindfold. At the entrance to another building, my specialist was waiting for me. I realized that "specialist" is just a euphemism for interrogator, the same way pimps are called procurers.

"Thank you, Seyyed," the specialist said to the guard.

I could tell by his scent and voice as he greeted the guard that it was Rosewater. He took my arm and gently led me down several hallways; we entered and exited, I thought, a few different buildings. Eventually, he brought me into a room. He shut the door behind us and sat me down in a chair. It was the kind with a writing arm, like I'd used back in school. The air-conditioning was on full blast, and the room was freezing.

I could feel him close behind me.

"Mr. Bahari," he said, his voice in my ear. "This is the end of the line for you. There is nothing beyond here. You have to reveal everything you know."

It felt strange to be speaking to another person under the darkness of the blindfold. "Can you tell me why I'm here, please?"

"You know why. Because you are an agent of foreign intelligence organizations," he began.

I was completely caught off guard. *Of what?* "Could you let me know which ones?" I managed to say.

"Speak louder!" he shouted. He bent closer toward me, his face an inch away from mine. "What did you say?"

"I was wondering if you could be kind enough to let me know which organizations," I repeated.

"CIA, MI6, Mossad, and *Newsweek*."

I thought at first that he was joking.

"Do you mean *Newsweek* magazine?"

"Yes. Your 'magazine' is part of the American intelligence apparatus."

I wondered if someone else was in the room—someone in charge of this incredibly ignorant man. "Let me explain," I said. "I'm a journalist for *Newsweek* magazine, which is almost eighty years old. It's not part of the American intelligence network. If it were, people would know that. Other magazines in the United States would report this. I can assure you of this because the media organizations in the West are very competitive and ruthless."

"Don't try to teach me a lesson about the media, Mr. Bahari. We know everything. We know what you did." Rosewater walked around me. The smell of his sweat overpowered the scent of his perfume.

"I'm sure this is all a misunderstanding. I'm an accredited journalist. I have been accredited by the Islamic Republic government for the past twelve years."

"So?"

"Well, that means that the government of the Islamic Republic has known what I've been doing for twelve years and that they haven't had any problems with my reporting. If they did, they would have revoked my press card."

Rosewater walked around me for a while, silently. When he stopped behind me, he flicked his fingers gently on my shoulder. "The very same people who gave you that press card will end up in a chair similar to this one," he said. "They committed an even more serious crime, by accrediting people like you." Every sentence was marked by a touch on my shoulder. "We have all of your colleagues here now, as well. All of your agents in Iran. They are all in this prison. Don't think you can cheat us or misguide us. We know everything about you. We know you are the mastermind of the Western media in Iran."

This was so unexpected that I had trouble following him. "Masterminding the foreign media?" I asked. "Me?"

"No, not you. My aunt!" he said sarcastically. "She is the mastermind of the foreign media in Iran."

I sat quietly in the chair, unable to speak. I wouldn't allow myself to entertain the idea that my stay at Evin might be less temporary than I had hoped. But the thought kept finding its way to the surface nonetheless.

No, I thought, *this man is just trying to scare me—so that when they release me a few days from now, I'll stop writing stories about the demonstrations.* I tried to convince myself that they would find out that I had done nothing wrong and would let me go before too long.

Eventually, Rosewater left the room and a guard came in. Through the crease in the blindfold I could see that he wore brown sandals.

"You can go to the bathroom now," he said.

Brown Sandals led me to a bathroom. He closed the door behind me and told me that I could take my blindfold off. There were five stalls in a row. Three of them had signs saying, "Guest Toilet." The other two had big "No Entry" signs with the warning "Guests will be punished if they use these toilets!" I obediently used a "Guest" toilet.

It took Rosewater quite some time to return to the interrogation room. As much as I wanted to remove my blindfold and look around while I waited, I didn't dare take the risk. I could see writing on the arm of the desk under the blindfold. It was covered in graffiti. Some of it had been written by former prisoners; some of it was in a child's hand.

Hassan is a horse. This was next to a blurry image of a smiley face.

God have mercy on me. This was written in Arabic instead of Persian.

Iran's judiciary, which is in charge of Evin, buys secondhand chairs from the Ministry of Education. At the beginning of the 1979 revolution, Khomeini declared that prisons would be transformed into schools in the Islamic government, that all of the anti-Islamic activists who entered prison would leave as supporters of the regime. The authorities in Evin seemed to take their leader's advice quite literally.

Eventually, Rosewater came back into the room. His steps were quieter than before. I saw, as he walked closer to my chair, that he was no longer wearing shoes, but black leather slippers with light gray socks. This worried me. I guessed it meant that he was settling in for the long haul. He paced the room, and each time he passed by, I tried to catch a better glimpse of his slippers. In Iran, low-ranking functionaries often wear shabby plastic sandals, and they usually have holes in their socks. I was hoping to find a hole in Rosewater's socks, indicating that the authorities were not taking my case too seriously, and had assigned it to someone with very little power. But there weren't any holes in his socks. In fact, his slippers looked as if they had been polished.

I heard someone else enter the room, and hoped that it was his boss, or someone I could try to reason with. The new man spoke to me, asking me questions I'd already been asked, but he was more mild-mannered and patient than Rosewater. *Good cop, bad cop,* I thought.

"Mr. Bahari, you know that the editors of most American newspapers and magazines are assigned directly by the CIA," the new man said.

Dumb and dumber, I thought to myself.

At this point, I had to accept that Rosewater was, in fact, in charge. I was playing chess with a gorilla. He could swallow my pieces at any point during the game. But I had to keep on playing.

"I'm sorry, gentlemen—the situation is much more complex than you think. I don't think the CIA would want to assign editors." I waited for a response, but none came. "If they were hoping to influence different media organizations, my guess is that they would attempt to do it through an orchestrated public relations campaign."

Rosewater left the room without reacting. When he came back, he put both hands on the back of my chair. "I don't trust anything you say, Mr. Bahari," he whispered into my ear. "From now on, most of our communication will be in writing. I am going to write down questions, and you will write your answers. Do you understand me?"

"Yes."

I considered this good news. New instructions meant that someone else—hopefully someone less ignorant than he—was supervising the whole thing.

"Face the wall and remove your blindfold," he said. He stood me up and moved my chair. "And keep your head down for as long as you are here." Then, as if sensing my question, he added, "However long that will be is up to you. People who have not cooperated have grown old, very old, here."

The thought of spending even one night in Evin frightened me. *He's bluffing,* I told myself, trying to concentrate on answering his questions. They were very general and simple: where I had lived, where I had studied, the names of people in my family. I finished and handed the paper back to him without moving my gaze from the wall.

"I cannot read this!" I heard the sound of paper being torn into pieces behind me. He threw the shreds over my head, like confetti. "Write in better handwriting!"

"I'm sorry, I cannot help it. I've always had bad handwriting."

"But you write so well for *Newsweek.*" He said the name as if it were a curse.

"Yes, but I use a computer to write. I rarely use a pen these days."

He ignored what I'd said and gave me another piece of paper. I sat in that chair for hours, answering his questions. I marked the passage of time by the call to prayer. Shia Muslims pray three times daily: morning, noon, and evening. Brown Sandals came to bring me back to my cell just before the evening prayer.

I had had nothing to eat except for the breakfast at my

mother's house. When I took off the blindfold inside the cell, my lunch and dinner were both there. The lunch was bread and *ghaymeh,* a Persian stew with lamb, split peas, dried lemon, and rice. I've always loved the taste of *ghaymeh,* especially the way my mother made it, with eggplant. I missed the bitter, sour taste of dried lemon. I grabbed the plate of *ghaymeh,* eager to devour it, until I saw that it had been there so long, it had almost congealed. Its smell nauseated me.

*   *   *

My father always hated *ghaymeh,* not so much because of the taste but for what he thought it represented. *Ghaymeh* is typically served to the poor during religious ceremonies, and my father hated organized religion and all its rituals. I sat down on the dirty green carpet and thought of him.

My father, Akbar Bahari, was born in 1927 in Bahar, a small town in a mountainous part of western Iran—that is how we got our surname. At the time of my father's birth, the majority of Iranians either were nomads or lived in villages. Most people in Bahar made their living by farming wheat or poppies or harvesting fruit. But my father's family was not like most others. My father's grandfather, Samad Roghani, whose surname means "oil seller," was a cooking oil merchant and, according to legend, one of the richest men in the region. Unlike most men of his generation, Samad had only one child, and when he died, in the late nineteenth century, he passed on his fortune to this child: Hossein Bahari, my grandfather.

Hossein Bahari was tall and handsome, with a thin mustache. In the photos I have of my grandfather, he looks like a Hollywood star of the silent era. Thanks to the cooking oil money, Hossein enjoyed the better things in life. He held big parties in his house, where people gathered to enjoy the local vodka and opium. In addition to the family fortune, he had also inherited his father's religious devotion and tried to be a good

Shia Muslim. He spent freely on religious ceremonies during
Shia holy days, and did almost everything by the book during
Ramadan. He fasted and woke up before the sunrise to pray,
while his servants prepared a big breakfast with eggs, milk, and
honey for the poor. In the evening, when it came time to break
his fast, he did it with vodka. Drinking vodka is, of course, forbidden in Islam, but I guess my grandfather thought that Allah
would pay more attention to his charitable contributions than
to his having a few drops—or bottles—of alcohol.

To add to these contradictions, my grandfather became a
communist during the Second World War. In 1941, the Allied
forces overthrew Reza Shah, the despotic but nationalist king of
Iran. They claimed that Reza Shah had got too close to Nazi
Germany, and they wanted to use Iran to provide help to the
eastern front. They replaced Reza Shah with his twenty-two-
year-old son, Mohammad Reza Pahlavi, who came to be known
as simply the shah, and who took control of the nation. The
Soviets and the Americans controlled the northern half of the
country, and the British occupied the oil-rich south. My father,
who was fourteen at the time, often spoke of the humiliation
and anger people felt as they watched soldiers from the British
Army marching through the streets of Bahar. "It was as if the
British owned our country," he'd say, recalling with obvious
pleasure how he gathered his schoolmates to throw stones at
the foreign troops.

The fall of Reza Shah in 1941 took the lid off Iranians' historic frustration with despotic rulers and foreign intervention.
Amid the postinvasion chaos, political parties mushroomed in
Iran, as prominent politicians started their own parties, promising freedom and independence. With the help of the Soviet
Union, which had long had designs on Iran's rich natural resources, the Tudeh Party of Iran was established. The Soviets
financed it heavily and aided its members with their organizational and intelligence skills, and the Tudeh customized its mes-

sage for different groups in Iranian society with great success. It also developed official and underground networks all over the country. By the mid-1940s many prominent intellectuals, artists, and authors were members of the Tudeh. As the sole voice of the proletariat, the party also attracted many workers and the unemployed.

Like many communists at the time, my grandfather, I believe, was not drawn to communism by stringent ideological beliefs. In fact, I doubt that he ever read Marx and Engels's *Communist Manifesto* or Lenin's *What Is to Be Done?* Rather, he deplored the widespread corruption of his government, hated to see his country occupied, and sympathized with the poor. In the face of these problems, he believed that the Communist Party presented the quickest way out of misery. At the time, the Tudeh Party shrewdly did not present itself as an atheist organization, and, in fact, a number of its leaders were practicing Muslims.

But perhaps my grandfather was just looking for a way out of his own misery. At the time, he had almost depleted his inheritance. My father's mother, Hossein's first wife, died when my father was only five years old, and soon after Hossein remarried. Hossein was not a very good husband to his second wife, or father to his four children. According to my father, he had a habit of coming home very late from political meetings, beating his wife and children on his way to bed, and sleeping until noon the next day. I think this is partly why my father spoke so often about him—he was adamant that his children not become anything like his father. "What kind of man mistreats his family?" my father would ask. "What kind of man doesn't take responsibility for his actions?"

My father loved my mother's cooking, and during meals that went particularly well with a drink—such as fried whitefish with rice, accompanied by yogurt with garlic and marinated vegetables—his grandiloquence could become overwhelming.

"You have to fulfill your responsibilities no matter how difficult it is," he'd tell us. And always, just to spice it up a little, he would add, "Otherwise you're worth less than shit!"

After my grandfather joined the Tudeh Party, his life gained a third ingredient, beyond the debauchery and the religious sessions: discussions about equality and independence. My father was forced to attend these party meetings and serve tea to the guests. "They were like religious ceremonies," my father would tell us over family meals. "In a religious ceremony, a mullah would talk about religious figures and battles at the time of the Prophet. In a Communist Party meeting, we would listen to the stories of the Great October Revolution of 1917, and the heroism of Soviet troops fighting the Nazis."

Following in his father's footsteps, my father became a Tudeh member in 1945, when he was seventeen. Joining the party gave him a means of satisfying a need of his own: getting into street fights as often as possible. My father was by all accounts a very talented young man, but he didn't like to study nearly as much as he liked to fight. After joining the party, he would organize the young Tudeh members and attack the members of other political parties. "If I had not become a communist, I would've become a thug," my father used to say.

After the war ended, my father decided that he'd had enough of Bahar. He worked for a few months in a mechanic's shop in order to save money and move to the capital, Tehran. There, his very first stop was the local branch of the Tudeh. Through the party, he found a job in a small factory. Soon he became a skilled metalworker. By 1949, his readiness to get into fights and his writing skills had helped him become one of the leaders of the Union of Metal Workers of Iran. The union was famous for its ability to organize strikes and for its members' ability to beat opposition groups to a pulp with metal rods.

My father was fanatical about communism. Most religious people I know follow the teachings of their religion (or what they think are the teachings of their religion) without putting that much thought into it. They attend services and join religious groups because they feel more comfortable surrounded by like-minded people. Many communists joined the Tudeh Party for the same reason. My father never denied that this was the case for him; he always said that the party was like a family to him. When he came to Tehran he did not have a penny in his pocket and spoke Persian with a villager's accent. The party gave him an identity, educated him, and provided emotional and intellectual support in a way his father never had.

Because of this devotion, my father never questioned any of the wrong or treasonous policies of the Tudeh Party. To this day, I cannot understand how he and many other Iranian communists supported the Soviet occupation of parts of Iran in 1945, when the American and British forces left after the end of the war. The Soviets took over the Iranian province of Azerbaijan, in the northwest, where they established the proxy People's Republic of Azerbaijan. To my father and many of his friends, the fact that the Soviets had shamelessly taken over a part of Iran was not important. After all, the Tudeh Party was part of international communism, and the Soviet Union was the big brother who knew better. It was only in 1946, after the Iranian prime minister's clever negotiations with the Soviets and threats made by American president Harry S. Truman, that Stalin ordered the Red Army to evacuate Azerbaijan. My father and his friends mourned the death of the thousands of communists who were massacred by the shah's army, including many of their close friends.

Things continued to get worse for Iranian communists. In 1949, there was an assassination attempt against Mohammad Reza Shah. The shah's bodyguards killed the would-be assassin immediately. There are still debates about the would-be assassin's political affiliation, but the attempt against the life of the monarch was blamed squarely on the communists, and the

Tudeh Party was outlawed. Many leaders of the party were arrested; others fled to the Soviet Union. Even so, the party's rank and file continued to hold public meetings under different pseudonyms, especially under the banner of the unions. The communist workers' unions held illegal meetings all over the city and prepared for an attack by the police and the army. "We all had a piece of wood with us, and as soon as the police arrived we would start beating them," a friend of my father's remembered, smiling affectionately at my father. "And your dad was always in the first row of any fight with the police." My father was arrested several times between 1949 and 1953, mostly during clashes with the police.

My father's time in prison seemed to have worked much like Mafia initiation rituals. Inside, he met Tudeh leaders who would indoctrinate him further in party politics, and he would leave jail with more responsibility than before. The Tudeh Party had a vast underground military network whose members even included bodyguards of the shah. "Some of the prisons were practically run by our comrades," my father said. "We could mingle freely with other party members; we had classes about the history of communism and poetry-reading sessions."

My father was not accustomed to being surrounded by such educated people, and he absorbed what they told him like a sponge. In prison, he forged many friendships that would last throughout his life. These men were like uncles to me. It was not unusual for me to come home from school and find a famous Iranian singer or writer sitting at our dining table. There was Mr. Hosseinpour, a poet whose long hair and thick mustache reminded me of a Soviet intellectual; he and my father had shared a cell for many months. My father and Mr. Banki, an engineer whose big cheeks shook whenever he remembered his torturers, recited poetry together during their daily walks in prison. Mr. Abdollah, an industrialist, shared a room with my father, once they were both out of prison, in an apartment given to them by the party.

Whenever three or four of them got together, they would tell stories. These aging men looked at their time in prison with pride and would talk about the torture they endured, and their near-death situations, the way some people talk about a culinary tour of France or a hiking trip in Peru. To a stranger—or to a son—the stories could be both fascinating and horrifying. As a young boy, I was also enthralled by the language my father and his friends used to describe their prison experiences. It was as if talking about a painful past gave them permission to use obscenities. "The motherfuckers punched my head as if it were a boxing bag," Mr. Banki would say.

"The bastards had no mercy," Mr. Abdollah would add.

"The prison was a shithole and stank like a pigsty," Mr. Hosseinpour would interject.

Eventually my father would conclude, "Those thugs tried to break us, but what they did just made us stronger."

These men, and many others who were not lucky enough to survive, endured imprisonment and torture because they stood for freedom. What was happening in Iran in June 2009 was a continuation of the same struggle. My father and his friends loved to recite the poem "The End of the Game," by Ahmad Shamlu, which Shamlu wrote about the shah.

How can you enjoy
trees and gardens
for you spoke to Yassmin
with shears.
Where you step
plants
refrain from growing.
For you

never believed
in integrity
of soil and water

As the Islamic regime consolidated its power after the revolution, the poem became not only about the shah anymore; it referred to all despots who have ruled my country. As I sat in Khamenei's prison, I thought of him while I recited the poem.

Alas! our destiny
was the faithless ballad of your soldiers
returning
from the conquest of the harlots' fortress.
Wait and see what the curse of hell
will make of you,
for the grieving mothers
—mourners of the most beautiful children of the sun and
    wind—
have not yet
raised their head from their prayers.

*   *   *

I had been reporting on the Islamic Republic for twelve years. I knew how irrational and dangerous the regime could be. The longer I sat in my cell waiting for someone to explain to me what was happening, the more concerned I became. In my better moments, the journalist in me found the experience, even the interrogations, fascinating. There were not many journalists that had got so close to the inner workings and secrets of this notorious prison.

I concentrated on remembering every detail for an article I imagined I'd eventually write: "Seventy-two Hours in Evin Prison."

That first night, I shut my eyes and tried to sleep. Immediately, I started to dream. I was with Paola in Hampstead Heath on a foggy London morning. We were lying on top of a hill. Paola was wearing her white pajamas and a white tank top. I was kissing her pregnant stomach and rubbing baby oil on it. In my dream, I did not miss any opportunity to kiss Paola. I told her about the absurdity of my seventy-two hours in Evin, and we laughed about Rosewater's absurd allegations. Then we were back in our flat in London, her dark blond hair spread across the pillow beside me. Then, suddenly, someone was banging on our door.

"Prepare yourself. You'll be going back to your specialist soon!"

In my dream state, I couldn't make sense of those words.

"Get up! You leave in five minutes."

"What time is it?" I asked, aware only of the throbbing ache in my lower back and the stiffness in my legs.

"If you were supposed to know the time, we would have put a clock in your cell," said the guard. I recognized the voice: it was Blue-Eyed Seyyed. "Now hurry up!"

I was led blindfolded through the courtyard again, and guessed it to be around four A.M. When Rosewater came into the interrogation room, I could hear him yawning. He once again told me to remove my blindfold and sit facing the wall. He then took a bite of something and chewed loudly.

"Would you care for some of this?" he asked me.

"What is it?"

"A salted cucumber."

"No, thank you."

He sounded insulted. "What? Do you think that interrogators don't wash their hands?"

I accepted the cucumber and took a bite of it. Rosewater placed another sheet of paper in front of me.

"I want you to write down the names of all of your friends and the countries you have been to."

I took my time listing all the countries I had visited. When I was nine years old, I spent a month touring Europe with Maryam and my mother. Because of the oil boom of the 1970s, Iran's economy was doing well, and the currency was strong. We visited twelve cities in nine countries. The trip opened my eyes to other cultures and people, and instilled in me a love of travel that persists to this day. As Rosewater hovered around me in the interrogation room, I remembered visiting the Houses of Parliament in London with Maryam and my mother. It was that day when I first learned of a concept called "democracy," and I fell in love with London because of it. As a child growing up in the shah's Iran, all I knew about politics in Iran was that the shah—or, as they called him on state television, His Royal Majesty the Shah of the Shahs—had all the power in the country and the people had none.

"So what do they do here?" I asked Maryam. "Why don't we have a parliament in Iran?" To my surprise, Maryam told me that we did.

"So why don't we hear about them?" I asked. Maryam and my mother exchanged an exasperated look. They didn't know how to explain to a child my age that the Iranian parliament in the time of the shah was just a charade, and that no one who was even remotely critical of the shah would ever be allowed to run for office.

"Well, it's different in Iran," Maryam said. "The parliament is not that active."

"Why?"

My mother was growing impatient. "Mazi *jaan*," she said, "don't repeat this to any of your friends or at school. We have a shah in Iran and everyone has to listen to him. Everyone—cabinet ministers, members of parliament, and all other people."

"And how's it here?"

"People vote for people they trust, their representatives, and they are the ones who select the prime minister," my mother said, obviously hoping that I would drop the issue. "In England, the queen has no power; she has to listen to the people. It's called democracy. In Iran, people have no power; they have to listen to the shah."

"But why?" I wanted to know, but my mother's patience had run out.

She smiled at Maryam and me. "Shall we go to Madame Tussauds?"

Now, as I wrote down the names of all the countries I had visited, I smiled at the memory. When I finished, I slowly listed the names of my friends, leaving out the Iranians. I wanted to avoid answering any questions about anybody the Guards might be able to locate and arrest.

"Mr. Bahari," Rosewater said after I'd handed him the paper. "Why is it that you do not write down the names of your Iranian friends?"

"I don't have that many Iranian friends, sir," I answered. "I spend most of my time outside Iran. I only come to Iran to work, and don't socialize much while I'm here."

He knew I was lying. I heard him take a piece of paper in his hands, and he began to read off a list of names of my friends, foreign and Iranian. I realized he must have got the names from my emails and phone. When I'd first arrived at Evin, the guards had requested that I give them the passwords to my email and Facebook accounts. They had also confiscated my London and Tehran mobile phones. I hadn't resisted—I had nothing to hide. "I want an entire *tak nevisi* on these people," Rosewater said now, meaning an explanation of how I knew each individual and the nature of my relationship with that person. As with his previous interrogations, he didn't seem interested in finding new information. He'd already made up his mind about me and what I'd done. He just wanted to prove a point.

"The more you tell us about the anti-revolutionary and sedi-

tious activities of each person, the more we can have an understanding," said Rosewater. "And a better understanding means
that you can have an easier time in prison."

He interrupted me as I wrote, asking me questions about
why I'd been to certain countries, how I'd met certain people.
Rosewater was particularly interested in anyone named Jonathan and Mary. He gave me a list of all the people I knew with
these names.

"Write down where you have met each one of them and how
you know them," he said.

I stared at the list. The Jonathans I knew included three
broadcasters and a cameraman. I knew more than a dozen
Marys from different periods in my life. I couldn't imagine why
he had singled out these people; there were no connections between them. I started with my friend Jonathan Miller, a correspondent for Channel 4 News. I explained that we'd worked
together on several programs about Iran and Iraq.

"Good," Rosewater said from behind me. "Now write down
which spy agency he works for."

"I beg your pardon, sir?"

"Am I talking Turkish here?" he asked brusquely. "Tell me
which intelligence agency this Jonathan works for."

"Sorry, sir," I said desperately. "He's not a spy. He's a filmmaker."

"You are lying, Mr. Bahari."

"No, really. I don't think he's a spy." I paused for a few seconds, then continued. "Even if he were, he probably wouldn't
tell me that." I explained that we had worked on a series of
programs about human-rights abuses in Iraq after the American
invasion, as well as on a few films shot in Iran. Rosewater
seemed to know all of this already. He mentioned a program we
had collaborated on about Hossein Ali Montazeri, an ayatollah
who was a vociferous critic of the Islamic regime. The film

showed footage of Montazeri questioning the legitimacy of the government.

"It's so interesting," Rosewater said. "You've worked on anti-revolutionary television programs together. His name is Jonathan. Yet you say he's not a spy."

"I don't understand the connection," I said. In school, one of my favorite subjects had been logic. I'd always thought I could follow people's reasoning, even if it was riddled with non sequiturs. But I had no idea what Rosewater was talking about.

"With friends like that and making films like that, how can you tell me that you are not a ringleader of the foreign media in Iran?" he asked.

Years of covering Iranian politics and trying to draw conclusions about the irrational behavior of the Iranian government had not prepared me for understanding Rosewater. All I could do was follow out a logical sequence of my own:

These people are in charge of my life.
They are ideological, ignorant, and stupid.
I am screwed.

*   *   *

Back in my cell afterward, I lay down again on the green carpet and talked to my father. "Mazi *jaan*, whatever you do, just don't name names," I heard him say in my head. My father had always told us about how prisoners who revealed information about one comrade would only be pushed to reveal more information about others. "Be careful, Mazi. You name one name, and the list of questions will go on forever."

Over the next two days, between interrogations, I did my best to remember the kinds of conversations I had had with my father, and I concocted further dialogues with him in my head. Meanwhile, Rosewater made sure that I understood that he was going out of his way to be polite and patient with me. "Please answer these as well," he would say sarcastically as he handed me page after page of questions about different Iranian journalists working for the foreign media. It was clear that the aim of the questions was to connect me to a vast array of journalists from different Western news organizations, in order to prove that I was the mastermind of the Western media in Iran. In response, I wrote out long, general answers that revealed very little.

Explain your relationship with Nazila Fathi of *The New York Times*.

Mrs. Fathi is a journalist for The New York Times. The New York Times *is a national newspaper, with headquarters in New York City. Its building is located around Times Square, at 42nd Street in Manhattan. It is privately owned, by the Sulzberger family. It publishes a daily edition, as well as a popular Sunday edition. . . .*

After writing down everything I knew about the paper, I would then add pages and pages of general ideas about the history of the media in the West, things I had learned in my journalism courses at Concordia University. On the second day, Rosewater began to take the pages away and provide me with new ones before even reading my answers. At first I still hoped that he was communicating with someone above him—someone who was, I prayed, supervising this charade; but I soon realized he was just busy interrogating another person in the room next to me.

"*Mardak!*" I heard him yell through the wall, calling the prisoner "little man." "I'll finish your life here. Do you think you can fool me?! Stop writing this bullshit and answer me." These words were followed by the sound of a man being slapped repeatedly.

Hearing this, I felt the sweat collect in the small of my back. I tried to keep my writing hand steady. Then Rosewater was back in the room, offering me a snack.

"Please, have some nuts, Mr. Bahari," he said, placing a plate of cashews and pistachios on the writing arm of my chair.

"Thank you very much, sir," I said.

"You are most welcome." He was breathing heavily. "Would you Americans treat your prisoners like this in Abu Ghraib and Guantánamo?"

I didn't reply.

"You know something, Mr. Bahari? It would be in your interest to just end this all and confess to masterminding the Western media in Iran. That's all you have to do. Tell us about it. Tell us your methods for directing the media." He picked a cashew from the plate. "To be honest, we're really quite amazed by you. We know that you operate in a certain way. Quite mysterious. Almost invisible." His tone was uncharacteristically controlled. I was not sure whether he really believed what he was saying or was trying to frame me. "We've been living with you for months. You didn't know that, did you? Well, it's true, so you better not deny anything. We know the answer to most of the questions we're asking. We just want to know how willing you are to tell us the truth."

I tried to keep my voice calm. "I think you have the wrong person here, sir," I said. "None of the attributes you mentioned fit my character. You make me sound like James Bond!"

Rosewater laughed heartily. "James Bond should take lessons from you, Mr. Bahari. The devil himself should learn playing mischief from you." He seemed to be enjoying this. "Surprise me, Mr. Bahari. Tell me something I don't know."

"I have nothing to hide," I said. "And I'm glad to hear that you know everything about me, because then you must know that I'm innocent."

"Oh, really?" growled Rosewater. "So why did you use a motorcycle to travel around Tehran?"

So Davood was right, I thought. *We were being followed.* "You know about the traffic in Tehran, sir. I always use motor-cycle cabs."

"And you always use the same person?" Rosewater said sar-castically. "Mr. Bahari, we've arrested your personal biker. Or shall I call him a courier? He's told us everything about you."

I wasn't concerned about what Davood could tell his inter-rogators, because there was nothing to tell, of course. But I was worried about Davood. What had I got him into? He had moved to Tehran to support his family with his motorcycle, and now . . . a chance encounter with me may have ruined his life. I tried not to imagine what Davood might be suffering at that moment.

"Sir, that poor man is just a motorcycle cabbie," I said. "All he did was take me from one place to another, and I paid him at the end of each day."

"I'll keep you posted about him, Mr. Bahari. We know that he's part of your vast network. He seems to have a lot to say about you." He tapped my chair with his fingers. "So tell us about the dinner at Nazila Fathi's house on the twenty-eighth of April."

The pen shook in my hand. For the first time, he was asking me about something that had actually happened. He was refer-ring to a dinner I'd attended with eight other journalists and photographers at my friend Nazila's house in Tehran several weeks before the election.

It had just been a friendly get-together, and it surprised me that Rosewater knew about it. Nazila had been the Tehran cor-respondent for *The New York Times* for years. She and her husband, Babak, had told me that they thought that their house was under surveillance but that they didn't know which branch of the government was staking them out.

"It was just a dinner. It wasn't anything special," I said as dismissively as I could.

"Who were the other guests?" he asked.

I told him the names of each of the guests except for two. One was a Spanish journalist whose presence there I had genuinely forgotten. The other was my *Newsweek* colleague Babak Dehghanpisheh. I didn't mention Babak's name in order to test Rosewater—I wanted to see if he knew as much as he claimed to. I was also worried about Babak and wanted to know whether they had arrested him.

"And?" he asked.

"That's it," I answered.

"This is a very dangerous game you're playing, Mr. Bahari," Rosewater murmured into my ear. "Very dangerous." He paused and then put a piece of paper in front of me. "You forgot your dear friend Babak Dehghanpisheh and a mysterious foreign woman."

So he knew everything. "Yes, I forgot to mention Babak. Of course he was there. And I totally forgot the Spanish journalist. I can't remember her name."

"Is that so?" he said. "You are part of a very American network, Mr. Bahari. Let me correct myself: you are in charge of a secret American network, a group that includes those who came to that dinner party."

"It was just a dinner."

"It was not a dinner! It was a *mahfel*!" This word, which means "cabal," suggested that I was part of a group of seditious reformists and journalists conspiring against the Islamic Republic. "A very American dinner," he went on. "A very American *mahfel*. It could have happened in . . . *New Jersey*."

The strangeness of the accusation was unsettling. New Jersey?

"You've been to New Jersey, haven't you, Mr. Bahari?" The thought seemed to infuriate him.

The worst thing that can happen in any encounter with Islamic Republic officials is for them to think that you're looking down on them, so I was careful to control my tone. "Well, yes, sir. New Jersey's not a particularly nice place," I said, trying to sound conversational.

"I don't care if it's nice. All I know is that it is a godless place, like the one you were trying to create in this country. With naked women and Michael Jackson music!" He paused. "Your own New Jersey in Tehran."

His questions were having a weakening effect. I felt dizzy all of a sudden. I tried to muster the strength to answer him. "I'm sorry. I don't understand."

"You were planning to eradicate the pure religion of Mohammad in this country and replace it with 'American' Islam. A New Jersey Islam. Tell me," he said, "did any of the women at the dinner party have their veils on?"

"No."

"Then don't tell me that you didn't have a secret American network. A *New Jersey* network."

The absurdity of his fascination with the Garden State almost made me laugh. But the fact that my life was in his hands horrified me. *Where is Paola?* I thought. *She is the master of divining theories about people's behavior. How would she define this Islamic Republic torturer's fascination with the birthplace of Frank Sinatra and Bon Jovi?*

"I have news for you, Mr. Bahari," Rosewater went on, his voice calmer now. "We will never let people like you change our country, to make it like New Jersey. I wish your American masters could hear me now. It will *never* happen."

I remained silent. The potent mixture of the Garden State and ideological zeal had numbed my senses.

"Now go back to your cell," Rosewater ordered, putting his hand on my shoulder, "and think about what I just said."

My father and Maryam had told me how they had cried in

prison for what had happened to our country. I'd never thought
they'd meant it literally. Yet when the guard shut the door of my
cell behind me that night, I could not stop my tears. I was not
missing my mother or Paola at that moment. I was shedding
tears for my country. I felt as if Iran, my country, had been invaded by monsters—men like Khamenei and his odious gang. I
thought of the first lines of the poem "Winter," by the Iranian
poet Mehdi Akhavan Sales.

They are not going to answer your greeting
Their heads are in their jackets

Nobody is going to raise his head
To answer a question or to see a friend
The eyes cannot see beyond the feet
The road is dark and slick. . . .

Akhavan Sales wrote this poem after the 1953 coup, when
the shah was silencing any voice of dissent. The poem was one
of Khamenei's favorites, and before the revolution, he often recited it to members of his cabal. I wondered if he still read it.

The breaths are clouds, the people are tired and sad
The trees are crystallized skeletons, the earth is low-spirited
The roof of the sky is low
The sun and moon are hazy
It's winter

*   *   *

On my fourth full day in Evin, I was allowed to call my mother.
"You have exactly one minute," Rosewater said in the interro-
gation room that morning as he handed me my mobile phone.
"Just tell her you're fine. That's all."

When my mother picked up, I had a hard time controlling

my voice. I could tell that she had been sitting near the phone, waiting for this call, every day. Her voice was steeped in relief.

"Mazi *jaan,* how are you?"

Rosewater's head touched mine as he leaned down to listen to what she was saying. I tried my best to not reveal the desolation in my voice. "I'm fine, Moloojoon."

She had been through this before, of course, and knew exactly what to say. "We've hired a lawyer for you: Mr. Saleh Nikbakht. He's trying to arrange a meeting with you." Nikbakht was one of the most courageous lawyers in Iran. He was famous for his persistence and for pestering judges to make quick decisions in favor of his clients.

"Khaled spoke to Paola," my mother said as Rosewater made a motion for me to end the call. I felt an immediate sense of relief. I had been sick with worry about Paola's well-being, and it was at least a little comforting to know that she wasn't under the impression that I'd simply vanished. It also meant that Khaled had done as I'd asked, as I'd known he would. In the updated list I had sent him a few days before my arrest, I had included Paola's name. The fact that Khaled had contacted her meant that he must have also contacted the other people on the list—and perhaps, I hoped, that meant that Paola, Khaled, and others were making as much noise about my situation as possible.

"Paola's fine," my mother assured me. "She's worried about you." Those were my mother's last words before Rosewater reached for the phone and ended the call.

"Do you know this attorney? This Nikbakht?" Rosewater sounded concerned.

I was lost in thoughts about Paola. Was her sister Barbara with her? Had she been in touch with anyone at *Newsweek*?

"Not really," I answered absentmindedly. I was sick of talking to Rosewater. I'd had more than enough of his questions.

"He's a really timid lawyer," Rosewater said, going on to

explain that my mother's hopes for me to meet Nikbakht were empty. Rosewater told me that because I was still going through interrogation, I would be denied access to an attorney. That would change only after the interrogation process was complete.

"Mr. Bahari, let me advise you on this matter," he said before exiting the room. "In our judicial system, it is the interrogator who makes the final decision. It is better if you cooperate with us, rather than rely on anyone outside of this room. You are here, and here, I am the only one who will make decisions about your life."

CHAPTER NINE

My lunch was once again waiting for me when I returned to my cell. But I couldn't eat. I picked at the piece of bread that came with the meal.

I thought of the conversations we had had with Maryam when she'd called us from prison. I'd always envied Maryam's sense of responsibility and her dedication to her family. She, in turn, had always wanted to travel and roam around the world as I did. We shared the same tastes in film and music. We both loved the HBO series *Six Feet Under*. Many nights, after everyone had gone to sleep, we'd watch the show together, then talk for hours about the intertwined stories of the characters' lives. Like the family in the series, Maryam and I felt the presence of our father in our daily lives. We, too, had had our share of fights with our father and at the same time respected his values and his free spirit. We had even both dreamt about our father as embodied by Richard Jenkins, the actor who plays the ghost of the father in *Six Feet Under*.

Yet our father had a more important presence in Maryam's life because of their shared experience of spending years in an Iranian prison. Now, as I watched a row of ants climb over the plate of *ghaymeh*, I remembered my long talks with Maryam and hoped that these recollected conversations would give me strength and hope.

Over the six years of Maryam's imprisonment, I was able to visit her only twice, as siblings were typically not allowed to see prisoners. The first time was two years after her arrest, when I was eighteen years old. When my mother, Khaled, and I arrived, after a seventeen-hour bus ride, the guard in charge would not let me in. "Only parents and children of the prisoners can come in," he said. He was a *tavab*, a prisoner who had repented and, therefore, had been given special perks and responsibilities inside the prison. At the time, among the families of prisoners, the word *tavab* was used as an insult: a *tavab* was someone with no moral principles who was willing to rat on his friends to save himself. Despite my protests, the *tavab* simply repeated the reason why I could not get in. I took a chair in the waiting room and, although I was not proud of this at the time, sobbed into my hands.

"Why is it so important for you to see her?" the *tavab* asked me, once the other families had gone inside.

"She is my sister." What else did I need to say?

"Too bad," he said. "The answer is still no."

Anger took hold of me. I stared the man in the eyes. "When you come out of prison, I will know what to do to you. You better watch yourself."

He walked out of the room, and when he returned, he told me the warden wanted to see me.

I was afraid, but I had no choice. I stood and followed the *tavab* to the warden's office.

"Who do you think you are, threatening this man?" the warden gruffly asked me. He got up from his chair and walked toward where I stood. "You want to be where your sister is?" With that, he started to slap my face. I wanted to fight back, more than I had ever wanted to fight in my life. But I couldn't. I just stood there and took it.

His slapping was not hard. He didn't want to hurt me; he wanted to humiliate me. *"Begoo goh khordam,"* he kept on telling me. "Say 'I ate shit.'" I was too proud to say that, so I said, *"Bebakhshid, eshtebah kardam"*: I apologize, I made a mistake. That was enough for him, and he stopped slapping me.

I was shown back to the waiting room. Not long after, the warden walked into the room and told me I could see Maryam.

"Five minutes," he said. "That's all we'll give you."

I don't know what made him change his mind, but I didn't care.

Five minutes with Maryam was well worth the humiliation. She was waiting for me in a private visiting room. Her body was draped in a hideous gray chador embroidered all over with the logo of the judiciary, but I could tell how thin she'd got. She looked skeletal. I couldn't stop crying, and Maryam took me in her arms to comfort me. I didn't tell her about the scene with the warden; in fact, we barely spoke at all. It was hard for me to speak through my tears, but I tried my best to answer her questions about school, and what films I had seen. All I wanted was to remain in her arms. When the *tavab* knocked on the door five minutes later, I realized I'd barely said a word to my sister. I kissed her cheek and left the room quickly. As I walked back into the sunshine that day, my legs and heart felt as if they were made of lead.

When Maryam was finally released from prison, in 1989, I was living in Montreal, where I was about to begin my university studies. The first time we spoke on the phone, I thought I was speaking to a zombie. I could hear the exhaustion and pain in her voice. I was desperate to go home and visit her, but that was impossible. When I'd left Iran, in 1986, I had avoided being drafted, and if I returned, I would be arrested immediately. As a former prisoner, Maryam could not leave Iran. The best we could do was speak by phone, and we did, once a week for six years, until they finally allowed her to travel outside Iran. We met in Turkey. When I first spotted Maryam walking toward me with my mother, Maryam's son, Khaled, and her daughter,

Iran, at the Istanbul airport, I was overcome with emotion. The last time Maryam had seen me, I was eighteen. Now I was twenty-eight. I had become a man.

We spent ten days together, staying mostly inside our hotel suite. Maryam and I both looked forward most to the hour when everybody else would finally fall asleep and we could have some time alone.

It was here that she first told me about the things they did to her in prison. It was hard for me to hear her stories. The Revolutionary Guards had ordered that she be kept in solitary confinement for one year. She spoke to nobody during that time, except the prison guards who would deliver her meals. At times, they would bring her to a room simply to beat her, most often with a cable on the soles of her feet. Thousands of people perished in Iranian prisons in the 1980s, and there were many times when Maryam thought she was going to die.

In 1988, five years into her sentence, many of her cellmates—even some with light sentences—were dragged from their cells and executed, in a nationwide massacre. This crime against humanity was precipitated by the fact that the MKO, the terrorist group based in Iraq, had organized an attack on Iran at the end of the Iran-Iraq War, in the summer of 1988. The leader of the MKO, Massoud Rajavi, sent thousands of his followers to attack Khomeini's defeated army. Rajavi had brainwashed them into believing that when they arrived in Iran, they would be greeted like heroes and be able to take over the government within a few days. But the Revolutionary Guards and the Iranian army repelled the attack in less than a week, and arrested and killed hundreds of MKO members.

Khomeini, like Massoud Rajavi, believed that murder was the most effective political tool. After the military defeat, to teach all political dissidents a lesson, he ordered the massacre. Within a few weeks, thousands of people who were suspected of supporting the MKO were rounded up and killed. Khomeini's henchmen also killed hundreds of people who supported other political groups, including the Tudeh Party. No one knows exactly how many people died during this barbaric slaughter, but Amnesty International recorded the names of more than 4,482 people. Maryam never understood why she was spared.

Her worst experience in prison happened not long after the massacre, when she had gone on a hunger strike in protest of abuse by the prison guards. One night, Maryam and several other prisoners were summoned to an area outside of the cells. They were then marched to a field and lined up against a wall. Maryam had no idea what was happening, and was too afraid to ask. Prison guards began to hand out blindfolds and asked the prisoners to repent. This was when she knew: it was an execution ceremony.

"I thought I was going to die, Mazi," she said, her eyes brimming with tears. "All I could feel was guilt. I felt guilty for putting our parents through this, and I felt responsible for what could happen to Khaled. I was a bad parent. A bad daughter."

The Revolutionary Guards who were in control of the prison ordered the prisoners to face the wall. And then the shots were fired. But Maryam felt nothing. It took her a few seconds to understand what had happened: this was a mock execution, and the guards had fired blanks. She felt confused by the fact that she was still alive.

Maryam's whole body shook as she told me about the mock execution. It was 1996 as we spoke, seven years after the fall of the Berlin Wall and five after the defeat of the Soviet Union. In those years Maryam had learned about the atrocities committed by the Soviet Union. She felt used by the Tudeh Party and the Soviets, and brutalized by Khomeini's regime.

"Why did I join that party? I hate that party," she told me in our hotel in Istanbul. "Nothing is worth dying for, Mazi. Nothing is worth what I went through."

It was November 2008, nineteen years after she was released

from prison, that Maryam called to tell me she had been diagnosed with leukemia. After we hung up, I felt shattered and hopeless. I left the small Soho editing room where I'd been working on a film for the BBC and called Paola. When she answered the phone, I could barely get the words out. "Why?" I kept asking her, as if she could give me an answer. That night we went to an Indian restaurant. I ordered the spiciest thing on the menu, hoping to feel something besides numbness.

Over dinner I told Paola I had to go to Iran to be with Maryam. "You should do whatever you think is best, Mazi," Paola said, holding my hands. My napkin was soaked in tears.

The next morning I called Maryam and told her I was coming back to Iran. She immediately said no. She insisted that she was doing fine, that the worst was over.

Three months later, I was in Washington interviewing former U.S. hostages held in Iran when my phone rang. I took the call outside. It was a friend of mine, calling to say that Maryam had died earlier that morning.

My life had not been the same since then. I'd been shattered, constantly needing to escape from the memories and emotions. Every now and then, I would blame everything on the Islamic government, which had separated Maryam and me for such a long time. But that was an easy way out. The Islamic government had been brought to power by the people—people like Maryam. I also thought there was no point in blaming everything on the government; instead I should remain the person Maryam wanted me to be: a good journalist.

I could do that outside, but now I was trapped in Evin, in the same situation that Maryam had been in for six years, and all I could do was think of Maryam. I picked at the fraying green carpet on the floor of my cell. Maryam had always loved to draw. In prison she hadn't had a pencil or paper to draw with, so, she had told me, she'd drawn landscapes in her imagination. "I could see the sky even though my cell didn't have a window,"

Maryam said. "I looked at the wall and tried to talk to it. I thought I was going crazy, but it helped me to survive the confinement."

I slowly chewed my bread, wondering how my sister would draw my cell, what she would say to these walls.

* * *

Later that day, Rosewater took me to the office of Evin's resident prosecutor, Judge Mohammadzadeh. Above the chair where Mohammadzadeh sat was a large portrait of Khamenei, smiling. He certainly looked satisfied with himself.

The guard sat me on a chair a few feet in front of Judge Mohammadzadeh, who was talking on a landline phone while continually silencing his mobile phone, which kept ringing. The person on the other end of the landline seemed to be important.

"Yes, sir, I shall do that, sir, of course, sir," Judge Mohammadzadeh said, with machine-gun speed. A man walked in and tried to get the judge's attention. Mohammadzadeh put the phone between his shoulder and cheek and took a file from a stack of papers. He handed it to the man, then shooed him away. I became engrossed in watching the judge. He was in his mid-forties, and his beard was short but very thick and as black as a crow's wings.

Finally, Mohammadzadeh put the phone down. He looked at me, and I noticed that under his very thick glasses, his eyes were crossed.

"And you are Mr.—?" he said, with a disingenuous smile.

"Bahari, sir."

A man I didn't know piped up from behind me. "The spy!" he said.

The judge looked at me again, more closely this time. "Interesting." He then read aloud from a paper in front of him, listing the countries I had visited and the names of my friends.

The man behind me spoke while the judge read. "He is a real

spy, Mr. Mohammadzadeh. He is the one who wrote all that crap about the supreme leader and the Revolutionary Guards. He is the one who filmed the attack against the Basij."

Mohammadzadeh didn't pay much attention to him. He was looking at the paper, shaking his head. "There is not even a single person among your friends whose name is Ghazanfar." He burst into laughter, and the guy behind me started to laugh as well. Ghazanfar is an old-fashioned name specific to peasants.

"His punishment should be death," the man said.

Judge Mohammadzadeh seemed to agree. "Here we sentence anyone who doesn't have a friend named Ghazanfar to death!" he said firmly.

I knew they were trying to scare me, to make me feel threatened, but what I mostly felt was annoyed. How sad that these people held positions of power in my country while hundreds, if not thousands, of educated, innocent people were locked behind bars. It was shameful. They were both waiting for my response to the unfunny Ghazanfar joke, but I said nothing.

"Okay," the judge said, sounding suddenly serious. "His punishment shouldn't be death. It should be life in prison." He looked at me and spoke. "I've seen the list of countries you've visited, Mr. Bahari. Seventy-six countries! You've had enough fun in your life, it seems. I think it will do you good to spend the rest of it in prison. What do you think?"

I thought of Maryam, who'd once stood in a similar courtroom, in front of a similar judge. "I don't know what to say to that, sir."

"Good. You have so much to answer for. You should save your breath." He flipped through another stack of papers before looking me straight in the eye. "What would they do if someone did this in America?" Mohammadzadeh asked, showing me a photograph someone had tagged on my Facebook page. In the picture, a young follower was kissing Ahmadinejad. I had seen the picture before but hadn't thought much of it, and I hadn't untagged it. "Through this picture you're suggesting that our beloved elected president is a homosexual."

That comment almost threw me off my chair. "Sir, but someone else tagged me in the photo," I said.

"So?" He obviously thought that by having the photo on my Facebook wall I had insulted Ahmadinejad.

"I didn't put the photo there. It's like if someone throws a gun into your house, are you culpable for having the gun in your house?"

From the blank look on Mohammadzadeh's face, I could tell he didn't know how Facebook worked and was not interested in listening to my answer. He leaned back in his chair. "You've been to America a lot. Where do you stay in America?" he asked me with a mischievous smile.

"It depends, sir."

"On what?"

"Why I'm there. Sometimes I stay with friends. Other times I stay in a hotel."

He regarded me over the papers. A slow smile crept across his face. "During these trips to America, do you have illicit sexual relationships with women?"

This question surprised and embarrassed me. "What do you mean?"

"You know. Do you? Do you have *that*?" He winked at me, lifted an eyebrow, then mimed grabbing a woman's breasts. And then made a motion simulating sex. "Do you do *that*?"

I didn't say anything. I just shook my head.

"Oh, come on, look at you. I'm sure you do something like that." He continued to make sexual gestures. The man behind me, lost in a fit of laughter, kept kicking my chair.

My face burned with shame for this man and this farce of a system: a Muslim judge presiding over the case of an innocent man in an Islamic country, asking me about my private life. "Sir, I'm a married man." The judge seemed disappointed—

even angered—by my answer. He wanted to hear my salacious stories, perhaps. So he could attack me for them, all the while enjoying what he was hearing. It was beyond hypocritical. It was sadistic.

Mohammadzadeh became serious again. "What does being married have to do with it? You look like someone who would do anything."

"I'm sorry about that, but I'm not who you think I am." I paused, then asked Mohammadzadeh, "Was I arrested for my work as a journalist or for having illicit affairs?"

Mohammadzadeh didn't answer me, but the guy behind me kicked my chair with all his force, startling me. "Look at you!" he said. "Even execution isn't enough for you. You should be more than executed. Guys like you deserve to be put in a hot tar bath by Saddam Hussein."

"Okay, okay," said the judge. "That's enough. Mr. Bahari, here are your charges: undermining the security of the nation; propagating dissent against the holy government of the Islamic Republic; insulting the supreme leader; and taking part in illegal demonstrations. Write down on this paper if you don't accept them."

The man behind me got up to pass a sheet of paper to me. I just stared at it. The charges listed there didn't register. I couldn't think of anything but the sexual masquerade I had just witnessed. *How can you call yourselves Muslims?* I thought. *How can you justify what you're doing?* I was burning with anger. I felt so sad for my country and terrified for myself.

"Hey!" the judge said. "Why don't you sign?"

"I'm reading the charges, sir. Just give me a second."

"What?! Give you a second?!" he howled. "May God be my witness, if you don't sign this paper now, I'll kick and punch you so hard that your mother will mourn you."

I wrote that I didn't accept the charges and stood up to hand him back the piece of paper.

"Get him out of here," Judge Mohammadzadeh said. "Give him back to his owner."

Outside, Rosewater was waiting for me. He was a proud owner. "This is just the beginning, Mr. Bahari," he said. "In fact, Mr. Mohammadzadeh is one of our kindest judges. The one who will be issuing a sentence for you will not be as nice. Do you have anything to say?"

"May God help me," I said. But only to myself.

*   *   *

In the interrogation room that night, Rosewater was not alone. The man he was with—a man whose voice I had not heard before—complained about my *tak nevisi,* the answers I'd written about my friends and acquaintances. When he came closer, I saw through the crease in the blindfold that he wore shiny, polished black shoes. His trousers were neatly ironed and creased. "Mr. Bahari, your answers are very general. We hope that you can give us more details," he said. He sounded more mild-mannered than Rosewater.

"I just write what I know, sir. If I were to give you more details, that would mean I'd be lying."

"Well," said Rosewater, who had been fairly quiet up to this point, "we have some interesting video footage of you. We think it may persuade you to be more cooperative."

I could not imagine what he meant. They had confiscated many videos from my house, as well as external hard drives with the unused footage of two of my films: one about AIDS in Iran and another about an Iranian serial killer who had murdered sixteen prostitutes. Although both films were banned in Iran, there was nothing in them that would incriminate me in any way.

I saw the flicker of a laptop screen through my blindfold. Then I heard someone speaking. It was a recording of another

prisoner's confession. "It's not that one," said the new interrogator. "It's the one marked 'Spy in coffee shop.'"

Before the elections, Tehran had had a vibrant café society.
Young men and women got together, their green bands fastened
around their wrists, talking about the campaign and what they
planned to do after Mousavi was elected president. I spent a lot
of time in different coffee shops in Tehran, conducting interviews, in order to get a sense of what young people were thinking. Perhaps they had filmed me at the time, speaking to friends.
This worried me. I was coming to understand just how ruthless
these people were—how willing they were to believe their own
lies, to construct their own version of the truth. I worried about
who else might be imprisoned somewhere in this building, behind these impenetrable walls, because of my reporting.

I was immersed in these thoughts when I heard the voice of
Jon Stewart from Comedy Central's *The Daily Show,* and then
that of Jason Jones, a *Daily Show* correspondent. "What is it
that makes these people evil?" Jones was saying. "I hadn't
signed up for Twitter, so the only way to find out was to go and
see for myself."

No, no, NO! I thought. *They can't be that stupid.*

Among the hundreds of journalists from news organizations
around the world who had come to Iran to report on the election was a team from Jon Stewart's satirical news show. I'd met
Jason; his producer, Tim Greenberg; and their translator, Mahmoud, about three weeks before the election. Over a few cups
of Turkish coffee, we discussed the situation in Iran and Jason
asked if he could interview me on camera in a coffee shop. Jason
was going to pretend to be a thick-skulled American, and their
goal was to present an image of Iran different from the one
typically shown on American television. I agreed, and for the
interview, Jason wore a checkered Palestinian kaffiyeh around
his neck and dark sunglasses. He pretended to be completely

ignorant about Iran and eager to find out just how evil Iran was. Introducing me, he joked, "He goes by the code name Pistachio."

"Why is this American dressed like a spy, Mr. Bahari?" asked the new interrogator.

"He is pretending to be a spy. It's part of a comedy show," I answered.

"Tell the truth!" Rosewater shouted. I couldn't believe it. He honestly seemed to believe what he was saying: that a spy had come to Iran and filmed me for a segment that had appeared on television. From the way he was speaking to me, I drew the conclusion that he was acting tough to impress the other man, who I assumed was his boss. "What is so funny about sitting in a coffee shop with a kaffiyeh and sunglasses?" he demanded.

"It's just a joke. Nothing serious. It's stupid." I was getting worried. "I hope you are not suggesting that he is a real spy."

"Can you tell us why an American journalist pretending to be a spy chose to interview you?" asked the other man. "We know that you told them who to interview for their program." I had given Jason and Tim a number of names of people I thought they'd be interested in. Others Jason had interviewed— a former vice president and a former foreign minister—had been arrested a week before me as part of the Revolutionary Guards' sweeping crackdown.

"It's just comedy," I said, feeling weak. I asked them to listen to the content of the interview. In it, I said that Iran and America had many things in common, like fighting drug trafficking and Al Qaeda. At the end of the interview, I concluded that George W. Bush's infamous statement about Iraq, North Korea, and Iran being the "axis of evil" was as idiotic as Iranians going around and burning the American flag.

Rosewater pulled a chair over and sat in front of me. "Keep your head down," he said. "Do you think it's also funny that you say Iran and America have a lot in common?"

I had to give a careful answer. "Sir, all I'm saying is that Iran needs America for its security as much as America needs Iran for the security of its troops and its interest in the region. We are living in a world where nations cannot live in isolation and prosper. Aren't we all interested in the prosperity of our country?"

"Why do you care about U.S. interests?" asked the new man.

"Don't you know," added Rosewater, "that Imam Khomeini called America the Great Satan?"

They didn't let me answer.

"The imam also asked, 'Why do we need to have a relationship with America?' " Rosewater's boss said.

"America cannot do a damn thing!" Rosewater said, repeating one of Ruhollah Khomeini's favorite phrases.

It was as if the two of them had been rehearsing this anti-American rant for months. They seemed to be enjoying it.

"Do you know why you told that spy about common interests between Iran and America?" asked Rosewater's superior.

He seemed to have an answer ready, but I had to defend myself. I thought of my father, who could communicate with anyone. "These men are weak, Maziar," I heard him say. "Appeal to their emotions. Gain their sympathy."

"Sir," I began, "many people die in plane crashes in Iran because the Americans do not sell spare parts from old Boeings to Iran, and Iran has to buy worthless defunct Russian planes. It saddens me to see so many of our compatriots die every year. We are an independent nation. Having relations with America doesn't mean that we must be American slaves. Venezuela, Syria, Russia, and China do not agree with the U.S., yet they maintain diplomatic relations. And sometimes they even cooperate with America. I advocate an equal relationship between Iran and the United States. A relationship based on mutual respect."

"And you want us to believe you?" the boss said.

"Mutual respect!" Rosewater mocked me.

"Mr. Bahari, the only reason you are searching for a common ground between Iran and America is that you want to find a way for them to infiltrate our country," the boss concluded.

"We have kicked them out through the door and you want to bring them back through the window," Rosewater added, finishing his thought.

"*Ahsant!* Bravo! Well said," Rosewater's boss declared.

Bravo for what? I thought. *For being a brainwashed moron?*

Rosewater finally said, " 'Tell America to be angry with us and die of that anger!' Do you know who said that?"

"Yes, Martyr Beheshti," I said. Mohammad Hossein Beheshti was the first head of Iran's judiciary after the revolution. Anti-regime terrorists killed him and several other officials in a bombing in 1981. I knew Beheshti's family. His son, Alireza Beheshti, had been a Mousavi adviser for years, and I had met with him a few times during the campaign. He'd been arrested a few days before I had.

"I find it ironic," I added, "that you quote a statement from the heyday of the revolution while you have arrested the son of the man who said it." The ridiculousness of using *The Daily Show* as evidence against me gave me enough courage to argue with my interrogators. "With all due respect, revolutions, like people, have to grow up, gentlemen," I said.

Rosewater was taken by surprise. He grasped my left ear in his hand and started to squeeze it as if he were wringing out a lemon. As the cartilage tore, I could feel the pain, like a slow fever, inside my brain. Rosewater let go of my ear and then whispered into it, breathing heavily. "Didn't you hear what the judge said?" It felt like my ear was broken. "I am your owner. This kind of behavior will not help you. Many people have rotted in this prison. You can be one of them."

"Mr. Bahari is wise," the other man said. "He will soon realize it's in his own interest to cooperate with us."

The man with the creased pants said something else to me as he left the room, but I didn't hear him. My ear was ringing with pain.

* * *

A few minutes later, as I walked once again under the darkness of the blindfold from the interrogation room to my cell, I was hit hard by the thought that I might not be leaving anytime soon. *How will I survive here?* I asked myself. As my father used to say: "You can prepare yourself to go to prison, but when you get there, all you can think about is *How can I keep from shitting in my pants?*"

The guard locked the heavy steel door behind me. I removed the blindfold and passed it through the slot. I was coming to understand the routine.

Routine. It was, my father had said, one of the worst parts of prison. As I put my hand to my ringing ear, I thought I felt my mother's soft fingers pressing the lobe tightly. I was eight or nine again, and she was gently scolding me. I had just returned from my friend Reza's house, where I had got into trouble, again. The truth was, whenever I visited my friends I felt different, and lucky. I could see that none of the colorful conversations we had around our dinner table happened in their houses. There were no expletives used, and no one reminisced about their time in prison, where there were famous poets and musicians there to commiserate with. Instead, their fathers spoke politely about their work and school or, if they really wanted to communicate with us, about football or films.

On this day, over lunch, Reza's father had been telling me and some other kids about a recent trip to the zoo, imitating different animal sounds. The man was treating us like children. Even though I was a child, that didn't mean I appreciated being treated like one. In our house, children would listen in on adults' conversations. I never thought that a conversation about politics, business, or prison was beyond my understanding. Reza's father's story bored me. "Is it right that animals choose their mates in the spring?" I interrupted. "Choosing mates" is a semipolite way of referring to sex in Persian. "Did you see them doing it?"

I'll never forget the look on his face. He dropped the spoon onto his plate. "Tsk, tsk, tsk, it seems that we have an impolite boy in the group," he said, shaking his head and looking me in the eye. My friends started to laugh. They were used to my wisecracks at school, where more often than not the teacher asked me to stand in the corner as punishment. Reza's father immediately took me home. When we got to my house, he asked if my mother would come to the door, and then sent me inside.

My mother came up to my room a few minutes later, where I was reading a book. "Where did you learn that term?" she asked me.

I told her that I had heard my father say "Fuck you" to someone and then I'd asked Maryam what "fuck" meant. She said it meant choosing mates. My mother gave me a bewildered— although not wholly disapproving—look. "Well, you shouldn't repeat what you hear at home to other people. Our house is different from others. Some of your friends' parents will not like to hear you repeat the things we speak about in this house." She then lovingly grabbed my ear. "Okay?"

It is not unusual for Iranian parents to tell their children to lie to strangers, especially in a political family like ours. From an early age, I had learned to live a double life. There was my life in the house, where I was exposed to ideas about the corrupt system that was ruling the country, and another life in which I was supposed to conform to what Iranian society expected of me. Sitting in my cell, I realized that this education had prepared me well for my current experience. From the moment I'd first smelled Rosewater, I'd known that I had to conceal my true self and my feelings toward him and his regime.

Now I would have to pretend that the arrest had changed me and that I would become a supporter of the regime, a hypocrite like most of its supporters. I would have to go along with his paranoia that the whole world has only one objective and that is to bring down the Islamic Republic, because trying to convince him otherwise was hopeless. Agreeing with what he said and somehow giving him enough to make him feel he'd achieved something in his interrogation with me was my only chance of getting out of this mess and joining Paola in London in time for the birth of our child. The difficult part would be doing all that while keeping my dignity and without naming names. As I struggled to fall asleep in my tiny cell, I wondered if that was possible.

CHAPTER TEN

It was the middle of the ninth night when Blue-Eyed Seyyed opened the door to my cell. "Get up! Specialist time!" he barked. I had had trouble falling asleep the previous night and as I fumbled with the blindfold, my body felt heavy and exhausted. Rosewater was waiting for me at a different door than usual, and did not offer his typical hello. Instead, he grabbed my arm and yanked me brusquely away from the prison guard. With his hand firmly on my arm, he pulled me down what seemed to be a path, with trees on both sides. Evin is near the mountains and so the nights there are cold, even in the summer. Tonight was particularly chilly. I welcomed the cold air; it helped wake me up and clear my head. I could hear Rosewater breathing heavily. The fact that this was not our usual routine worried me. I thought I should find a way to talk to him.

"I'm sorry if you don't get much sleep because of me," I said with a smile. I expected one of his sarcastic responses. But he sounded serious.

"The fun is over!" He pushed me harder with every step. "Islamic kindness is over." His breath was heavy on my neck. "You little spy, we will show you what we can do with you. You are going to see what we are capable of." He shoved me inside a room where people were speaking in hushed tones. The smell of sweat, feet, and rosewater was strong.

Rosewater sat me down and pushed my head close to a table. "Keep your head like this," he said.

A few moments later, the room erupted in a cacophony of greetings.

"*Salaam, Haj Agha!*"

"Hello, Haj Agha!"

Typically *Haj Agha* is a term of respect used for someone who has made the pilgrimage to Mecca, but among Iranian officials, it signifies seniority. Haj Agha took my hand.

"Salaam, Mr. Bahari. Do you know why you are here?" He sounded like a high-ranking Iranian official.

"No, sir," I answered. "I'm still not even sure why I was arrested in the first place."

"Well, we know exactly why you're here," Haj Agha said.

"But, sir—," I said, raising my head to speak. Rosewater's beefy hand forced it back toward the table.

"I told you to keep your head down!"

"Whatever you do, keep your blindfold on, Mr. Bahari," Haj Agha said. "Do not even open your eyes." He was giving me this warning, I thought, because he did not want to be recognized. Maybe I was correct, and he was a regime official.

"Is the car here yet?" Haj Agha asked someone in the room. Then he addressed me again. "Mr. Bahari, you're suspected of espionage. You have been in contact with a number of known spies." He named a few of my friends, mostly Iranian artists and intellectuals in exile. "A car is coming to take you to the counter-espionage unit. There, you will be interrogated more . . . shall we say, aggressively? Sometimes up to fifteen hours a day. We are done playing games with you. It is time for you to talk." I could sense him moving closer to me. "Our agents there are prepared to subject you to every tactic necessary. The investigation can take

between four and six years." He paused. "If you are found innocent, you will, of course, be freed and we will offer you our apologies. But if you are found guilty, you could be sentenced to death."

My heart sank with every word. This was the end of my
magical thinking.

This prison, these people, these questions—this would be my
life for the foreseeable future. I tried to quiet my mind, but I felt
as if the earth had opened and I was being swallowed by it,
powerless against everything. The black velvet blindfold became damp, and I didn't know if it was with my sweat or my
tears.

"Would you like a cup of tea?" Haj Agha asked.

A cup of tea? "Yes, please. Thank you." I could barely get
out the words. I was lost in thoughts about my mother, about
Paola, about our unborn child. How could I have put them in
this situation? I felt the beginnings of a migraine creeping slowly
up the back of my neck.

"Unless . . . ," said Haj Agha.

"Unless what?"

"Unless you would be interested in a deal, Mr. Bahari."

"A deal?" I felt the blood move through my body again. Of
course. I knew exactly what kind of a deal he wanted to make.
I thought of all my friends who had been forced to confess on
television. They were all freed eventually, and the dream of
being with my family again was my only consolation as I remembered their tired and broken faces as they'd read their
scripted confessions.

"Yes, a deal," said Haj Agha. I could hear the smile in his
voice. "We believe in Islamic kindness, Mr. Bahari. I've heard
that Mrs. Paola is pregnant. Is that true?"

Hearing Paola's name come out of this man's mouth made
me want to jump up and strangle him. "Yes, sir," I said, through
gritted teeth.

"How many months?" he asked.

"Five months."

He went on, speaking about the benevolence of the Islamic system and how the supreme leader regarded all of us, even the mischievous ones, as his children. But I was not listening. I was thinking about Paola, and about my father. I could hear Paola's words: *Come home, Mazi. We need you.* That was where I wanted to be. I wanted to spend my life with Paola and our baby, away from these hypocritical bastards and their "Islamic kindness."

I had tried to be a balanced reporter. I was in favor of democracy and human rights, but I had always tried to present the point of view of the Iranian government in my work, to the point that I'd even been accused of being an agent of the government. All I was asking was to be left alone, to do my work in peace. But instead the Revolutionary Guards had jailed me and were tormenting me. To my horror, I was disillusioned with my country. *We deserve this,* I thought. *This regime, this close-mindedness. Everything that is wrong with this country, this nation has brought on itself.*

In that moment of despair, I wished that these bastards had been hanged by their turbans, that the people had the guts to take arms against these monsters. I wanted to leave Iran and never look back. I felt betrayed by my own country, by my own people. I just wanted to be back with Paola.

My violent thoughts horrified me. I hated myself for feeling this way about Iran. I shut my eyes as tightly as I could. I could see my father sitting at the head of the table shaking his head, chastising me. "Please, Baba Akbar," I implored him in my thoughts. "Please let me be with my family." I looked my father straight in the eye and said to him, in my head, "I'm not going to name names. I will harm no one."

Then I took control of myself and addressed Haj Agha.

"With all due respect, sir, I don't like to talk about my family. I would like to know what kind of a deal you have in mind."

"I can understand your emotions, Mr. Bahari," Haj Agha said in the most melodramatic tone imaginable. "We do not want to harm you. We do not want your wife to raise the child alone. I do not want your child to grow up an orphan. Is it a boy or a girl?"

I forced myself to answer his questions as diplomatically as I could, trying to keep from him what we both knew was true: my family was my main vulnerability. "We don't know the sex yet. In fact, we were planning to find out together this week, but instead I have the privilege of being in your presence."

"And you have a mother who has lost two children and her husband in the past four years," he went on. Each time he mentioned Paola, my mother, my sister, or my brother, I felt as though a knife were twisting in my body.

"The deal you mentioned, sir? Could you explain, please?"

"Mr. Bahari, you're a well-known filmmaker and journalist. In fact, I saw you last month on television talking about the art of documentary filmmaking." He was referring to an interview I did with Iranian state television in May 2009. "Young people are tired of old faces. They need to hear from people like you." He paused. "Don't you agree?"

"You are very kind, sir," I said. "What do you want me to say?"

"Nothing special. We just want you to speak about your experience of working with the Western media and its role in the velvet revolution," he said. The term "velvet revolution" originated as a way to describe the peaceful revolutions that had brought down socialist dictatorships in Czechoslovakia, Ukraine, and Georgia from 1989 to the early 2000s. Khamenei had accused Iranian reformists of being "velvet revolutionaries," which, according to him, meant being a stooge of the West.

"But, sir, I don't know anything about it." I was desperate to make a different deal. The thought of condemning my work and my colleagues on television repulsed me.

"That is fine, Mr. Bahari," Haj Agha said benevolently. "We will work on it together." He explained to me, in careful detail, the role the West had played in creating and encouraging the demonstrations after the elections. The media, he said, was a major factor in this, and a big part of the capitalist machinery. I was to explain how a velvet revolution had been staged—by foreigners and corrupt elites, using the Western media—and how only the wisdom and munificence of the supreme leader had thwarted this latest attempt.

"Do you agree with my points, Mr. Bahari?"

I had tried my best to listen to what he was saying—knowing that I was about to be used to shore up an illegitimate government that I abhorred—but I was distracted by thoughts about Paola. What was she doing right now? How was she feeling with the pregnancy? Were she and Khaled in frequent communication? "Of course, sir," I said automatically.

"Good. Then you can repeat this information in front of television cameras tomorrow," Haj Agha said.

Our conversation was interrupted by the morning call to prayers from the courtyard. It must have been around five A.M. I could hear the other people in the room stand and gather their things to pray.

Haj Agha wanted to wrap things up. "Well, Mr. Bahari, I have a few pages of notes for you. You can practice in your cell." He pushed several pieces of paper toward me. "I suggest you read these words carefully so you can repeat them as naturally as you can." He grabbed my hand and held it. "You'll have a haircut tomorrow, and a shave." Before saying good-bye, he made his last point.

"If it doesn't look natural, we will not broadcast it. The

counterespionage unit is always ready to greet you." He let go of my hand. "Have a good night, sir."

* * *

Jafaa. In Persian, this very poetic word refers to all the wrongs you do to those who love you. According to Haj Agha, I was guilty of *jafaa* against Khamenei. Now I was to repent. But it wasn't Khamenei's forgiveness I needed for what I was considering doing. It was everyone else's: all the people I loved.

I moved to a corner of the cell and curled myself into the fetal position. I screamed into my blanket, trying to muffle the noises so no one would hear me. My father and my sister had not been high-ranking members of the Tudeh Party, and they had not worked for the media. They had never been forced to confess. They had endured years of imprisonment—as painful and torturous as it was—with their integrity intact. I needed their help.

I called in my mind for Maryam. "Maryam *joon,* you are a ghost, why don't you come and help me?" I cried. I shook with pain and anger. I was a coward. I was weak. I was going to confess.

"Just don't name names, Mazi *jaan,*" I heard my father say. "No one believes in the *koseh she'r*"—the bullshit—"that you're going to say." I smiled. How I missed my father and his swearing. "Everyone knows that these bastards will do anything to force you to confess," my father said. "Just say whatever they want and get out of here as soon as you can."

I got up and began to pace the room. I was so tired. My steps were slow and clumsy. Six forward. Six back. "I have to sleep," I told myself. I couldn't allow them this—I couldn't become a zombie.

Instead, I lay down, closed my eyes, and carried the green carpet of my cell to our bedroom in London. There, I placed it on top of the bed I shared with Paola. When I opened my eyes, she was in the living room, wrapping Christmas gifts. I walked as silently as I could into the living room and stood there for a few moments, watching her. Her long hair was tied into a messy bun.

She was startled when she turned to find me standing there. "Gosh, Mazi," she said. "You scared me. What are you doing?"

"The strangest thing just happened to me," I told her.

She stopped wrapping the gifts and turned to me, a look of concern on her face. "What? What's wrong?"

"I realized something just now. I have a huge chip on my shoulder."

"What are you talking about? No, you don't."

"No," I said. "I really do. I think I need your help."

"What do you mean? A chip on your shoulder about what?"

"I'm not sure," I said, walking toward her. "Come here. Feel it." I put my hands around her waist and extended my right shoulder toward her so she could see the bump under my sweater.

"What is that?" she asked.

"I don't know. Get it off, though."

She smiled at me with a look of amusement and curiosity as she slid her hand under my sweater and pulled out the small jewelry box holding her engagement ring. When she looked back up at me, there were tears in her eyes. Before long, we sank onto the green carpet together, and though it took many hours of lying there, holding each other as tightly as we could, we finally fell asleep.

CHAPTER ELEVEN

I had come to find breakfast the best part of my day. Every sip of tea was like an escape, and I spent a lot of effort trying to make the cup last as long as possible, while also keeping it from becoming cold. It was a very delicate balance. That morning, as I sipped, I waited to see what would be served with the thin lavash bread given to me in a plastic bag: jam or cheese. The guard slipped the plastic bag through the lower slot. Today it was cheese.

I again read the handwritten notes Haj Agha had given me. He apparently had a lot to say about velvet revolutions. The gist of Haj Agha's argument was that such changes of government could not happen without the help of the Western governments, especially that of the United States, and the financial help of rich Zionists. It seemed that Haj Agha didn't understand that by comparing the green movement in Iran with the revolutions in Eastern Europe, he was essentially saying that the Islamic regime was a dictatorship like the former totalitarian socialist states. Though it's true that the CIA and MI6 had been involved in changing regimes in a number of countries during the Cold War and it's likely that they did whatever they could to help the dissidents in Iran, it was absurd to blame millions of people's disenchantment with their government on foreign intelligence agencies. Demonstrations such as the ones I'd witnessed sprang from the people, not from outside. Anyone on the streets of Tehran after the election would have known just how spontaneous—even leaderless—the protests had been. But Khamenei claimed that they had been orchestrated by foreigners. He and his ministers wanted to maintain the fallacy that the people had reelected Ahmadinejad. The legitimacy of their government depended on it.

Haj Agha was quite sure that the Western media had been the main vehicle used to provoke the demonstrations, and that reformism, both before and after the election, had been fabricated by the West. To him, the green movement was driven by Westernized urbanites trying to bring decadence and moral corruption to Iran, and they couldn't have done anything without the support of the West, especially Americans. Everything he said echoed a familiar fear of the regime. Khamenei liked to warn Iranians about a "cultural NATO" as threatening as the military one—a network of journalists, activists, scholars, and lawyers who supposedly sought to undermine the Islamic Republic from within.

Though I knew my testimony was intended to prop up a despised regime, I told myself that I could talk about Haj Agha's idea of velvet revolutions generally, without hurting anyone. As I was taken outside for my *hava khori,* or a short walk in a courtyard between two high walls, which I was afforded for an hour each day, I thought that I could even embellish and exaggerate his concepts so that they would sound more ridiculous. That way, when people heard or saw the confession, they would know it was coerced.

When my *hava khori* was over, I was called inside to the communal guest bathroom for a haircut and shave. The man who cut my hair had a round face, thick glasses, and a short beard. His prison uniform was the same as mine.

"Why are you here?" he asked.

"I was arrested after the demonstrations," I answered.

He told me that he had heard the news of the demonstrations and arrests on state television in his communal cell. The state TV called the demonstrators terrorists, and said that only those who caused death and destruction had been arrested. The barber seemed to believe everything that was said on television.

"You don't look like a killer," he said. "Did you throw Molotov cocktails at the police?"

"I'm a journalist," I said. "I didn't attack anyone. Why are you here?"

"Five kilos of heroin," he answered nonchalantly. The majority of prisoners in Iran are drug smugglers.

I knew that possession of more than a kilo of narcotics could lead to a death sentence. "Five kilos of heroin and you're still alive?" I marveled.

"Yeah," he said, as he trimmed my sideburns. "There were ten of us. All neighborhood friends. So they divided the sentence between us and none of us were sentenced to death."

The journalist in me was very curious. "Why did you smuggle drugs? Couldn't you find another job?"

"Like what?" he asked, brushing the hair from his apron. "I don't have any education, I don't have rich parents, and I don't know anyone. I thought I could sell heroin, make the down payment for a car, and start working as a cabbie."

His simple reasons for taking such a risk were disarming. Before saying good-bye to him I had to ask a final question: "Who would you vote for if you were outside?"

"Ahmadinejad," he said. "Who were the other candidates?"

The haircut was followed by a dress rehearsal for my confession. They took me to the same room where I'd had my mug shot taken on the first day. Brown Sandals arrived, carrying about ten shirts, and asked me to choose one. Most of them smelled of sweat and only a few of them fit. I settled on a blue short-sleeved shirt. Then they gave my glasses back to me.

Rosewater was in the room, behind me. "Put on your blindfold and wait at the door," he instructed. A few minutes later, he led me down a series of hallways, stopping at different checkpoints along the way. I'd learned to recognize certain rooms by their flooring. The room I was finally brought to was one in which I had once been interrogated. Haj Agha was waiting for me. He took my hand and shook it.

"You know, Mr. Bahari, I really enjoyed meeting you last night," Haj Agha said.

"The pleasure is mine, sir," I said as if I meant it.

"In my line of work I have to meet many people who don't understand ideas very easily. You seem to have an intellectual predisposition, and seem able to grasp these complicated concepts in a short time."

"Well, thank you, sir," I said. "It was a very eye-opening conversation we had last night."

I knew I had to walk a fine line between flattering Haj Agha and mocking him. But he was so full of himself that he had no room for humor, and was oblivious to mine. "Give your answers as clearly and articulately as you can," Haj Agha said. He added, "Of course, in your own words."

"Of course, sir," I said. "But would it be possible to keep the notes for reference?" I wanted to hold the notes on my lap so that the interviewers—and hopefully the viewers—would realize that the answers I gave had been fed to me.

"I can understand that it might be difficult to remember all that information, even for a man of your intelligence," he said. "In order to have maximum exposure, you will be doing several interviews, one right after another. To make it easier for you, we have grouped the information in a series of questions on like topics and given them to the interviewers." He said this so I understood that he was in charge of everything: the counter-espionage unit, state television, my life. "We think this will help give the interviews a natural flow." Haj Agha wished me good luck. "I'm really happy you're doing this, Mr. Bahari. I don't think the counterespionage interrogations would have been a very pleasant experience."

Rosewater made me stand up and led me to a room. He stood outside and directed me to remove my blindfold. The room had a sink and a bed. I guessed that this was the room where the interrogators took naps. He gave me a bar of soap and a disposable razor to shave with, and spoke to me from the hallway: "Don't forget to give clear examples of individuals, spies who pretend to be reporters, spies who pretend to be politicians, Maziar." This was the first time he'd called me by my first name. "Haj Agha has high hopes for you," he said. "You can be freed in a couple of days if you perform well. We need names." He then left me in the room to rehearse.

You can be freed in a couple of days if you perform well. These were the only words I could hear as I read through Haj Agha's script again. Outside the room, the camera crews were moving in their equipment. I could hear the familiar noise of tripods being set up, the lights adjusted, and tapes placed in the camera. The crew members spoke about shot sizes, testing the sound, and daily life. *I used to be one of them,* I thought. I missed my camera equipment. One of the cameramen complained that his wife was not helping him much in the house.

"She works during the day and when she comes home she just watches television," he said. "She doesn't even iron my shirt. I even have to cook for the children."

"How old are they?" another guy asked.

"My daughter is twelve. My son is ten," said the cameraman. "And, you know, during the demonstrations after the elections I always had to carry the camera on my shoulders. My back is killing me, but my wife doesn't care."

"I was lucky," said someone else. "I was working in the studio during the demonstrations. I have four daughters. One of them cooks, another one washes, the third one cleans the house, and the fourth one irons my shirts!"

"Lucky you!" another said. They all laughed and went on telling stories as I tried to read Haj Agha's script.

Suddenly the men became quiet, as if uncomfortable with the presence of a stranger in their midst. The unwelcome guest was Rosewater.

"I guess I'm lucky that I don't have any children," he said, with an obvious sadness in his voice. "I don't have any such stories to tell."

"Don't say that," someone said. "Children are the best things that can happen to you."

"They're God's gifts," said the man with four children.

Suddenly the door opened. I knew by then not to look up. "Put this on," a voice instructed, and a black blindfold was thrown onto the ornately patterned Persian carpet in the middle of the room.

Rosewater led me to Haj Agha's office and instructed me to remove the blindfold after he left. There were three camera crews in the room. I was told to sit in a single chair placed in front of a red curtain hung at the back. I understood from this that the "journalists" interviewing me would not be in the shots.

The first interview was with a reporter from Channel One of the state television network. He held a photocopy of the same script I had. Talking to a prisoner under duress can be the most shameful thing a journalist will ever do. I stared at him, willing him to look me in the eye. I held the blindfold on my lap so that he could clearly see it.

"So," I asked him, "we're both journalists. Do you do many interviews in prison?" He fumbled with the papers in his lap. "Oh, those?" I said. "Those are the questions you have to ask me. I have a copy of them too, as well as the answers I'm supposed to give you."

He finally looked up at me with an expression of helplessness in his eyes, as if telling me, "I know what I'm doing is wrong, but I have to feed my family."

Even though the interviewer had the script, Rosewater kept passing him more questions from behind a screen. He also guided me on how to answer. Each time I did not answer the questions according to Haj Agha's notes, Rosewater would remind me of the counterespionage unit. "Mr. Bahari, maybe we should wrap up the interview and follow the other option?" he would say, then direct me to look at the script. "Maybe we should repeat the question again," he would tell the TV crew.

The second interviewer was from Press TV, the Iranian government's English-language satellite channel, which has offices all over the world. While the Iranian government was harassing and imprisoning journalists, its reporters could work freely in Western countries. The Press TV reporter didn't seem to have any problem with this. He was a particularly nasty character and spoke with an English accent.

"If you're a journalist, what are you doing here?" he asked me in English with a smirk on his face.

I'd like to ask you the same question, I thought. I smiled at him and said, "I am here because I am a journalist."

No one in the third and last crew even bothered to introduce himself.

"Where are you from?" I asked the interviewer as he sat down and hooked up his microphone.

"*We* are supposed to ask the questions," he said. I later found out that this crew was from the Fars News Agency, which is owned by the Revolutionary Guards.

All the so-called journalists I spoke to that day were at the service of the government. A free press was an alien concept to them. To Haj Agha, Rosewater, and the journalists, this was a normal state of affairs; they were utterly convinced that the same situation existed in the rest of the world.

I don't know how many hours passed while I sat in that chair, answering their questions, telling them what they wanted to hear. Their questions, written by Haj Agha, were mostly about the evil Western media, and my answers, also written by Haj Agha, verified that their information was correct. As the day wore on, my thoughts drifted to Paola. I imagined her, pregnant with our baby, walking around our London neighborhood. She had on a long white maternity shirt and a floral skirt. As soon as this was over, I would go back to London, spend the summer with her, and finally get around to reading my pregnancy and parenthood books. I was really looking forward to that.

"One characteristic of the velvet revolutions is their relation to the media. International media pave the way for such revolutions, and without their presence, these revolutions cannot happen," I heard myself saying.

I had very little idea of how to handle babies in their early months. Ever since Paola had told me she was pregnant, on that humid day in a small village in Cambodia, I'd been keeping a list of the baby books I wanted to read. I needed guidance on so many things: changing nappies, sleep patterns, being a good dad. The pile of books on my bedside table was tall, but the list of books I'd yet to buy was even longer.

"Can you give us a few examples?"

What to Expect When You're Expecting. Be Prepared: A Practical Handbook for New Dads. "BBC. CNN. Euronews. *New York Times.*"

"Are you forgetting one?"

My Boys Can Swim! The Official Guy's Guide to Pregnancy. "*Newsweek.*"

When it was over, they unhooked my microphone. Rosewater led me back to my cell.

"Names, Maziar," he said. "You forgot names."

I smiled. I nodded. I turned my back to him. And inside, I seethed.

CHAPTER TWELVE

Bang.

Bang.

Bang.

I hit my head hard against the faux marble wall, again and again, ignoring the pain that crept up my neck. I deserved the pain. I had betrayed my family, my colleagues, myself. My father.

What had I admitted to? What had I told them? I stood up and paced through the silence of my cell, and tried to speak to Maryam. After the confession, they had forgotten to take my glasses away from me again, and for the first time since I'd arrived, I could see every detail of the cell. In focus, it seemed less clinical—less impenetrable. The walls were covered in tiny, spidery cracks I had missed before, as well as dozens of scribbles: *Your interrogator is more afraid of you than you are of him, that is why he forces you to wear a blindfold. This too will pass. Moghavem bash."* Be strong.

Near where the wall met the floor, I found dozens of straight lines, marking the number of days different prisoners had spent in my cell: Twenty-two days. Ninety days. It had already been ten days, and I couldn't begin to imagine spending even another night in this place. But, I thought with relief, I didn't have to.

The confession was worth it, even if I felt I'd let everyone down. Now I could go back to London, and be with Paola, and nothing was more important to me than that.

It was hard to gauge how much time I spent pacing the small cell—maybe several minutes, maybe hours—but eventually, I fell to the floor again and curled the blanket around myself. I needed to sleep so that I'd be as alert as possible when the prison guard came the next morning to take me back down the same steps I'd climbed that first day in Evin. I pictured it all as I drifted toward sleep—getting my clothes back, seeing the fullness of the sky, finally calling Paola from my mobile phone—and even in my dreams, I expected to hear a knock on my cell door signaling that the process had begun, and I could go home.

*   *   *

But that knock on the door didn't come.

For several days, they ignored me. *Why don't they interrogate me anymore?* I thought. *Have they forgotten about me?* The only human contact I had was with the prison guards who silently slid my food through the slot in my cell door or led me out for my daily walk and to use the toilet. Gradually I even came to miss Rosewater and his idiotic questions. Every day, I waited for him to call for me. I sat on the floor, listening for footsteps, and passed the time by counting things in my head. How many schools had I attended? How many houses had I lived in? How many women had I dated? How many cities had I visited?

The knock finally came on the fourth night, well past midnight.

"Specialist time," I heard a guard say from outside my cell, in a sleepy voice. I'd barely slept since the confession, and I jumped up to take the blindfold he extended through the bottom slot. It was Brown Sandals. I was so happy that they'd finally come for me—that I was going to see Rosewater—that I momentarily forgot the rules. "Don't the interrogators have regular working hours?" I joked to Brown Sandals, before immediately regretting it. I didn't know what his reaction would be, and I didn't want any problems before getting released.

"Tell me about it," he replied. "But don't forget that they wake me up, too. I was having a nice dream."

This was a welcome surprise: a friendly exchange with a guard. It could only be a good sign, I thought. They were preparing to see me off, and no longer considered me a threat. I went with it, knowing that the fastest way for two men to bond is through sexual innuendos; it doesn't matter whether you're in an office in New York or a notorious Iranian prison.

"Don't worry," I said, "you'll get back to whoever you were dreaming about as soon as you go back to sleep."

Brown Sandals laughed. "Don't be naughty now. I only have clean, wholesome dreams." He sounded like many jolly, middle-aged government employees I'd talked to in the past. He could have been an accountant, or someone in charge of a small local park. I wished I had talked to him earlier. It was only later that I learned that even though the Revolutionary Guards have their own detention center inside Evin, the prison guards work for the judiciary and are not as indoctrinated as the members of the Revolutionary Guards.

He led me through the courtyard toward the building where I had been interrogated. I figured that they wanted to give me one last talking to, and warn me against any further reporting in Iran, before they let me go. I recognized Rosewater from his slippers and, of course, his smell.

"Hello, Mr. Bahari," Rosewater said. "Long time no see. Are you ready for freedom?"

"Yes, sir," I answered quietly. I didn't want to sound too enthusiastic. "I've been waiting for you."

Rosewater led me by the arm to an interrogation room I had

never been to before. I couldn't ever really make sense of the layout of the prison and would soon understand that keeping me disoriented was part of their strategy to control me. I was never supposed to know where they were taking me, or what they would ask. One of the first things I would do when I got home, I thought, would be to check out the aerial view of Evin on Google Earth. Rosewater sat me in a chair.

"How are you, Mr. Bahari?" he asked from his side of the room.

I would be fine if I could just get out of here. "I'm well. Thank you, sir."

"Do you think we're stupid?" I bit my tongue. Of course I could not answer that honestly. I sensed him quickly crossing the room. His face was near mine. "Are you deaf? I'm asking you a question!" he screamed into my ear.

This wasn't the scenario I had been picturing. I felt a trickle of sweat slide down my side, and I tried to steady my voice. "I'm sorry. I don't understand." *Had they just used me to get the confession and now they want more?* I pushed away that thought. Rosewater moved away from me but remained in the room. I could smell his stench. "I don't understand," I whispered.

"You know what we do with people who think we're stupid?" He came near me again, and then he began slapping my thighs with all of his might. Over and over again, until the skin on my legs began to sting.

"You little man, you think you're dealing with a bunch of villagers? Do you think you're smarter than us? You don't know who you're dealing with." His blows came quicker, and my legs stung so badly it felt as if he had stuck them with needles. Finally, he left the room. I curled over my legs, wanting to protect them. I tried to ease the pain by rubbing my legs, but even the slightest touch through my uniform hurt.

Rosewater came back into the room in a rush, bounding

toward me, and I sat bolt upright. "You either cooperate with us or every day will be like this," he said. With that, I felt the crack of a belt on my legs—so hard that I cried out in pain. "Shut up, little man!" he screamed as he hit me again. "Why've you gone mute all of a sudden? You spouted all that nonsense in front of the television cameras. Why are you deaf and dumb now?"

"But, sir, Haj Agha instructed me to say those things," I stammered through the pain.

"I told you to name names, didn't I? Didn't I?!" He began punching me on my shoulders, so hard that I could feel his wedding ring press into my skin. Rosewater was a big man with strong arms, and I braced myself for each blow. But I was glad that for a moment he had stopped slapping my legs. I had been doing push-ups on a regular basis since my teenage years, and my shoulders have always been strong. The punches to them hurt less than the slaps to my legs.

I started to moan. "Please, please, sir. That hurts," I said. My trick worked. He punched my shoulders even harder, forgetting about my legs.

"The whole country is in a turmoil because of you," he said. Drops of his sweat fell onto my neck. "How can you answer all of the mothers who've lost their children because of you? How can you answer for all the blood you've shed since the election?"

The pain in my shoulders began to crawl toward my neck and into my head. I've suffered from migraines since 1994, and they were often made worse by any physical suffering and stress. Feeling the beginnings of a migraine now and wanting to protect my shoulders, I turned my face toward him, trying to block his punches with my cheek. "Turn your face away, you little spy," he yelled and began to slap my thighs again.

I closed my eyes under the blindfold.

"But, sir, please tell me, what have I done wrong? I said what you asked me to say."

"I'm the one who asks the questions," he yelled, beating my legs with the belt.

Rosewater grabbed my hair, jerking my neck violently. "Get up," he ordered. But I couldn't. My legs were numb and my shoulders were throbbing. He practically had to pull me from the chair by my hair. "Go back to your cell and think about what happened tonight," Rosewater told me. He punched the back of my head, and I winced. "I haven't even started yet. This will happen to you every day if you don't cooperate with us."

As a guard led me back to my cell, I tried to figure out what had happened. This wasn't the plan. This wasn't what we had agreed to. I had said what Haj Agha had told me to say. Why weren't they letting me go?

"It's time for morning prayers," said the guard, whose shoes I did not recognize. "Do you want to use the bathroom and do your ablution?"

Of course, I thought. *The only reason Rosewater stopped beating me was because he had to prepare to pray.* The rage I felt at his hypocrisy frightened me.

"No, I don't," I said. "But I need two migraine pills. I need them right away."

The guard locked me in my cell and went to get the painkillers. I pulled down my trousers and looked at my legs. They were so bruised, they looked nearly black.

*   *   *

A few hours later, I paced the cell—back and forth, as quickly as I could—waiting for what was going to happen next. Rosewater wanted names, but what names? Reporters? Politicians? Friends? The noise of the air-conditioning unit was so loud, I had trouble staying focused on my thoughts.

I remembered Maryam telling me about the time they took her to the torture room and beat her without reason. "It was toward the end of my sentence," she said. "I think they just wanted to teach me a lesson before releasing me so I would never forget what prison was like." I tried to convince myself that Rosewater was doing the same.

But a voice inside me suspected otherwise: that they'd never had any intention of keeping to our agreement. What had happened last night was, I somehow knew, just the beginning. But how far would they go? I'd heard too many stories, and I couldn't block the horrifying thoughts from my mind: Fingernails pulled out. Electric shocks to the testicles. "The first thing he did with the pliers was squeeze my earlobe," my father would say. "If you think that's painful, just wait. Nothing hurts more than when they use those pliers to pull out your nails. The man who tortured me pulled out each of the nails on my right hand slowly, one by one. He told me that he had all the time in the world." My father related this story many times throughout my life. As a child, I would study his hand, trying to picture it disfigured. I was in awe of him. How could he resist such pain? I didn't know if I had his strength, but remembering my father's words gave me hope: "They thought that by exerting maximum pressure, they could force me to reveal all the information I had about my comrades. But I never did."

The metal slots of the other cell doors started to open and close, startling me. It was time for breakfast. I had always looked forward to the click-clack sound of the slots opening and closing. This meant it was time to eat and, especially, for tea. But that morning, the sounds of metal against metal made the panic I felt more intense. I waited for the lower slot to open and my breakfast to appear, but it didn't. Instead, Blue-Eyed Seyyed opened the door. For some reason, he was the only guard who didn't mind showing his face to the prisoners. He placed a blindfold on the floor along with my food and poured me a cup of tea. "Have your breakfast as soon as you can. Your specialist wants to see you right away," he said as he closed the door. "I'll be back in ten minutes."

I stared at my nails as I held the cup of tea. Would I still have them at the end of the day? I felt Maryam sitting in the corner of my cell, watching me. Dropping to the floor, I started to do push-ups. *What if they pull my nails and lash my feet, how many push-ups will I be able to do then?* I thought.

"None," Maryam answered. She had told me about a friend of hers in prison who'd lost her toe after a bad beating. "She had lied to them about her husband's whereabouts, and when the prison guards found out, they punished her by lashing her feet for almost an hour," Maryam had related with tears in her eyes. She'd said that when they brought the woman back to their shared cell, the soles of her feet were so badly damaged that she couldn't walk for days.

The thought of Maryam getting knocked around by an animal like Rosewater brought forth the tears that I'd been holding back since the beating. As I did my push-ups, I watched the carpet under my face grow dark with my tears. "Maryam *joon,* I will be strong," I said. "But how will I survive this? How much worse will it get?"

"Who are you talking to?" Blue-Eyed Seyyed was standing at the door to my cell. I ignored him, sat up, and took a sip of tea. "Come on, it's time to go," he ordered.

Rosewater didn't say anything when Blue-Eyed Seyyed handed me to him. He silently took my arm, as if leading a lamb to the slaughter. I could sense his anger in the force of his breaths and his grip on my flesh. He sat me in the chair in the interrogation room and removed my blindfold. From this corner of the room, all I could see was the badly painted white cement wall in front of me. Rosewater tapped me gently on the shoulder. "Maziar, you have a choice here. You can be my friend or my prisoner," he said. His tone had changed. It was as if we had entered a new phase of our relationship and now that he had beaten me, he felt more comfortable with me. "Do you understand me, Maziar?" Rosewater asked as he circled around me, marking his territory, dragging his slippers on the floor like a common thug.

I hope he's not going to urinate on me, I thought. "Yes, sir," I said.

"Friend or prisoner?" he repeated.

"I'm sorry," I said quietly. "Maybe I don't understand."

As he placed a blank piece of paper on the chair's writing arm, he said: "This is friend." He then moved back and suddenly slapped my right cheek with all his might. It sent a shock down my spine, and I felt dizzy. "And that is prisoner," he added calmly. "Mr. Maziar, you can choose to rot here by repeating your *koseh she'r,* your bullshit." He took a deep breath, as if to calm himself. "Write your answers clearly and honestly. Did my slap hurt you?" he asked gently.

I didn't reply. I sat in the chair with my legs crossed, trying to think of a way to reason with him, to ask him what had changed. Rosewater kicked my feet. One of my slippers flew across the room. "Never cross your legs in front of me, you little spy." He then grabbed my hair and forced me out of the chair. "Go pick up your slipper," he yelled, making me crawl across the floor to retrieve it.

After I took my seat again, he sat in a chair behind me. I could hear him writing something. For several minutes, he sat silently, writing. As much as his beatings and screaming were upsetting, this erratic behavior worried me even more.

I finally heard him pull his chair closer to mine. He then calmly placed a few pieces of paper in front of me. On them, he had written the names of six prominent pro-reform politicians—Mehdi Hashemi, Mohammad Khatami, Mehdi Karroubi, Mir Hossein Mousavi, Grand Ayatollah Hossein Ali Montazeri, and Grand Ayatollah Youssef Sanei—and the same question next to each of them: *Explain the nature of your relationship with this person.*

As on the first day of interrogations, I could see that the questions were supposed to place me in a certain scenario. I took the top off the ballpoint pen and had started to write when Rosewater hit me in the neck. "Give me the papers," he said. "Before you start to write *koseh she'r*, Maziar, I have to make one thing clear." He slapped the back of my head. "We know that you're working for an enemy agency and that your job is to connect various reformist politicians with the Western powers." He spoke with more confidence than I had heard from him before. "We know that you've been working as an agent of a foreign intelligence agency since you arrived in Iran and have had, at least, two missions: to put the reformist elements in Iran in touch with foreign embassies and to incite a velvet revolution in Iran."

I was dumbfounded. He'd delivered these ideas the same way a narrator might recount the plot of a film or a play. The leaders of the Islamic regime had clearly already written their story about their opponents, and somehow I had been named as a major character.

"We know that you've been in touch with each of these elements, and have been a conduit between them and foreigners. If you're honest with us and tell us the truth, we will let you go tomorrow. I personally guarantee that, Maziar." He breathed into my ear. "But if you think we're a bunch of idiots and believe you can fool us, I personally guarantee that I will stand you on a chair, put a noose around your neck, and kick the chair from under your feet. I will make sure that your body rots while it hangs, and I will put your remains in a bin bag and throw it at your mother."

I raised my head and looked him in the eye. For the first time since I'd seen him, I didn't feel anger toward him. Instead, I felt pity. Rosewater was simply a foot soldier for Khamenei, there to help back up his story: that, as Khamenei had said repeatedly after the election, the green movement was not a popular uprising but a foreign plot concocted by the enemies of Islam. Rosewater was not important to the regime. He was simply a man whose ideology had led him to become the person who met my stare: a vicious ideologue who believed his path to heaven was lined with all the innocent people he'd beaten.

He punched my forehead, bringing stars to my eyes. "Put your head down!" he bellowed, punching my head again. "Didn't I tell you that while you're here you should always keep your head down?" He stepped away for a second and then said, "You're very lucky, Maziar." As a migraine began building, I found it hard to make sense of his words. It felt as if the pain were dripping down the inside of my body from my head.

"Can I have some water, please?" I asked him.

"Of course," he said and poured me a paper cup of water. "Do you think we're like you Americans in Abu Ghraib and Guantánamo who torture people by keeping them thirsty? We have something called *ra'fateh Islami*"—Islamic kindness—"in this prison. Something you Americans have never heard of." He genuinely believed that calling someone an American was an insult, and always said the word with a sneer.

Rosewater sat down on the chair behind me again. When he stood up and placed another sheet of paper on my chair's writing arm, he was breathing very heavily.

He'd made a diagram, a big circle with a smaller circle inside it. The names of the six people he had mentioned were on the periphery of the inner circle. Rosewater explained that the circle as a whole represented the Islamic system. The smaller circle indicated the minority of people who'd been fooled into supporting the reformists, thereby interfering with the wishes of the majority of the people who supported the system. "This line that creates this little circle in the middle of the big ocean of the Islamic system is the dust and dirt that eventually will be thrown

out of the ocean by the big waves of people," Rosewater explained with the pride of a bad junior poet who thought his
idiotic metaphor made sense.

"Do you mean the six people you mentioned are the obstacles between the Islamic system and the people?" I asked, trying
to make his point clear.

"*Ahsant.* Bravo! So you are not as stupid as I thought. That
is why I said you're lucky. Our system has chosen to bestow its
kindness upon you."

"The problem, sir, is that I really don't know any of these
men that well, and I haven't put any of them in touch with anyone." My voice was faint with the pain of my migraine. I cleared
my throat and tried again, hoping to hide from him how much
I was suffering. "In fact, I've always avoided foreign embassies
in order to avoid getting myself into situations such as this. I
know the rules, sir, and I've always obeyed them—"

Rosewater didn't let me finish. Instead, he began to slap me
once again on my legs. "*Nemidooni? Na?* You don't know anything? Is that right?" As quickly as he'd started beating my legs,
he stopped. "Well, listen," he said abruptly. "How about I get
you some tea and dates so we can have a friendly conversation."

It was hard to make sense of his actions, but when he left the
room, I savored the few minutes I had alone. When he returned,
I could smell the fresh tea.

"Mr. Bahari, you're an intellectual and knowledgeable person, so surely you know who the dirtiest family in this country
is, correct?" I knew he meant the family of former president
Akbar Hashemi Rafsanjani, whose name had become synonymous with financial corruption since the beginning of the revolution. There were rumors that the family had a monopoly on
everything from oil tankers to pistachios to shrimp.

Akbar Hashemi Rafsanjani and Ali Khamenei had been
friends since 1957, when they were young clerics in Qom. Both

joined Khomeini's movement in the early 1960s. Rafsanjani was always known as one of the smartest and most diplomatic of Khomeini's acolytes. When Khomeini died in 1989, Rafsanjani lobbied for Ali Khamenei to become the supreme leader. Rafsanjani became president. With Khamenei's support, Rafsanjani asked the parliament to dissolve the duties of the prime minister and merge them into those of the president. Rafsanjani wanted to amass enough power to effectively be the leader of the country, and manipulate the supreme leader, but Ali Khamenei outmaneuvered Rafsanjani.

Rafsanjani started diplomatic rapprochement and tried to open the Iranian market to the rest of the world. In a country with endemic corruption and cronyism, Rafsanjani's reforms created a new class of nouveaux riches, while leaving millions of Iranians, including many war veterans, poorer. At the same time, Rafsanjani had little respect for democracy and human rights. Many political activists were imprisoned and tortured during his presidency, and dozens of writers and intellectuals were assassinated by government agents. While Rafsanjani's economic policies alienated poor and devout Iranians, his cultural policies angered the reformists. This led to the landslide election of the reformist Mohammad Khatami, who promised equality and freedom, in 1997.

Rafsanjani's mistakes suited Khamenei just fine. Khamenei allied himself with the most ideological members of the Islamic government, including many commanders of the Revolutionary Guards, and tried to marginalize Rafsanjani. While Rafsanjani insisted on the necessity of economic development and political moderation, Khamenei reminded people of the ideological goals of the revolution. The two men's lifestyles contrasted sharply as well. While Rafsanjani's daughter became an outspoken member of the parliament and his sons became rich businessmen, Khamenei famously ordered his six children (four sons and two daughters) not to take part in politics or economic activities in order to avoid any rumors of nepotism or financial corruption. Khamenei's supporters grew to despise what they perceived as Rafsanjani's revisionism and decadence, and to revere Khamenei's simple lifestyle and his ideological zeal.

Yet Rafsanjani remained an influential figure in Iranian politics. By the time of the presidential election in June 2009, many religious figures and politicians who rejected Khamenei's tyrannical rule had allied themselves with the more moderate Rafsanjani, who was supporting Mousavi. Even many former Guards commanders who found the radicalism of the new generation of the Guards dangerous supported Rafsanjani. Because of Rafsanjani's prominence, Khamenei and the new generation of the Guards didn't attack him directly. Instead, after the 2009 election, they tried to incriminate his son, Mehdi Hashemi.

Rosewater answered the question about the dirtiest family himself. "It is, of course, the Hashemi Rafsanjani family," he said. "Our holy Islamic system wants to give you a chance to reveal what you know of this dirty family, Maziar. We know that you were in contact with Mehdi Hashemi. We know that you were active in his circle. We just want you to give us one example of when and how you put this dirty element in touch with foreign agencies."

"But, sir—" Rosewater slammed the back of his right hand against my mouth. I tasted blood, and spit it into the empty cup.

"Be quiet and listen," he said. "Remember: you and I are going to be friends." He then reminded me of the *Newsweek* interview I had done with Mohammad Khatami, who many saw as the spiritual leader of the green movement, a month before the election. During his tenure as president of the Islamic Republic, from 1997 to 2005, and even after leaving office, Khatami was regarded as the most important reformist figure in

Iran. During his presidency, Khatami spoke to Ali Khamenei on the phone on a daily basis, as the supreme leader criticized almost all of Khatami's decisions.

In 2009, four years after his term as president came to an end, he was still popular among many young Iranians, and Khamenei rightly thought that if Khatami became president again, he would try to rally the youth against him. According to my friend Amir, Khatami had wanted to run for president again in 2009 but the supreme leader had explicitly warned him against doing so. When Khatami had not paid attention to Khamenei's warnings, the supreme leader's office had sent threatening messages to Khatami that if he continued his campaign, he could be assassinated and his advisers could be harmed.

"We would like you to tell us how and why the agency told you to interview Khatami," Rosewater explained.

I was exasperated. "But which agency, sir?" I asked.

Rosewater slowly approached me. "What's in this cup?" he asked.

"Blood," I answered.

"Do you think I cannot make you bleed more?" I didn't answer. "Answer me. I asked you: DO YOU THINK I CANNOT MAKE YOU BLEED MORE?!" he screamed.

"Yes, sir," I conceded. "You can."

"So do what I'm telling you to do." He tapped gently on my shoulder. "The Koran says: the hypocrites are even worse than the infidels. We have a chief hypocrite in this country, and that is Khatami. You brought up the dirty idea of vote rigging with Khatami one month before the election, Mr. Bahari," Rosewater said. Khamenei had called the reformists' claim that the election was fraudulent "a great sin." I could see that my having reported on the possibility of election fraud infuriated Rosewater. "This is very interesting, since at the time, no one else was talking about the possibility." This wasn't true, of course. Since

Ahmadinejad's first presidential election, in 2005, the idea that he would rig the 2009 vote had been widely discussed. I wanted to remind Rosewater of this, but I remained quiet. "We simply want you to tell us how the agency came up with the rumor of vote rigging, and how you guided Khatami to answer your question about vote rigging," Rosewater said.

"But Mr. Khatami says in the interview the votes will *not* be rigged," I pointed out. Khatami had told me it was impossible, given the system of checks and balances in place. I braced myself for another blow to my head, but it didn't come.

"I know that," Rosewater replied. "But he let you ask that question and allowed you to publish it. We both know that in a Q&A, the question is often more important than the answer. Now, we're just getting started. Let's talk about Mehdi Karroubi." He let out an exaggerated laugh. "Karroubi is a joke. A moron!"

Look who's talking, I thought.

Karroubi was known as the old man of reformism. While Mousavi was regarded as the gentle face of reformism, Karroubi was famous for his bluntness. After Ahmadinejad's first victory in 2005, in an open letter published in the reformist press, Karroubi accused the supreme leader's son Mojtaba Khamenei of vote rigging. In the letter, addressed to Ali Khamenei, Karroubi wrote that Khamenei's son worked with the Basij and the Revolutionary Guards to tamper with the ballot boxes and raise the number of votes for Ahmadinejad. At the time, all my sources in different government ministries told me that Karroubi was right on target, but they also told me that this could not happen again. I did one of the first foreign press interviews with Karroubi in March 2008, for *Newsweek*. During the interview, he openly talked about his plans to topple Ahmadinejad in 2009.

"And you, Maziar, made Karroubi look like an intellectual

by calling him 'Iran's organized reformer'!" Rosewater punctu-
ated each word in the phrase I'd used as the title of my interview with a blow to my head. My migraine pain was so intense,
I felt nearly ready to vomit. "You then went on to ask him,
'Don't you think those who rigged the last vote can do it
again?'"

He took a deep breath. "*La elaha ella Allah*. There is no God
but Allah. The things you've written make my blood boil. Why?
Why did you want to corrupt our youth by instilling the idea of
vote rigging in their heads? Why, Maziar?"

Before I could answer, Rosewater began to rail against certain clerics, those he believed were agents of the West. Chief
among them were Grand Ayatollahs Hossein Ali Montazeri and
Youssef Sanei, whose names he'd written on the paper. In 1988,
after Khomeini ordered the massacre of thousands of members
of the MKO and other groups, Ayatollah Montazeri spoke out
against the summary trials and executions. Prior to this, Montazeri had been regarded as Khomeini's successor, but his criticisms of Khomeini cost him that position. In a rare interview I'd
done with Montazeri for Channel 4 News, he'd expressed his
doubts about the legality and the Islamic pretenses of the Islamic Republic.

Youssef Sanei was regarded as the most media friendly of the
grand ayatollahs in Iran. While other grand ayatollahs rarely
gave interviews, Sanei was regularly quoted by the foreign
media and even had an album in his office where, after interviewing him, journalists wrote down their impressions of the
ayatollah's views. I was given unprecedented access to Sanei
when I was allowed to film him in the privacy of his home for
my documentary *The Online Ayatollah*.

The films I'd made about Montazeri and Sanei were among
the DVDs the arrest team had confiscated from my house.
"These films are evidence that you have been in touch with the

spiritual leader of these hypocrites, who pretend to be Muslim clerics but are acting against the supreme leader of the Muslim world," Rosewater said.

The call to evening prayer sounded outside. Rosewater had to pray. He marked the end of the session with a sharp slap on my neck. I breathed a sigh of relief, anticipating a break from this madness.

Back in my cell, my lunch was waiting for me on the floor, covered with ants. I tried to sleep, but was soon called back to the interrogation room. Rosewater once again made me sit facing the wall, and slowly removed my blindfold.

"Maziar, you may think I'm a violent person, but please understand my position here," he told me. "We have a divine government in our country. We have a leader whose wish is our desire. If he tells us to die, we die. If he tells us to kill, we kill. And you worked with people who want to annihilate our leader and destroy our holy system of government. How can I forgive you? You know, Maziar," he continued, "many of my colleagues wouldn't let you live for a second in this place, but I believe in remorse. I think you can repent, and I saw how you went halfway toward remorse when you confessed in front of the cameras a few days ago. But then you got cold feet and didn't want to continue. My punches are meant to motivate you to move on the path of the righteous, on the path that our master, Grand Ayatollah Ali Khamenei, has determined for us."

Rosewater put a thick green folder on the arm of my chair; it had my name on it. "This is what we have against you, Maziar. We have pictures and evidence of you working with foreign embassies, my friend. My *mohareb*"—anti-Allah—"friend. But I promise, if you collaborate with us and give us information about these men, I will throw away this file and we can forget about everything." Rosewater put his hands on my shoulders and started to gently massage them.

"We need you to go on television again. We need you to clearly explain how you put anti-revolutionary elements with foreign agents." Rosewater then handed me his drawing with the two circles. "Friend or prisoner? It's your choice, Maziar. You can be out of here in a week's time or you can rot here. Now go back to your cell and think about it."

CHAPTER THIRTEEN

The next morning, Brown Sandals came to my cell early, and with my breakfast, he gave me a pen and six pieces of paper with the names of the reformist leaders on them. "These are for *tak nevisi,* writing information about individuals," the guard said.

"*Tak nevisi* can save you, Mr. Bahari," Rosewater had told me repeatedly.

I looked at the pen and the papers. I had no inner conflict about what to write. Despite the ache in my body and the bruises that now covered my skin, I was not going to follow Rosewater's orders and lie about my connection with the reformists, or say that I had put them in touch with foreigners. I threw the papers into a corner and stroked the pen in my hand. It was the first time I'd been alone with a pen in the twenty days I'd been in Evin. What a tremendous gift.

Then I moved to a corner of the cell and pulled back the green carpeting, exposing the gray tile floor underneath.

The living room of my parents' house was in the shape of a square, which I now drew clumsily. The dining table was at the upper left, with eight chairs around it. The table was wooden and round, the kind you find in elegant Chinese restaurants. A buffet was next to the table, and a large silk carpet was hung on the right side of the buffet. It depicted the eleventh-century Persian poet Omar Khayyám being handed a glass of wine by a beautiful woman. The silk carpet had a golden frame. Maryam and I had always hated that tacky silk carpet, but my father had loved it. I loved it too right now, and I wrote out the words of one of Khayyám's poems:

> *Ah, my Belovéd, fill the Cup that clears*
> *TO-DAY of past Regrets and future Fears—*
>   *To-morrow?—Why, To-morrow I may be*
> *Myself with Yesterday's Sev'n Thousand Years.*

I saw my family sitting together. In this mixture of memory and fantasy, it was lunchtime, and my father had taken his usual seat at the table, a glass of illegally produced vodka in one hand. My mother was in the kitchen, and the smell of simmering herbs from the north of Iran filled the large apartment. She was making *ghormeh sabzi,* a lamb stew with kidney beans and vegetables. As I drew my mother in the kitchen, standing by the stove, I could smell the simmering dill, parsley, leeks, and spinach and taste the tender pieces of lamb steeped in the herbs.

In the living room, Maryam was sitting to my father's left, watching the news on the television that was in a corner on her right. Next to Maryam was her husband, Mohammad. Unlike Maryam and me, Mohammad is a great listener. My father had loved telling his life stories to Mohammad, time and time again. I was across from Maryam. I played with my food as I told my family about the forced confessions of a friend on television. "I don't see anything wrong with making televised confessions," I said. "No one believes his words anyway. So I think he made the right decision in order to be released." I tried to avoid my father's stare.

My father looked at me as he squeezed the juice from a grapefruit into his glass of vodka. My father suffered from hyperuricemia, a high level of uric acid in his blood. The doctor had told him to eat grapefruit and stop drinking. He'd chosen to follow only one recommendation.

"You may think it's normal to give in and do what they ask you to in order to avoid torture," he said, pausing to take a sip of his drink, "but you're just setting yourself up to be fucked."

He had such a way with words. Thinking of Baba Akbar, I felt the familiar mix of anxiety and admiration. I'd never known if his next sentence would hit me below the belt or not. My mother always came to my rescue. She would change the subject so radically that my father would be forced to stop his condescending comments. "I didn't know that the life expectancy in Burundi is only fifty-one years old," my mother told me. "You've been to Burundi several times—are they really poor?" But this time, Baba Akbar didn't want to change the subject.

The sound of steps coming down the hall pulled me out of my fantasy. I covered my drawing with the carpet and waited. The steps continued past my cell.

In my fantasy, my father continued to lash out at me as my mother cleared the dishes from the table. This time, Maryam defended me. "Each person is different, Baba Akbar," she said. "What did your generation achieve, anyway, that you're so proud of it? You thought of dying as a value. Young people these days appreciate being alive. They don't believe in martyrdom and stupid concepts like that. I think it's about time you should change as well." In my fantasy, Maryam stood up and left the room.

I returned to my drawing under the carpet, and when I had finished with the apartment in Tehran, I moved on to our flat in London. I drew each room, each piece of furniture. Paola and I had just renovated the apartment and had added an extra bathroom. I made sure to draw the new bathroom in detail. Even though the new bathroom was smaller than the old one, Paola and I liked it much better. I missed the new bathroom. I missed Paola. When I was done, I drew her. I laughed out loud at the image—knowing she'd be mortified by my amateurish depiction. I took my time drawing her body, imagining the shape of her belly at this moment. How big had she become? She'd barely been showing when I'd left London a few weeks earlier. I wished I had read those books before I left—then I would know more about what was happening to her.

I started to hum songs as I drew more things—maps and images of every house I ever lived in, schools I'd attended, cities I had visited. I couldn't believe how much I was enjoying myself. Suddenly, I panicked. What if they found me drawing my houses and accused me of practicing drawing the map of Evin for an intelligence agency? Who knew what they would accuse me of, if they found the drawings. I spat on the maps and frantically tried to wipe them away, but this only made a big blue ink mess on the tiles. My fingers were dark blue with ink, which I tried to wipe on my prison uniform. What had I done? What if they opened the door and found this mess? I rubbed my fingers against the tiles to get rid of the ink. Despite the blasting air-conditioning, sweat dripped down my back.

"What are you doing, Mazi *jaan*?" I heard my father ask in my head, in his usual sarcastic tone. "What is this mess you've made here?" He smiled.

"What if they find the drawings?"

"Maybe they will. Maybe they won't," I heard him say calmly. "Remember that for these hypocrite bastards, instilling in you the idea that they control your life is much more important than what they can actually do. They want you to be afraid of them even in your dreams. What if they find the maps? They are already accusing you of espionage. What more can they do? Screw them. Relax and be yourself."

I pulled the carpet back over the drawings and stared at the sliver of blue sky and the slice of a tree I could see through my tiny window. Sunshine was reflecting off the leaves. There was a slight summer breeze outside, and the leaves moved in a gentle rhythm. I was lucky to be alive. I was lucky to be able to enjoy the blue sky, the breeze, the summer. I played Miles Davis's rendition of Gershwin's "Summertime" in my head.

I closed my eyes, and I slept.

*   *   *

"Do you have your papers ready?" A guard was standing over me, nudging me awake.

I felt panic rising inside me, until I remembered that I had covered the drawings with the carpet. I hadn't even begun to answer Rosewater's questions. "Almost. I need just half an hour to finish," I said.

"Hurry up—your specialist wants them back."

I set about answering the questions as quickly as I could, writing just the truth and no more: I had no personal relationship with any of the people he'd named and knew them only in my capacity as a reporter. I gave the answers back to the guard and prepared myself to be called to the interrogation room and, I was sure, receive another brutal beating. But I didn't hear back from Rosewater that day at all. The next morning, a guard came to my cell to tell me that I was being moved. When I walked into the new cell, my heart sank. It was just three doors down from my old one, but less than half the size: maybe twenty square feet. It had no window and was much dirtier than the first. One of its two light bulbs was broken.

Rosewater did not call for me that day, or the next day, either. Losing the sunlight meant that I had no idea of the passage of time except for when they sounded the call to prayers at different times of the day. I knew that the smaller cell and the solitary confinement were part of my punishment, but I somehow found a renewed sense of strength. I spent hours exercising. I knew I was losing weight. My stomach had become flat, and my ribs were more prominent. I started a rigid yoga, stretching, and strengthening program to help me pass the time. I lay on my back with my eyes closed, kicked the air with my legs, and pretended that I was jogging with Paola along the route we usually ran back in London: past houses and shops on the way from our flat in Belsize Park to Primrose Hill, into Regent's Park, around the lake, and back to Primrose Hill. In my head, as in the past, we always ended our jog in a coffee shop around the corner from Primrose Hill. I took my time as I mentally followed the path.

Two days after I had moved to the new cell, I was doing my bicycle moves when the guard finally opened a slot in my cell door and said that my specialist wanted to see me.

Rosewater sat me in the chair. He left my blindfold on.

"What do you think this country is, you little spy? A stable full of animals and whores, like Europe? We have a master in this country. Do you think of anything except yourself and your carnal desires, you little man?" He began to kick my feet. "You know what you are, Maziar? You are a *mohareb*," he said, "you are at war with Allah. And you know what the sentence for a *mohareb* is, Maziar, don't you?" I did know. It was death by execution. I said nothing. "I'm sure you know that, you little spy."

He then grabbed my hair and pulled me from the chair, and out of the interrogation room. "I can't look at your face anymore," he sneered. He led me to the courtyard that separated the interrogation rooms from the cells. "Face the wall! Think about those six godless anti-revolutionary elements when you're back in your cell," he said. "Don't let yourself rot here while they're having fun outside, Maziar. They don't care about a worthless spy like you. You shouldn't care about them, either."

For the next week I was beaten by Rosewater on a daily basis, and despite his endless questions about my relationships with the six reformist politicians, I never answered them again. As I sat silently in the chair day after day, I wondered if he honestly believed the words he was saying or was simply acting on orders to break me through torture and threat of execution. Because he was always careful to avoid injuring my face, I also guessed that they planned to parade me on television and force me to repeat my statements about the Western media's animosity toward the Islamic Republic.

After a while, his behavior became more erratic. In the beginning, other interrogators had periodically joined Rosewater in the room, but since the day he had started to beat me, he was always alone. He had to play the bad cop and the good cop at the same time. After hours of kicking, slapping, and punching me, he would bring me fresh apricots and tea and sit beside me, asking about my family and my personal life.

"You know, Maziar, I like you," he'd say. "I think you're a good person but you were tricked by the agency to act against our holy system of the Islamic Republic."

"But which agency, sir?"

"Don't worry about these things right now. We're having a friendly conversation. You know better than me which agency you're working for, so don't make me use my hands again."

"But, sir, please show any evidence you may have and I can prove that it's a misunderstanding."

"Maziar, please, relax. Stop worrying. Have an apricot. Tell me about your life. How many brothers and sisters do you have?"

I was aware that he already knew the answers to these questions, and it pained me more than his punches to have to speak to him about the people I loved. On his lips, the mention of their names was even more obscene than his physical torture. Rosewater sighed melodramatically. "So sad, Maziar. I really don't want you to join your father and your siblings in the hereafter. Think about how much your mother needs you. Who is going to take care of your mother if you rot in prison or, God forbid, get executed?"

I did everything I could to keep Rosewater from seeing how effective this psychological manipulation was. During our conversations, I would sit calmly and say as little as possible. This just enraged him further, and he'd respond with some of his hardest punches. Most of the time, I was able to keep it together. But sometimes, in the coldness of that interrogation room, under the darkness of the blindfold, all of the emotions I had been holding back in the five months since Maryam had died spilled forth, and with each blow to my body, I cried harder than I ever had in my life. I did not want my mother to go through yet another loss. At times, I thought of confessing to his ridiculous accusations just to stop him from speaking about my family and to put an end to the hurt I must be causing my mother and Paola.

Back in my cell, I punched the walls until my hands were bruised and cried Maryam's name out, asking for her help. My pleas were lost in the noise of the air-conditioning, so the prison guards couldn't hear me. "Maryam *joon,* why don't you help me?" I screamed. "Is this the way they treated you? These bastards, these sisterfuckers, these animals!"

* * *

One morning, Rosewater was in a particularly foul mood. He had brought the Persian translations of many of my articles. Though I rarely use exclamation points in my writing, the translations included dozens of them, one after almost every sentence. For a reason I couldn't fathom, Rosewater hated exclamation marks, and seeing them in the articles enraged him. "Why do you use so many exclamation marks?" he screamed at me.

"Sir, the translator added them. They are not in my original, English version."

"You're lying," he said. "Why would someone put in exclamation marks if you didn't use them originally?" He grabbed the belt and swung it across my thighs and back; then his voice took on a different tone. "*Agha joon,* you know that I'm doing this for you," he whispered, addressing Khamenei. "*Agha joon,* I'm your servant, I sacrifice my life for you. You know that I'm only thinking about your happiness and your satisfaction." He grabbed my hair and started slapping the back of my head.

I heard a ringing that I thought was only in my ears, but it continued even after Rosewater stopped hitting me.

"Hi, sweetheart," I heard him say. "I can't talk right now. Is it urgent?"

I couldn't make sense of the change in his tone of voice. Was what urgent? Who was he calling sweetheart?

"No, I'm not sure when I'll be home, love. Is everything okay?" Only then did I realize that he had answered his mobile phone. He must have been speaking to his wife.

"Oh," he asked gently, "is she all right?" With that, he left the room and closed the door.

I buried my throbbing head in my hands. Who was this man? How could anyone beat another person the way he was beating me, then speak so lovingly to his wife? I remained as still as I could, trying to overhear his conversation. And then it struck me: Rosewater was just a man. Despite the power he had over me, he was just a man with a job. Like most people, his main priority was to keep his job and provide for his family.

As the air-conditioning clicked off and I heard Rosewater's laughter from the hallway, I knew what I had to do. I had to allow him to be successful in that job: I had to give him enough information so that he could prove to his bosses that he was making progress, but not so much information that I would harm my contacts or the people close to me.

It all seemed so simple, suddenly. While I could not admit to what they were asking from me, I did have something they wanted: a connection with the international media. I would vow to work with them and help spread their propaganda.

Despite the pain everywhere he had punched me, I felt a smile creeping across my face. Finally, I had a job to do.

CHAPTER FOURTEEN

Over the next few days, Rosewater's telephone conversations with his wife became more frequent. From what I could understand, his wife's mother was ill. Different doctors had made different recommendations, and Rosewater's wife had become desperate. He always tried his best to calm her, but he often didn't succeed.

"You know I would be there if I could, *azizam*, my dear," Rosewater told her once. "But I have so much to do here. They've given me all the difficult cases."

His wife was not happy with his excuse and wanted to know when he was coming home. "I said, I don't know!" he exclaimed abruptly before hanging up on her.

"Are all women as demanding or is it just Iranian women?" Rosewater asked me before slapping my head one more time.

I came to the slow realization that devising the plan had been the easy part. Enduring the pain that went with executing it was not nearly as simple. Rosewater's moods were becoming more unpredictable, his outbursts more vicious. But he seemed to have realized that beating me was not enough. He had to take his psychological torture to the next level.

One day he asked me, "Don't you have any friends or relatives?"

"What do you mean?"

"There are campaigns for everyone in this prison—even the most unknown of the prisoners—but nothing for you," he laughed. "It seems that people have forgotten about you, Maziar."

A former guerrilla fighter who became an interrogator after the revolution once told me about the effectiveness of white torture. In white torture, the interrogator uses only psychological menace, refraining from physical contact. According to him, Assadollah Lajevardi, the man responsible for managing Evin Prison in the 1980s, realized, after a few years of experimenting with different methods of physical torture, that making threats against a man's life or against his family was much more effective than pulling out his nails or lashing him. Lajevardi had spent many years in the shah's jails and knew about the value of solitary confinement; among all the methods of white torture, keeping a prisoner in a cell by himself, without any access to the outside world, was the most effective.

I could testify to the validity of their argument when Rosewater left me in my cell for days at a time. As I sat in my new cell, surrounded by gray-and-white marble walls, with no window to the outside world and nothing to read except for the Koran and a book of prayers, I sometimes felt that I was in a grave. I continued to exercise for many hours each day, but no amount of exertion could help me from feeling abandoned.

I knew Rosewater was lying when he told me that everyone had forgotten about me, but as I stared into the abyss of my small cell I sometimes thought the worst. *What if Paola is not campaigning for me? What if* Newsweek *doesn't care about me? How about my friends at Channel 4, the BBC, and other media organizations?* I thought about my nephew, Khaled, who now lived in Australia, and the list of people I'd given him. Had he contacted all of them? Was he making as much noise as possible to bring attention to my case? If he had, why hadn't any news of their efforts reached me? I wondered what Paola and

Khaled were doing as I did hours of sit-ups and push-ups in my tiny cell.

I couldn't escape from the loneliness of solitary confinement, not even in sleep. I would dream about sitting in my cell alone for days, forgotten and abandoned. I would cry for help and try to open the door, but no one could hear me. My cries often woke me up, and seeing the locked metal door, I didn't know if I was awake or still trapped in the dream. This went on for days, and I prayed for Rosewater to call me, even to beat me. At least it was human contact. At least that meant that someone cared where I was.

One morning, I woke up and stared at my eyeglasses, lying beside me on the blanket I used as a pillow. *This is not a life,* I thought as I rubbed the glass. *I'd rather kill myself and disgrace these bastards than waste away alone here, eventually dying in anonymity.*

I looked at my glasses for a long time, examining the frame and the lenses. I wondered if I could remove the frame carefully, so as not to shatter the lenses. I could then break one lens and slide the broken glass deeply, but gently, into my wrist. The thought was so vivid that I could clearly see the blood dripping slowly from my body until it covered the green carpet, turning it dark brown.

Then I heard Baba Akbar's voice in my head. "Don't be silly," he said. "You shouldn't do their jobs for them. If they want to kill you, they can easily do it themselves."

My father's authoritative voice snapped me out of my reverie, just as it had when I was in school and he would catch me daydreaming when I was supposed to be studying. "Back to the books," he would say. "You can always daydream, but you have an exam tomorrow."

I abandoned my suicidal thoughts and remembered what my father had told me about his torturer, a savage named Zibaei. It took Zibaei a while to understand that physical torture was not effective. "I kept on passing out while I was being tortured," my father used to tell me. "And when I didn't pass out because of the pain, I pretended that I'd passed out so that the torture would stop. I just couldn't live with myself if I revealed any information about my comrades."

Even though my father and his comrades were all atheists, most of them came from religious families where sex was taboo. Their interrogators knew this, and used it against them. Two of the main methods of torture favored by the shah's henchmen after the 1953 coup d'état were rape and touching the prisoners' genitals. It took the shah's intelligence almost two years to realize that threats of execution and denying prisoners the chance to see their families were far more effective.

"The interrogator pretended to be my friend, and asked about my family," my father told me. "He asked if I missed my wife and child. I didn't answer at first, because I knew he was going to use it against me, but when I finally said yes, he allowed Moloojoon to bring Babak to see me." My father always had to hold back his tears when he remembered these meetings with my mother and my older brother, who was a toddler at the time. "Then the next week he told me that if I didn't name my comrades and tell him where they could be hiding, I would never be able to see Babak and Moloojoon again." At that point my father's large eyes would well up with tears. "Bi sharaf ha," he'd say. "They had no dignity."

I grew up hearing my father's friends praising his strength in prison, maintaining that the only reason he managed to escape execution was that he'd had a cousin in the army. But many other Tudeh Party members broke under physical and psychological torture. Between 1954 and 1956, the shah's intelligence found the coded list of Tudeh Party members and its underground military network, and eventually deciphered the codes. By 1957, when the last execution of a Tudeh Party member under the shah took place, most leaders of the party had either been killed, imprisoned, or lived in exile.

As much as remembering my father's courage gave me strength, I knew that what I was facing in Evin was very different from my father's experience in the 1950s. My father had had concrete information about a number of individuals and their whereabouts. The torturers wanted him to tell the truth in order to save himself. I was being tortured to lie about myself and others to preserve the regime's and Khamenei's narrative about the election. My father used to say that he felt sorry for the shah: "He is a pathetic man who believes in his own lies and the lies others tell about him." In that moment, as I remembered my father's struggle, I was sorry for Khamenei, another pitiable despot.

*   *   *

I'd been in prison for a month when one night, after evening prayers, Rosewater took me to a new interrogation room.

"How are you, my friend?" he asked in a tone that reminded me of the one he'd used during the first days after my arrest. "Maziar, I have to tell you something that may make my bosses really upset." He paused for a few seconds. "But I have to reveal it anyway."

The dishonesty in his voice betrayed the fact that he was trying to manipulate me, but I wanted to hear what he had to say. "My bosses are not happy with your performance and want to make an example of you." He then brought his head forward and whispered in my ear. "I'm not supposed to tell you this, but they think that by executing you they can teach others an important lesson."

I felt a chill in my spine as Rosewater asked me to remove my blindfold. There was a basket of fruit and vegetables on the table. He pulled three small cucumbers from it and peeled them slowly. He then placed them on a small plate with a few apricots and slid it to me, along with a plastic salt shaker decorated with red dots.

"Would you like a Nescafé?" he asked. "I know you foreigners like coffee. I'll make you a Nescafé," he said as he left the room.

A Nescafé?! I thought. *What the hell is he up to?* The word "executing" hung in the air, and I felt weak and nauseous. I took a cucumber from the plate and sprinkled salt on it, but I tasted nothing. Rosewater came back into the room and put a cup of hot water and a packet of Nescafé on the table.

"Milk and sugar?" he asked.

"No, thank you," I said. I don't like instant coffee.

"I can't believe you don't put milk and sugar in coffee," Rosewater noted with genuine surprise.

I couldn't help myself from asking him: "Why do they want to kill me?"

"Don't worry about that, Maziar," he said. "Why don't you put milk and sugar in your coffee?"

"I can't drink Nescafé, sir," I lied, not knowing how to tell him that I found its taste revolting. "I'm allergic to Nescafé. What can they achieve by killing—"

Rosewater slapped me in the head. "What do you mean you're allergic to coffee? You speak constantly of meeting people for coffee in your emails! What, my coffee isn't good enough for you?!" He seemed genuinely insulted. He slapped my head again, the way Iranian potmakers slap the clay before they shape and glaze it.

"All right, I'll have a Nescafé," I said. My head was bursting with migraine pain. "And I'll have milk and sugar."

He prepared the cup of Nescafé and eventually regained his composure as he stood behind me. "My superiors have decided to sentence you to death this week, so that the other people involved in sedition can learn a lesson from it," he said as he took more fruit from the basket on the table. "In an emergency situation like this, it takes only a few days from trial to execution. It will be very similar to a court-martial. Because of what you've done to provoke the public against the holy Islamic Republic, the supreme leader, and Allah, you're considered a *mohareb* and will be sentenced to death by hanging." He put both of his hands on my shoulders. "Don't be mad at me, Maziar. I'm just the messenger. I really don't want it to happen. I'm doing my best to prevent it." He walked behind me for a few minutes and then placed an apricot on my plate. "Maziar, I really think there's a chance for you to repent."

I knew that the time to present my plan to him had finally come. "Sir, I have already repented. I've made certain mistakes in the past, but please allow me to rectify them. I can be a useful person for the Islamic system." I worried that my voice sounded too desperate.

"How?" Rosewater was curious.

"I can reveal all the secret ways that the Western media manipulates our youth and tries to topple our government. I can do more interviews. I can repeat exactly what Haj Agha told me about the media to more reporters if you want."

Rosewater wasn't taking the bait. Clearly, he had specific orders: I was to incriminate Rafsanjani, Mousavi, Khatami, Karroubi, Montazeri, and Sanei. "Are you going to tell us how you put them in touch with foreign agencies?" he asked. Then he came closer. "Maziar, I'll make a deal with you. If you can incriminate three of these six traitors, I will personally make sure that you'll be freed tomorrow."

He wanted to make a deal. It was a welcome new beginning.

When I'd been a university student in Montreal, I had worked as a carpet salesman. One thing I'd learned was that when someone was ready to make a deal with you, you shouldn't accept his first offer. "But, sir, that would be lying. I don't know any of these people, and I can't lie about them."

Rosewater tapped my neck with an open palm. His hand felt like a noose. "It seems that you want to die, Maziar." He then sat on the table in front of me and started eating a salted cucumber. "One morning, just before the morning prayers, the guard will wake you up and ask you if you have any final requests. A few moments after that, you'll find yourself in front of the noose, and a few seconds after that, you'll find yourself hanging in the air." He slowly crunched the cucumber between his teeth. "Did you know that it takes, on average, three to five minutes for someone to die after being hanged? Those are the most painful, excruciatingly painful, moments in your life. Those are the moments when you regret sitting here in this chair and not cooperating with me. There's the noose and there's you, Maziar. I'm between you two. Help me help you." He stood up and paced the room; he opened the window to let some air in. "I've made arrangements so you can see your mother and brother-in-law for the last time. This will happen in a couple of days."

Hearing that I would be able to see Moloojoon and Mohammad soothed my pain. I lowered my head and willed myself not to cry out my mother's name. I could feel cold drops of sweat on my back. "Moloojoon," I said silently to myself. "Maryam. Paola. Moloojoon."

Rosewater gently patted me on my back. "What are you humming, Maziar?" he asked with a laugh. "Go back to your cell, and think about what we just discussed."

It sometimes surprised me that in my imaginary conversations, my mother's voice didn't come to me as often as my father's and Maryam's. But I knew that I didn't need to hear her voice to be inspired by her strength. Just as she had shielded me from many dangerous things throughout my life, Moloojoon now shielded me from Rosewater's torture. I could stand his verbal and physical abuse because I knew Moloojoon protected me.

As I looked forward to my mother's visit, I remembered the way she had supported me during my difficult school years. I'd never been interested in my studies. My mother was often called to my school after I was caught missing classes to go to the library to read old newspapers or, during lessons, when I was caught reading novels or books about politics or cinema instead of listening to my teachers. Whereas other parents might have been infuriated by such rebellious behavior, my mother, who had been a primary school teacher for twenty-seven years, until she retired in 1973, always defended me. "You just don't understand the youth," my mother would say to the headmaster. "You don't know about their ideas, their needs, and what a difficult time they have in this society. So you just kick them out of your institutions and think your problems are solved."

The incompetent school administrators never knew how to rationally answer my mother. But in their minds, the fact that I had such a strong mother was just one more reason to expel me and not have to deal with me for another year.

*   *   *

In the days before the visit of my mother and Mohammad, I was allowed to call home twice, for a few minutes each time. Rosewater wanted to know which of my friends were in touch with my family. Each time I called, Rosewater would put his head against mine and say, "Ask who's been calling your family."

Rosewater didn't know that my mother was too smart for this. "No one," she would answer. "No one is calling us except for Paola and your nephew."

I couldn't even imagine what my mother was going through. But her trembling voice calmed me down. I remembered the times when Maryam used to call us from prison in Ahvaz—how Moloojoon would cry immediately before and after talking to Maryam, always in her room, so she wouldn't upset anyone else. But when she talked to Maryam she would muster every ounce of courage and strength she could for the duration of the call. Afterward, I often thought that my mother's soothing words and her compassionate, strong tone helped Maryam endure prison.

On the morning of the visit, I was given a haircut and allowed to shave. As the barber cut my hair, Rosewater stood behind me and gave me instructions on what I should and should not say during the meeting. I could not ask my mother anything about the lawyer she had mentioned or my case. "Nothing about your friends outside of Iran and nothing about political events in the country," Rosewater said. Our conversation had to be limited to family matters and my mother's and Mohammad's health. Someone was going to be assigned to sit at the table with us, to monitor our discussion. "A word out of normal family greetings and conversation and I will stop the meeting," Rosewater said. "Do you understand?" he yelled before slapping me on the back of my head.

"Is he your interrogator?" the barber asked after Rosewater left the room.

"Yes."

A look of sympathy passed his face. "Poor you."

They blindfolded me, led me to a car, and drove me the few minutes from the building where my cell was to the visitors' hall. Rosewater stayed next to me every step of the way, and used the opportunity to give me further warnings. "Remember your mother's face, Maziar. This may be the last time you see it. Imagine how she will feel in a few days' time while you are walking to the noose because you chose not to tell us which foreign agency you're working for."

The visitors' hall was a large space with white walls lit brightly by fluorescent bulbs. There were about twenty white round plastic tables, each with four white plastic chairs around it. The hall was very clean, and it seemed that the judiciary, which runs prisons in Iran, tried to make sure that visiting families were left with a good impression of life inside Evin. A few men in relatively clean blue uniforms were mopping the floor. There were no uniformed guards in the hall, but there were security cameras all around us.

A few prisoners sat at the tables, sharing meals with their families. I didn't see any familiar faces. I sat down with the guard assigned to monitor our conversation. A chubby middle-aged man with a small mustache, he wore his white shirt with the tails outside his pants. He smiled and offered me a small pack of salted sunflower seeds. As we waited, the man explained that, in the past, the space had been divided into cubicles. "But because of Islamic kindness, the government decided to get rid of the cubicles so the prisoners and their families could enjoy a larger space," he told me.

There was no trace of irony in his voice. It seemed perfectly fine to him to arrest, jail, and torture innocent people as long as you gave them a haircut, provided a nice place for them to meet their families, and offered them a snack.

I kept my eyes trained on the door, waiting to see my mother's face. Since I'd said good-bye to Moloojoon on the morning of my arrest, more than a month before, I'd been haunted by the sad look in her eyes. Remembering this now, I felt tears begin to roll down my cheeks. "Mr. Bahari, you're a grown-up, you shouldn't cry like this," the guard said. I wanted to tell him to go to hell, but instead I asked him to take me to the washroom so I could wipe my face. I didn't want my mother to see me crying. In front of the sink, I tried to remember a funny scene from a film to help me stop crying. But as I attempted to summon a scene from *Wedding Crashers* or *The 40-Year-Old Virgin,* instead I kept thinking of how Rosewater had beaten me for not liking Nescafé.

Since damaging her back carrying a heavy box of Tudeh Party leaflets while she was pregnant with Babak in 1953, my

mother has had a difficult time walking up stairs. In order to
reach the visitors' hall, she had to climb a steep flight of stairs,
and when Moloojoon finally entered the visitors' hall, I could
see that she was in pain. I felt guiltier than ever for putting her
through this experience again—of having to visit someone she
loved in prison.

During our telephone conversations, I'd known that my
mother was trying hard to appear strong, just as I was—desperate to keep from her the fear and loneliness I felt each night,
alone in my cell; the way my thoughts still often wandered to
my eyeglasses and the idea of slitting my wrists. But the façades
we'd both been working to present crumbled as we hugged each
other.

"*Mazi jaan, Mazi jaan, cheh ghadr laghar shodi,*" she said,
immediately noticing how thin I'd become. Her eighty-three-
year-old body shook with the strength of her sobs.

Mohammad, always the epitome of calmness and strength,
stood by my mother's side. He tried to calm both of us down,
and encouraged us to take a seat. We did as we were told, but
we couldn't stop crying. At first, my mother didn't notice the
prison guard sitting at our table. When she finally saw the man,
she gave him a uniquely insulting look.

"Who is this?" she asked me loudly so the man could hear
her. Then she turned to him, asking, "Do you have any children?" The man, clearly surprised by my mother's uninhibited
disgust, said he was not married.

"Why not? I thought your mothers forced you to marry
early," she said, referring to the religious families of many government supporters. I tried to change the subject.

"How are you, Moloojoon? How are you feeling?" I asked.

"I'm fine," she answered dismissively before turning once
again to the guard. She clearly wanted to shame him for his
career choice. "Why is it you don't have a family of your own?"

"Don't worry about this gentleman's family," I said. "I'm

sure he has good reasons for not getting married. Have you been in touch with Paola?"

"Yes, she's called me a few times." Paola doesn't speak Persian, so she had asked my half-Iranian friend Lizzy to translate her calls. "*Paola, mahshareh,*" my mother said, calling Paola "amazing." I understood immediately what this meant: Paola was campaigning for me and staying strong. Years of visiting political prisoners had taught my mother how to communicate her ideas in one or two words. It was all I wanted to hear, and my mother knew that.

Because we couldn't speak about anything related to my case or the lawyer my mother had hired, we spent the fifteen minutes of our visit talking about different relatives and distant cousins. I actually began to feel sorry for the prison guard, so every now and then I explained whom we were talking about. At times, to our surprise, he would offer a comment about our family affairs.

"Are you still in solitary confinement?"

"Please, talk only of family subjects," the guard said.

"Of course," my mother answered. "But you keep on interrupting us." I gave the guard a "she's out of control" smile and tried to change the subject, asking Mohammad about the swine flu epidemic that had started a few months before my arrest. My mother interjected before Mohammad could respond.

"The real swine flu is this government that has plagued the country for the past thirty years," she said.

"Moloojoon!" I tried to look upset, but inside I was proud of her. The guard was dumbfounded by her audacity. He sat quietly during the rest of the conversation. When we said goodbye, my mother hugged me and whispered into my ear, "Don't worry about anything. Paola is doing all she can to get you out." Mohammad didn't have any special message for me. Looking at his calm and peaceful face, I was confident that all that could be done for me outside of the prison was being done.

I was hoping to return to my cell, where I could cherish the memory of my mother's voice and face, but instead I was taken directly to an interrogation room, where Rosewater was waiting for me. He pulled a chair up next to me and whispered, "I feel sorry for you, Mazi." It was the first time that he'd called me Mazi, and I figured he'd eavesdropped on our conversation and heard my mother address me that way. When my friends and family call me Mazi, the nickname is familiar and affectionate. When Rosewater said it, it sounded obscene. "You are the most miserable of creatures, Mazi. You're rotting in this prison for people who are laughing at you. Haven't you come to your senses after seeing your mother's sad face? Don't you want to cooperate?"

After everything that had happened that day and the last few days, I felt on the verge of a mental and physical collapse. I knew that I was never going to cooperate with Rosewater, but the pressure was becoming unbearable. I lowered my head and whispered my own mantra: "Moloojoon, Maryam *joon,* Paola, Moloojoon, Maryam *joon,* Paola." Saying these names gave me strength.

"What are you whispering?" Rosewater said, pulling my hair. I didn't pay attention to him and kept on repeating the names of my loved ones. "What are you whispering, I asked," he demanded, hitting me on the back of my head. I continued, ignoring him. Rosewater rolled up the papers on which I was supposed to write my confessions about the reformist leaders and hit me on the head with them. "*Bad bakht,* you miserable man, you're gonna die here, you *bad bakht,*" he repeated as he swatted at my head and face.

In order to protect my face I raised my hands, but he shoved them away with such force that I fell from the chair. I was on the floor, but that didn't stop him from striking my head with the rolled-up papers. I looked at his face, red with anger as he bent over to hit me in the head. "*Negah nakon!* Don't look at me!" he ordered, continuing to punch me. "*Bad bakht khodam mikoshamet*. I will kill you myself, you miserable man." He then kicked me a few times in the back. I lay on the floor, breathing heavily. His mobile phone was ringing, but he didn't answer.

A migraine crept over my head as Rosewater's spit began to dry on my face. I felt sullied and violated but also encouraged: I hadn't signed the false confession. In that moment, I was proud of myself. When I returned to my cell afterward and lay on the green carpet, I felt my father's presence beside me. I knew that he was proud of me, too.

*   *   *

I once filmed a man hanging from a noose. He was Saeed Hanaei, a religious serial killer who had murdered sixteen prostitutes in the city of Mashhad, in northeastern Iran. I had interviewed him inside the Mashhad prison a few months before his death, and knew that he had no remorse about strangling those women to death. Hanaei told me that he wanted to rid the earth of corrupt elements; he knew that his killings had paved his path to paradise.

When I woke up a few hours later that night, feeling the familiar ache in my back and legs from sleeping on the floor, I couldn't get the image of Hanaei's death out of my mind. As I tried to fall back asleep, I worried that my nightmares would be riddled with images of a dead man hanging from the noose. But I didn't dream of Hanaei. I dreamt of Rosewater. We were alone in a prison sometime in the future, and this time, I was interviewing him. Unlike the serial killer, Rosewater regretted his past deeds and was uncomfortable talking about them. In my dream, I could see Rosewater's face. His big head was covered with drops of sweat, his stubble was longer, and his thick glasses were foggy with steam. The school chair in which he sat was too small for him, and he kept fidgeting in his seat.

It was my turn to ask questions. I stood in front of him and stared him in the eye. It was surprising, what I found there: not the gaze of a monster but signs of humanity. "Do you really believe that I am a spy?" I asked him.

He didn't answer and looked down, trying to avoid my stare. "I have to make a living," he said quietly. "I don't make any decisions."

"Why are you accusing *me* of espionage?"

"I'm sorry about that," Rosewater said.

"Why me?"

"I don't know. I'm sorry." Rosewater's expressions reminded me of an interview I had seen with a South African torturer after the fall of the apartheid regime. Faced with questions about his crimes, the man had no answer, except to blame it on others and say how sorry he was.

"Why did you beat me? Why did you slap, kick, and punch me?"

Rosewater's head was still down. "I don't think you're a spy," he said. "But they told me they needed a spy. It was my job to force you to become one, even if it was through lies." Each word caused Rosewater more regret. I was not sure if he was acting or if he really felt guilty. He seemed to be struggling with an invisible force that was pushing him off his chair. I wanted to punch him the same way he had beaten me, and to stomp all over his body, but at the same time, the thought horrified me.

"Stop interrogating him," my father's voice said to me. "He's making you into a monster."

Suddenly, Rosewater was far away from me, on the other side of the room. I tried to get close to him, but he was already on the floor and someone or something was killing him. He was dying fast. By the time I reached him, he was already dead. His body was rotting. Maggots were crawling all over him. I heard loud laughter in the darkening room.

I woke up feeling nauseous. I threw up in the plastic bag in which my breakfast had been delivered that morning. I sat in the corner of my cell, sweating and shivering.

*   *   *

A week later, I was walking as fast as I could with my blindfold on during my *hava khori*. My body was still hurting from Rosewater's beatings and many nights of fitful sleep, and the fact that I hadn't seen him in several days made me anxious about what they might have in store for me.

"You exercise too much," Blue-Eyed Seyyed said, leading me back to my cell afterward. But this time, he didn't shut and lock the door behind me as he usually did. Instead, he looked around my small cell. "We think you need a smaller place. Pack your stuff. You have to change cells."

My "stuff" included two blankets, a bottle of water, the Koran, and a book of prayers. I was desperate for anything to read, but both books were written in Arabic, which I didn't know. I gathered them and followed him up a flight of stairs. Despite what Blue-Eyed Seyyed had said, the new cell was much bigger and, most importantly, had a window. Left alone there, I could hear two other prisoners speaking to the guard. I immediately recognized their voices: former vice president Mohammad Ali Abtahi was in the cell next to mine, and former deputy speaker of parliament Behzad Nabavi was in the cell across the hall.

They were both among the most outspoken and influential figures in the reformist movement. Mohammad Ali Abtahi, a rotund man in his early fifties with a permanent smile, was an open-minded cleric. Abtahi had been reformist Mohammad Khatami's vice president for eight years. He was also the first prominent Iranian politician to start his own blog, in which he criticized the conservatives who ran the courts and the army.

Behzad Nabavi had spent many years in prison before the revolution and had held a number of high-ranking positions in the early years of the Islamic regime. Prior to the election, *Newsweek* had asked me to compile a list of the most influential Iranians. According to a pro-Ahmadinejad conservative pundit I interviewed, Nabavi was "the most devious element in Iranian politics.

"I'm sure he's behind all the conspiracies against the supreme leader," the pundit said. Khamenei must have thought the same thing. Nabavi had been among the first group of people arrested after the election, on Khamenei's specific orders. Nabavi later claimed that his arrest warrant had been issued weeks before the election, and that the Guards had only been waiting for an opportunity to jail him.

I didn't know why they had put me on the same level with such influential figures. I sat on the floor, gazed out the window, and searched for the strength to look on the bright side. After all, my cell was larger and cleaner, and I could see the sunlight again. I carefully rolled the blankets into a wide pillow, like the ones that covered our big bed in London. Placing the pillow on the floor, I leaned back into it, closed my eyes, and focused on the sun.

*   *   *

A few days later, on the morning of August 1, 2009—forty-two days into my stay at Evin—I was dreaming the most beautiful dream. I was in Croatia, making love with Paola. We had just finished one of my favorite dishes in the world: Croatian grilled calamari, accompanied by a cold glass of white wine. We were lying on a sandy beach and her soft skin was slowly growing dark with the sun. I rubbed the beads of sweat that covered the small of her back.

The top slot of my door opened. "*Shazdeh, pasho.* Get up, my prince." It was Brown Sandals. "Put these on." A new prison uniform and my blindfold landed on the floor of my cell. Brown Sandals waited outside while I changed. I wasn't sure what was going on, and my thoughts remained with Paola in Croatia.

"I feel privileged to be in the company of Mr. Abtahi and Mr. Nabavi," I said as I dressed, hoping to get any information about why I had been moved. I was shocked when Brown Sandals answered me.

"I heard you're going to be tried with them," he said. "And they said that you need to get a haircut."

Outside the bathroom, a few other prisoners were waiting for a haircut. When it was my turn, a prison guard sat me down, kept my blindfold on, and, in a matter of seconds, trimmed my hair and beard.

"Do you use gel?" he asked.

This is amazing, I thought. *They deny you your basic rights and then, when they want to put you on trial, they offer you hair gel.*

"Sure, I'll have some," I said.

After my haircut, I was taken outside. I could hear dozens of other men being moved around as well. There was a cacophony of guards shouting orders, wardens looking for keys, and people asking where they should stand or sit down.

I was eventually separated from the group and taken to a dark room; there I was asked to remove my blindfold. Before me was a breakfast of flat bread and cheese, and a small cup of tea. I was starving, but I could barely chew the food. Was it true that I was going to be tried today? Was I about to be killed? I felt the bread lodge in my dry throat.

Suddenly, Rosewater was behind me, his hand on my shoulder. "You thought I was joking about your trial?"

I couldn't answer him.

"You'll have a trial today and then an interview," Rosewater said. "Then I'll suggest a sentence to your judge, based wholly on your performance. We need names today, Maziar. We need a lot of names."

I was left alone in the dark room for hours after that. I heard the call for morning prayers, but no one came to take me to the bathroom. I'd had two cups of tea and really needed to use the toilet, but I'd been told to sit in my chair and not move.

After what felt like an eternity, a guard finally came for me. He put handcuffs on me and sat me in the back of a car, blindfolded. I was allowed to remove the blindfold only when we reached Chamran Expressway, about a mile south of Evin. There were three armed guards wearing civilian clothes in the car.

"Where are we going?" I asked.

"Sshhh," one guard said. "You'll find out soon."

It was the first time I had been out of Evin since my arrest six weeks earlier. I tried to absorb every scene and face I was seeing. I knew that I'd be back in my cell soon enough, and I was desperate to keep as many fresh images of the outside world as possible in the depository of my memory. Everything looked so bright: the colors were more vivid than I'd remembered, and I felt that even the wind was a colorful shade of blue. One of the guards' mobile phones rang.

"No. Tajbakhsh is not with us," the guard said. "We have Bahari."

Hearing the name Tajbakhsh felt like one of Rosewater's slaps on the back of my head. *What the hell?!* I thought. *Is Tajbakhsh still in Iran?*

Between 2003 and 2007, the Iranian-American scholar Kian Tajbakhsh had worked for the Open Society Institute (OSI), an organization run by the billionaire George Soros that promotes democratic values in former communist countries and many other nations. Tajbakhsh had held this position with the official permission of Iran's Ministry of Foreign Affairs until, in 2007, he was arrested by Iran's Ministry of Intelligence and held for four months in Evin. His arrest and that of two other scholars were part of the first wave of incarcerations of those accused of fomenting a velvet revolution in Iran.

The OSI's role in the soft revolutions in Georgia, in 2003, and Ukraine, in 2004, was not a secret. The organization had offices in both countries, and in both had openly endorsed a move to a more democratic state. But OSI had never received official permission to open offices in Iran, and Tajbakhsh worked only within the framework set for him by the Iranian government. Nonetheless, at the time, Tajbakhsh was forced to make a television appearance in which he admitted to being guilty of working with Soros to undermine the regime. The other two scholars left Iran immediately after their release, but Tajbakhsh stayed in Iran. He loved his country and wanted to raise a family there, and he believed the assurances of the Ministry of Intelligence that if he didn't get involved in politics, they would allow him to continue his job as an urban planner. I thought Tajbakhsh would have left the country immediately when he noticed that the situation was becoming more repressive. I later learned that after the election in June, the Revolutionary Guards had arrested Tajbakhsh in his house, in front of his wife and their two-year-old daughter.

The Guards had chosen three people to connect the reformists with foreign governments. I was supposed to be the media connection, Tajbakhsh was the connection to foreign nongovernmental organizations (NGOs), and Hossein Rassam, a political adviser to the British embassy, was the connection to foreign embassies in Tehran.

Part of Rassam's job as political adviser was to meet different political figures in the country and write papers for the British embassy staff based on those conversations and his own analyses. Rassam had held that position for years with no interference, until two weeks after the election, when he was arrested and charged with espionage. By arresting the three of us and parading us in front of television cameras, the Guards hoped to convince Iranians that the postelection unrest had been provoked by foreigners.

Rassam was going to be tried on a later day, but Tajbakhsh and I were among the first to be put on trial. I was taken to the Imam Khomeini Judicial Complex, in central Tehran, and led to a small office in the back of the building. As I followed the guard, I caught a glimpse of Tajbakhsh in a smaller room across the hall. He was sitting at a small table with Rosewater, going through a series of notes. I was surprised to see Rosewater there, and his presence confirmed one of my fears: that he was a high-ranking member of the Revolutionary Guards, responsible for high-level prisoners. I wished for the chance to speak to Tajbakhsh, but knew it would not come. He was being guarded by several men.

One of the guards in the room where I was taken had been part of the team who had raided my house and arrested me. He'd been in charge of keeping an inventory of my confiscated DVDs and equipment.

"How are you, Mr. Bahari?" he asked with a smile. "How is your mother? Have you seen her since that day?" I thanked him and said that she'd visited me a few days ago.

"Mr. Bahari's mother is a very strong woman," the guard told another man. The mention of Moloojoon's name made me really proud. There was a newspaper lying on the table, and I managed to read one headline before the guard grabbed it: something about the dangers of swine flu for pilgrims in Mecca.

"I guess the swine flu is a real problem," I said to the guard, hoping to distract him so I could focus on watching Rosewater and Tajbakhsh in the other room. From what I could hear, Rosewater was telling Tajbakhsh what to say.

Rosewater glanced up and caught my eye. "Don't look!" he yelled as he jumped up and ran at me. I lowered my head, preparing for his punch. Instead, he leaned over me and moved his jacket so I could see his gun in its holster.

"Do you know him?" Rosewater asked, referring to Tajbakhsh.

"Not personally," I said. "Is it Kian Tajbakhsh?"

"No, it's my aunt!" he answered.

Rosewater told the other guards in the room to leave. "Listen, Maziar," he said. "There are dozens of former ministers and members of parliament in the courtroom right now. They're all admitting to their crimes and dishing the dirt about each other. Why do you think you're so different from them?" He ran his fingers through my gelled hair. "Nice haircut," he said. "It will be such a pity if the last time your mother sees her beautiful son is on television." Then he slapped me hard on the head.

"Listen, you *bacheh khoshgel*"—you pretty boy—"you either name everyone on the list I gave you and apologize to the supreme leader for breaking his heart, or you're going to be sentenced today and executed a few days from now." He slapped me on the head again and opened the door. "It's your choice to live and see your mother, or die for Mousavi and Rafsanjani." He shut the door behind him.

I was eager to know what was happening inside the courtroom. I would later learn that the reality was far more absurd than anything I could have imagined. The "trial" was the first in a series of show trials that the Islamic government would stage after the election. A number of sources told me that the trials were produced on Khamenei's direct orders, meant to show the strength of the regime and disgrace the reformist leaders who were paraded in front of the press in their prison uniforms.

The scene was something out of the Soviet Union in the 1930s. Stalin himself had staged similar show trials, in which a couple dozen high-ranking former Communist Party officials were put on trial for treason and allegedly planning to assassinate Comrade Stalin. The difference was that the culprits in Stalin's courts had clear, albeit fabricated, charges against them; the incrimination procedure was thorough. In Khamenei's version, the charges could be anything from possession of a satellite television, to throwing stones at the Revolutionary Guards, to being in contact with the CIA. The Guards had collected more than a hundred prisoners of different backgrounds and political affiliations under the same roof. There were former ministers and parliamentarians, as well as a number of young kids who had done nothing more than attend a demonstration. It seemed as if everyone had been arrested for the same reason: to show the widespread nature of the *fetneh*—the sedition, as Khamenei called the postelection demonstrations. But there was not enough time to try each prisoner, leaving the prosecutor to read a long statement that sounded like the same propaganda and nonsense the Iranian people had heard too many times before.

I realized that I was not going to be tried on that day. I was part of the post-trial show. The Revolutionary Guards had decided to stage a press conference with four supposed leaders of the velvet revolution: Mohammad Atrianfar, a former security official and deputy minister of interior who had also been in charge of a number of reformist newspapers that had been shut down; Mohammad Ali Abtahi; Kian Tajbakhsh; and me. Tajbakhsh and I were told to sit in the courtroom as Abtahi and Atrianfar were taken behind a podium for the press conference.

It was difficult for me to watch Abtahi and Atrianfar during their press conference. I had interviewed each of them several times. Once jovial and chubby, Abtahi looked defeated and broken. He was less than half of his previous size. With a lifeless expression in his eyes, he made scathing comments about Mousavi and Khatami, and explained why the reformists had failed to gain widespread popular support and so had had to stage a velvet revolution. Abtahi's basic point was that the reformists did not understand how much Iranians admired Khamenei and, as a result of this miscalculation, devised misguided strategies to gain people's votes before the election or overturn the results after the election.

Atrianfar took a different approach: he spent a significant amount of time praising Khamenei's greatness. A clever type who knew how to switch sides, Atrianfar understood that all tyrants are susceptible to flattery, and so he compared Khamenei to Imam Hossein, the grandson of the Prophet Mohammad and one of the most revered figures of Shia Islam. Atrianfar then likened himself to an enemy of the imam who later joined Imam Hossein's army.

My turn was to come after lunch. We ate chicken kebabs and drank *doogh,* a salty yogurt drink similar to lassi, inside the courtroom. Rosewater told me to look down during lunch. He then gave me his drink, saying he had to watch his blood pressure. "Names, Mazi, names," he reminded me. Before the interview, Tajbakhsh and I were given dress shirts to change into.

I knew what I had to do. Watching Atrianfar's shameless praise of Khamenei had convinced me that I should follow him, and instead of naming names, as Rosewater wanted me to, I would offer my apologies to the supreme leader and repeat the paranoid but general theories Haj Agha, Rosewater's boss, had outlined about the evil Western media.

When at last we were up in front of the cameras, I remained as quiet as possible throughout the press conference and allowed Tajbakhsh to do most of the talking. We both concluded by saying how sorry we were to have made mistakes and asked Khamenei to forgive us. Afterward, Tajbakhsh and I gave our shirts back and put on our prison uniforms. We exchanged sorry looks. We were two broken men.

I was separated from Tajbakhsh and led back to the car that would take me back to prison. I hadn't named any names. I knew what awaited me.

*   *   *

A short time later, I sat quietly in my chair in the interrogation room. Rosewater walked over to me. From beneath my blindfold, I could see that he still had his formal shoes on. He stood in front of me for a while, then walked away. Then I could feel him standing behind me. He punched my shoulder so hard that I immediately felt my right hand go numb.

"You will be executed within the next twenty-one days," he said. I knew that twenty-one days from now was the start of the holy month of Ramadan, during which Muslims fast and no execution can be carried out.

Rosewater punched my shoulder again. I could feel the impact of his ring on my bone. "I will make sure you die before Ramadan, Mazi," he said. He stood in front of me and grabbed my nose with his fingers. "But I will also make sure that I smash your handsome face first."

CHAPTER FIFTEEN

It was a hot early August day, and we were in one of the inter-rogation rooms where there was no air-conditioning. That always put Rosewater in a bad mood.

His first question surprised me: "Who is Pauly Shore?"

Those unfamiliar with Mr. Shore are not missing much. He's a B-list actor who played a school outcast, a university party animal, and an unemployed male stripper in a series of come-dies in the 1990s. I, along with ten other pathetic souls, was a member of the Pauly Shore Alliance on Facebook. I had joined the group with a friend, as part of an inside joke.

"Why?" I replied.

Up to that day, except for the *Daily Show* interrogation, Rosewater had asked me only about politicians and journalists. He placed a piece of paper in front of me. At the top he had written *Describe your connection to Pauly Shore.* "I want to know everything there is to know about him."

Where does one start? I wrote down that Shore is a come-dian and was in a series of comedies I had watched while at university. I named a few of his films: *Encino Man, Son-in-Law,* and *Jury Duty.*

"Everyone you know seems to be a comedian," Rosewater said. "We'll investigate this Pauly Shore." I wondered which lucky fellow in the Revolutionary Guards would be assigned that crucial task.

Rosewater wasn't finished. "What is your connection to Anton Chekhov?" Despite its absurdity, I'd sort of expected this question. I was a member of two fan clubs on Facebook: Pauly Shore's and Anton Chekhov's. My inquisitors were really grasping at straws here.

"Anton Chekhov is dead, sir," I answered. "He was a Russian playwright who lived in the late nineteenth and early twentieth centuries."

"Was he a Jew?" Rosewater asked angrily.

"I don't know. I don't think so."

"He sounds like a Jew to me," he said impatiently.

"Well, in Russian, *ov* denotes belonging to a place. It is similar to *zadeh* in Persian."

Rosewater was silent.

"But I don't know. He could be Jewish. Many Russian writers and intellectuals, as well as revolutionaries, were Jewish at that time."

"And many of them were Zionists. Herzl was a Russian," Rosewater said, referring to Theodor Herzl, the founder of the Zionist movement.

"He was Hungarian," I replied and immediately regretted it. I didn't want to sound defiant, but sometimes his idiocy was too much to bear. And anyway, at this point, what did I have to lose?

"Oh, really?" He grabbed my neck from behind and squeezed with all his might. "You know so much about the Jews, don't you?"

He put a blank piece of paper on my chair and slapped the back of my head. "Write down everything you know about Anton Chekhov and don't write *koseh she'r,* bullshit!" Rosewater exclaimed. "We're going to investigate every Zionist you know, Mr. Maziar. We're going to show you that despite what you may think, we are not stupid. We know that your Chekhov was Jewish and that you are a Zionist."

After, presumably, Rosewater found out that Chekhov was not Jewish, he did not bother with any more questions about people with surnames ending with *ov*. That included my Israeli friend David Shem-tov. I don't think you can find a more Israeli name than Shem-tov, but I could just imagine the Revolutionary Guards researchers saying to each other, "Chekhov, Molotov, Shem-tov, they are all the same!"

I had grown up listening to anti-Israeli propaganda on Iranian television, but it was only in Evin that I discovered the real depth of the Islamic government's hatred, paranoia, and lack of understanding of Israel, and of Jewish people in general. The Iranian government claims Israel is its main nemesis. If the United States is the Great Satan, Israel is the "Even More Devious Satan." I was coming to understand that Rosewater, who was likely being fed anti-Israeli propaganda on an hourly basis, believed every conspiracy theory pertaining to the Jewish people. To Rosewater, a Jew could not be an ordinary person. To him a Jew meant a Zionist, a spy—someone who has no other occupation than conspiring against Islam and Muslims. I don't think he had ever met a Jewish person in his life. But he thought that he knew everything about the Jews and Israelis.

"Write down the name of every Jewish element you've ever met in your life!" he demanded one day.

I took the pen. *In the West it is not customary to ask about people's religious affiliations. It will be very difficult for me to answer your question because I cannot guess the religious background of every person I've ever met in my life.*

He tore my answer into pieces and threw them in my face. Grabbing my hair from behind, he forced me to pick them up from the floor. "Do as I ask! Tell me the names of the most evil, irreligious bastards you have ever met. They were all Jews!"

In order to satisfy him, I wrote down a list that included

journalists, university students, and teachers and former neighbors of mine in Canada and the United Kingdom.

"I thought you said you've never met any Jews in your life," he declared proudly. "But there are ten names here. You have to detail all the information you have about these elements."

I knew that Rosewater would be well rewarded by his bosses if he could connect me to shady dealings with Israel, but there was nothing to be found. Ever since I had returned to Iran, in 1997, I had made sure to keep my distance from any association with Israel. I knew that being connected to Israel could easily put me in jail or, at the very least, end my career in Iran. I even refused to cover the Palestinian-Israeli conflict—the most pressing issue in the Middle East—in order to avoid having to travel to Israel.

Rosewater's ideas about the Jews and Israel came directly from Khomeini's writings and speeches. After seizing power, like all Middle Eastern tyrants, Khomeini had sought legitimacy through demonizing the Jewish state. In turn, Israel—by committing atrocities against the Palestinians and setting up illegal settlements—kept providing Khomeini and other Middle Eastern dictators with ample reason to condemn it.

Despite Rosewater's hatred of the Jews, his attitude to Israel was one of awe and envy. While he clearly had contempt for anything to do with Israel, he frequently demonstrated his admiration for the methods Israel used to defeat its enemies. He once told me that all my friends in the West who have criticized the Islamic government or have acted against it would someday be brought back in a bag "just like that Nazi guy in Argentina, what's his name?"

"Adolf Eichmann," I said.

"Yes, Eichmann. The Nazi leader," he said. "If the Israelis can kidnap one of their enemies, don't you think we can do the same thing?" He took my right earlobe and pulled it as hard as he could. "We are much stronger than Israel. The Islamic Revolutionary Guards Corps has networks all around the world. Hezbollah and Hamas are only two of them. Nobody should think they're safe anywhere in the world."

*   *   *

I'm sure that the irony of comparing his government's ability to hunt its opponents with the Israelis' pursuit of a Nazi criminal was lost on Rosewater. Unlike Rosewater, most Iranians aren't anti-Semitic.

I, for one, had been fascinated by Jewish history and culture all my life. When I was between the ages of five and ten, my family lived in a neighborhood that had many Jewish people. One of Tehran's two largest synagogues, some Jewish butchers, and the main Jewish school were very close to our house. As old communists, my parents didn't have any predilection for or prejudice against the Jews. But other kids in the neighborhood would tell me that Jews were different from us. We didn't know how they were different, exactly, but we always knew who the Jewish kid in the class was. That didn't stop us from being friends with them. When I later moved to Canada, many of my Jewish friends told me that they had been taunted at school for being Jewish. I couldn't remember that ever happening in Iran.

Jews settled in the Persian Empire more than two millennia ago. Many Iranian Jews trace their roots in the country to 2500 B.C., when the Persian king Cyrus the Great provided refuge for Hebrew people fleeing from Babylon. The Jewish prophets Ezra and Isaiah called Cyrus "the one to whom God has given all the kingdoms of the earth." Cyrus's name is repeated twenty-three times in the Old Testament, and he is the only Gentile to be designated as a messiah—a divinely appointed leader—in the Torah. Outside of Israel, Iran still has the largest Jewish community in the Middle East. Even though many Iranian Jews migrated to Israel and other countries after the revolution, there are still twenty-five thousand Jews in Iran.

As a child, being told that Jews were different made me think about my own identity. Why did they buy their meat from a different butcher? Why did the men and boys wear yarmulkes? I remember being fascinated by the word "Jewish," especially when I understood that many of the people my parents, my siblings, and I admired—Karl Marx, Bob Dylan, Paul Newman—were Jewish, and that my hero, Charlie Chaplin, sympathized with the plight of the Jews. Chaplin's *The Great Dictator* is still one of my favorite films.

In 1993, I decided to make a film about Jewish immigration to North America as my senior-year project. I chose the story of the SS *Saint Louis,* a ship of Jewish immigrants who left Germany in May 1939. I found a number of the ship's survivors in different countries around the world, and interviewed them for the film. After *The Voyage of the* Saint Louis became quite successful in festival circuits, and was shown on television in many countries, I was interviewed several times about why I, a Shia Muslim, had made a film about a group of Jewish refugees. I always emphasized that one of my main reasons was to show that many Iranians care about the plight of other peoples. In October 2005, many Iranians were surprised and disgusted when Ahmadinejad called the Holocaust a myth and questioned the number of Jews killed during the Second World War.

I was always very proud that I was possibly the only Muslim filmmaker who had ever made a film about the Holocaust. In fact, in 2008, when the International Documentary Festival Amsterdam organized a retrospective of my work, I insisted that they show *The Voyage of the* Saint Louis in order to prove that not all Iranians are as ignorant as our president.

My words came back to haunt me as I sat blindfolded in my chair in front of Rosewater. Before he started asking questions, his mobile phone rang. It was his wife again. He squeezed my right ear with his free hand as he answered the phone.

"Hello, dear, how are you?" He sounded relaxed as he spoke. "I'm so sorry, *azizam*, my dear, you know that I've been busy. . . . I know it's the anniversary of our marriage." Rosewater squeezed my ear harder. I started to moan. "Shut up!" he yelled at me and then calmly told his wife, "I'm sorry I won't be able to make it tonight, but I'm going to be finished with this guy very soon." He let go of my ear and punched me in the head. "And I will make sure we have a nice celebration together. Now I have to go."

After he hung up, he slapped me on the back of my head a few times. "*Zendegi baraam nazashti*," he screamed. "You've ruined my personal life. You little Jew lover! Why didn't you tell me that you made films about the Jews?!" Rosewater roared as he repeatedly punched me in the head. He placed a printout of my interview with the International Documentary Festival Amsterdam on my chair. "Why didn't you tell us that you've cooperated with the Jews? Who gave you the money?! Tell me!"

Rosewater continued to slap and punch my head. It was as if by doing that he could rid me of my sympathies for Jewish people. He finally pushed me to the floor and kicked my back and legs.

"Tell me which agency you work for! If you don't tell me, I will let you rot here. I will put your bones in a bag and throw it at your mother's doorstep. You Zionist spy!"

*   *   *

In my cell that night, I woke up with my head pounding. I reached for the three sleeping pills and four migraine tablets I'd hidden under the green carpet. We could see the prison doctor twice a week. He had allowed me to take a migraine pill only when I was in pain, but sometimes I pretended to be suffering so that I would have enough pills for when I needed them. I knew it was dangerous to take them all at the same time, but the pain was so bad it felt like my head was going to explode.

So what if it was dangerous? I wanted to end the pain. I'd do anything to end the pain.

I went to sleep immediately, but within minutes a prison guard woke me up so I could use the toilet before morning prayers. After he led me back to my cell, I lay down and tried to go back to sleep. I pushed the carpet aside and put my throbbing temple on the cold tiles. I fell asleep within a few seconds.

Two women approached me. Their skin was tanned and smooth, their faces kind and beautiful. They were smiling at me the same way Maryam often had. They came to me from an endless white background. We were in an open space with no horizon. I watched their long dark hair blowing around their faces. I could feel the cool breeze on my skin. I was floating just above the ground, still suffering from my migraine, but their smiles soothed my anguish and pain.

Then they were at my side, lovingly touching my forehead with their cool, soft hands. After months with no human contact other than Rosewater's beatings, their touch felt like balm on my skin. They helped me stand and led me gently toward a white bed in the endless white background. I was floating in the air. Their hands remained on my forehead and soothed my pain. I felt safe on the bed because I had them at my side.

"Who are you?" I asked the women.

"Sisters of mercy," they answered.

"Like Leonard Cohen's 'Sisters of Mercy'?" I asked with a smile.

As I said those words, I heard a voice. It was Leonard Cohen singing one of the most beautiful songs ever written.

Oh the sisters of mercy, they are not departed or gone.
They were waiting for me when I thought that I just can't
*   go on.*

And they brought me their comfort and later they brought
   me this song.

I don't know how long the dream lasted, but I didn't want it
to end. I knew what emotions awaited me when I woke up—the
fear, the shame, the hatred—and I wanted this feeling to last
forever. I felt better. I felt safe. And, though only in my dream,
I once again felt free.

*   *   *

One day, I overheard a conversation between a female guard
and a woman who sounded American.

"*Roosari, roosari,*" the guard kept telling the prisoner.
"Head scarf, head scarf."

Later on, I heard a male American voice in the hallway. "Can
I use the bathroom?" the American prisoner asked in English.

"Yes, yes, yes," the guard answered, clearly not understanding what the prisoner was saying.

"Sir, I need to use the bathroom," the prisoner repeated desperately.

"Yes, yes," the guard said.

I wanted to help.

"He needs to use the *mostarah*—the toilet," I told the guard.
"I can translate for you two, if you'd like."

"I can't let you do that," the guard answered. "He and two
others are the directors of the CIA in Iran."

I knew that this couldn't be true, and it was only after I was
released that I found out that the American voices belonged to
two of the three young American hikers who were arrested in
late July 2009 on the border between Iran and Iraq. But the
experience really shook me. Other than the few conversations
I'd had with my mother, I hadn't heard a female voice in what
felt like ages, and it made me think of Maryam more than ever.

I also began to think that the Iranian government had started a new stage in its war against opposition activists and their foreign supporters—possibly arresting some foreigners in the country, simply for being foreign. Having no contact with the outside world, I fought not to imagine the worst.

At times, alone in my cell for days, I became terrified that I was going crazy. My conversations with Maryam and my father were becoming more frequent and made less sense. I started to have nightmares about the bruised soles of Maryam's feet after her lashings and my father's broken, bloodied nails.

It was the pen that saved me. I had stolen it during an interrogation session. When Rosewater had briefly left the room, I'd slipped the pen into the waistband of my uniform. I had heard that if you had a pen in your cell, you would be punished, but I didn't know what the punishment was, and I didn't care.

A day or two after I stole the pen, Rosewater suspended my *hava khori* privileges in order to punish me for my refusal to name names. For almost a month, I was allowed to leave the cell only three times a day, during the times of prayer, to go to the bathroom. The pen became my closest, and only, friend. At night, when I knew the guards were asleep, I would design crossword puzzles on the wall and on the floor under the carpet; I had first developed the skill while sitting through boring lessons in school. It surprised me that I could still do it, and, desperate for some diversion from my loneliness, I would create puzzles for hours—first in Persian, then in English. I further challenged myself by making the puzzles more difficult, designing them around certain themes and subjects: politics, history, pop music, and geography. I couldn't believe my good fortune when one day the plastic cups we had previously been given with our meals were replaced by paper ones. I'd drain the water from each cup, then carefully unglue it and lay it out to dry. At the end of the day, after the paper was covered in crossword puzzles, I would shred it into small pieces, form tiny balls, and play a solitary game of basketball. I'd designate one of the tiles of the faux marble wall as the net, and try to hit that tile with the paper balls. I was so distracted by my puzzles and basketball games that I hardly noticed that Ramadan had begun and I had not seen Rosewater for two weeks.

I had survived. At least for now.

* * *

On the second day of Ramadan, I was transferred again, to a smaller, windowless cell. Eventually they reinstated my *hava khori* sessions, and I was able to walk in the courtyard for fifteen minutes every three or four days. Twice I was allowed to call my mother. Before the guard grabbed the phone from my hand each time, she told me that Nikbakht, the lawyer she had hired, was still trying to see me. I prayed that this was true, and during the day, as I exercised on the floor and jogged around Regent's Park with Paola, I attempted to convince myself that they wouldn't really execute me. The Islamic government was irresponsible and stubborn, but it was not yet lawless. For a high-profile case like mine, the judges would at least pretend to observe legal procedures. If they were going to kill me, they would at least allow me to see my lawyer before passing a sentence.

"I hope you're right," my father said to me that night, as I tried to stretch the ache from my legs and back. "Time will tell."

* * *

From the day I'd arrived in Evin, I'd feared spending the month of Ramadan there. As a nonreligious person, I didn't know how I'd withstand the experience of not being able to eat all day. Maryam had told me about prisoners being punished for eating during Ramadan while she was in jail, but to my surprise, on the first day of Ramadan, Brown Sandals came to ask me my

plans: Would I be fasting or did I have a medical excuse to ex-
empt me?

"I've had ulcers in the past," I quickly replied. "I'd like to
fast, but doing so usually makes them worse."

He accepted my excuse without asking questions, and I felt
an enormous sense of relief when breakfast, lunch, and dinner
were delivered to my cell that day at the normal hours.

Ramadan is the month when Allah gives his servants the opportunity to repent and carry out good deeds, for which he be-
stows multiple rewards. As Muslim scholars explain, fasting
during Ramadan doesn't only mean not eating; it also includes
refraining from anything that is not in line with praising Allah.
Muslims are expected to have only clean thoughts and engage
only in chaste deeds during Ramadan. They should also avoid
using profanities and obscene gestures, which is why I was partly
confused—and wholly horrified—by the turn of events that occurred on the third day of Ramadan, when Rosewater finally
called me back to his interrogation room. After his failure to
connect me with the reformists, foreign intelligence agencies, or
the Jews, I was not sure what Rosewater's modus operandi
would be the next time I saw him. He greeted me by placing a
thick pink folder on my chair.

"*Chetori, gherti?*" he said, asking me how I was doing while
also referring to me with a derogatory term for a superficial
person who thinks only about fashion and his or her appearance. "Do you know what's in this folder?" he asked, slapping
the back of my head. Since it is also a rule that during Ramadan
Muslims must refrain from fighting, I'd been hoping that these
sessions would take place without their typical violence. I was
wrong. "This is the documentation of all your dirty, improper
conducts."

He opened the folder and showed me its contents. There
were printouts of hundreds of my email messages and the Facebook pages of different friends, as well as a long list of the

names of people I knew, in messy handwriting. They were all women.

"Do you think you can get away with *kardan*"—with fucking—"any woman you want, *gherti*?" He sat on the table in front of me. "I want you to go through this list of women and point out to me which ones you screwed. Then you will tell me how much you paid each woman for doing her."

If he hadn't been hitting the back of my head, I wouldn't have been sure whether or not he was serious. "No, sir. You have it wrong. These are not girlfriends. These are just women I know professionally, and some who have added me on Facebook, some of whom I've never even met."

"Oh, really?" Rosewater said. "Why don't you have the name of my aunt here?"

"I'm really not sure what you're getting at, sir," I somehow found the courage to say. "Did you arrest me for improper relationships or the other charges you've brought against me?"

"What did you say?" He kicked my leg. "We're getting really cheeky here, aren't we? Do you think that because you haven't been executed yet, our plans are to leave you alone? Well, my friend, let me explain. This is what we've decided: you're not only a spy but also a *mofsed fel arz*."

I had always dreaded that expression, which means "someone who corrupts the earth." Corruption can be by means of actions or thoughts, and can include anything the Islamic regime deems unsavory. Thousands of people have been executed for this charge since the establishment of the Islamic Republic.

The surprise I'd felt at Rosewater's stupidity turned to fear. While I knew he didn't have any evidence that I had engaged in espionage or acted against national security, I had had premarital relationships, and it wouldn't have been too difficult to find the names of my previous girlfriends. I decided to answer absurdity with absurdity. "Sir, I've only had a relationship with one woman in my whole life," I said. "And that is my wife."

"Who is this, then?" Rosewater asked as he started playing a video behind me.

I heard Paola's voice. "No, no," she was saying.

I realized what the video was. I'd recently bought a cheap laptop in London and had wanted to test the camera. I'd filmed Paola, who was having a bad-hair day, without her knowledge. When she realized I was filming her, she covered her face with her hands. "No, no," she said, trying to duck behind me and out of view of the camera. The sight of Paola in our flat in London nearly brought me to my knees. I missed her so much. I held back my tears, as well as my anger at Rosewater for even looking at Paola.

"That's my wife, sir," I managed to say. "I would appreciate it if you didn't look at my private videos."

I felt his knee hit me hard in the small of my back. "I do whatever I want. Don't ever raise your voice again." He sat heavily on a chair and played the video of Paola again, from the beginning. When it finished, he replayed it once more. I could tell by the tone of his voice, and his slow, steady breath, that he was enjoying watching my unveiled beautiful blond wife in a private moment.

"This is not your wife," he kept saying. "I'm going to watch it again. You take a look at that list of names in the folder." I breathed as slowly as I could, trying to fight the nausea settling in my throat, as Rosewater slid his chair closer to the video.

"Now, as I said. We are going to go through the names one by one. Begin by telling me how and where you met each woman," Rosewater said. Of course, I didn't even recognize many of the names on the list, but Rosewater wasn't buying that. Every time I wrote next to a name that I didn't know a particular woman, he responded by slapping me.

"Mazi, *bacheh khoshgel*, pretty boy. We both understand that the best way to get close to your female sources for espionage and other purposes is through sexual intercourse," he said knowingly. "Stop wasting our time. Stop trying to fool me. Here—" He placed a clean sheet of paper on the writing arm of the desk. "I want you to put down the names of your 'special' friends." He picked up the list of names. "Let's start here. Shirin Ebadi. You have four phone numbers for her. When and where was the first time you had sex with her?"

Shirin Ebadi was a Nobel Prize laureate, and one of the most prominent human-rights lawyers in Iran. "I've never worked on any project with Mrs. Ebadi," I said.

"*Sheytoon*, naughty boy, I'm not asking about 'projects.'"

"Sorry, I don't understand your question."

"Don't just sit there!" I heard my father whisper. "Find an answer to this moron's question."

"Sir, I think Mrs. Ebadi is a respectable married woman," I said. "If I remember, I interviewed her for—"

He didn't let me finish. He raised his right leg and kicked me hard in the right shoulder from behind. "You've never fucked her?" he yelled. "So why do you have four numbers for her? Why don't you have four numbers for my aunt?" I began to feel sorry for the poor woman. I wondered what she would do if she knew that her nephew was using her name so gratuitously.

"Sir, I have ten numbers for Mr. Ahmadinejad's office," I replied sarcastically.

As I expected, this brought another blow to my body. He continued to beat me, and each kick came with greater force, sending waves of pain so bad I felt nauseous all over again. He yelled at me all the while, but he no longer seemed to make any sense at all. I thought of Zahra Kazemi, the Iranian-Canadian photojournalist murdered in Evin. I had to find a way to appease him and stop the beatings.

Rosewater's attitude about sex revealed more information about him than he was ever able to extract from me. As he went through my list of friends and colleagues, it seemed genuinely inconceivable to him that a man and a woman could be friends or work together without having a sexual relationship. The scenarios he made up became ever more grotesque, and he seemed to believe in the truth of his own inventions.

On the sixth day of Ramadan, he arrived in the interrogation room particularly interested in how I'd met Malu Halasa; we had worked together to coedit *Transit Tehran,* a compilation of the work of Iranian writers and photographers. I told him we had met at a party.

"A sex party?" Rosewater asked.

This was the umpteenth time he had referred to sex parties, but he seemed to be in a gentler mood that day. I knew I needed to take advantage of this. "I've never been to a sex party," I said. "I don't know what one is exactly."

"Tsk, tsk, tsk, Maziar," he said sarcastically. "Don't play games with me, or you will make me angry again. Don't tell me that you don't know about these parties where men and women start with dinner and drinking alcohol and then go to the swimming pool, where they eat chocolate off each other's bodies."

I sat silently, trying to picture it. How on earth does one eat chocolate off another person's body in a swimming pool? I had a picture in my mind of chocolate floating on the surface of the water, and then I began to imagine the mixed taste of chlorine and chocolate.

I realized what he was doing. Most of the people he interrogated were no doubt devout religious men. For these people, sex is a highly taboo subject, and this line of questioning would likely make them feel very uncomfortable. In fact, I later learned that many reformist leaders who broke in prison and confessed to treason did so as a result of the constant psychological pressure from sexual innuendo. In some cases, Revolutionary Guards had genuine pictures of reformists having extramarital affairs.

In others, interrogators fabricated documents and used them to force witnesses to lie about illicit affairs.

While this constant psychological pressure about sex proved effective against religious men, it was going to be quite useless in breaking me. Although Rosewater threatened several times to send explicit details of my sexual relationships with Shirin Ebadi and other Iranian female activists to Paola, I wasn't nervous in the slightest. Paola knew all about my previous relationships, and I didn't have any affairs to be worried about.

The longer this line of questioning went on, the more I began to realize that something else was at play. Rosewater wasn't only hoping to break me psychologically; he was also aroused by thoughts of my sex life. He was asking me about pool parties where men lick imaginary chocolate off Barbie-like blond Western women because he couldn't be there himself. And he ached to be there. His religion had promised him that he could do all that, and much more, when he got to paradise, but he had to control himself until then. He hated me for being able to enjoy on earth things that were, for him, reserved only for a time after death.

I knew dozens of men like him. He reminded me of kids from traditional backgrounds in my secondary schools who'd thought that people in north Tehran, families who led more Westernized lives, acted out pornographic films daily. Much of their information about sex and the West came from pornographic magazines and films they watched again and again, illegal videotapes they'd bought on the black market. From Rosewater's line of questioning, I could see that much of his knowledge about the rest of the world also came from porn. In fact, I was coming to suspect that Rosewater mistook porn films for documentaries and, as such, honestly believed that most women in the West were sex therapists, horny secretaries, or naughty cheerleaders and that mailmen, milkmen, and

plumbers had sex with their willing clients after each delivery
or repair job.

*   *   *

"Who is Debbie?" he asked me one day.

"Debbie?"

"Yes, Debbie the *Cleaner*?" He nearly purred the last word.

Debbie was a housekeeper Paola and I had hired in London.
I didn't know her surname, so in order to remember who she
was in my mobile phone I'd saved her name as Debbie the
Cleaner. "She cleans our house," I answered. "Why?"

"Are you going to tell me that you didn't have sex with her?"
Rosewater asked.

"Sir, she's an older married woman from the Philippines," I
answered.

"Filipino?!" he asked with interest. "So you're telling me
that all the news about women from Thailand doing those dirty
things is false?"

"I said the Philippines, not Thailand," I corrected.

"Same thing," he sneered. "I'm sure you know all about
Thailand as well. I know your kind."

Paola and I had spent three weeks in Thailand and Cambodia in March 2009, and I had a number of photographs of us
there together, which by now he'd surely seen. There seemed to
be no doubt in Rosewater's mind that we had traveled to South-
east Asia for perverse sexual pleasures. "Why did you go to
Thailand?" he asked.

I was going to explain that Thailand was a transit stop to
Cambodia, but I had been through days of beatings, and my
body ached. I was also tired of these very personal questions. At
that moment, I had an idea: maybe it was time to give him what
he wanted, in a tactical move to distract him from my personal
life.

"I'm ashamed to say why, sir," I answered quietly.

"What do you mean?"

"It's a really personal and shameful thing to say."

Rosewater's interest was clearly aroused. He came closer to me and put his hand on my shoulder. "You can tell me anything you want, Maziar," he said, his voice soft and gentle. "This is just between us." He took the paper from my desk and crumpled it into a ball. "You don't even have to write it down."

I bowed my head and, somehow, found the ability to cry on cue. "But, sir, it's a shameful thing to say."

"What is?"

"I like sexual massages."

He was quiet for a few moments, but I could hear him breathing heavily. "What do you mean?" he asked, his voice faint.

"Well, sir. As you know, I suffer from terrible migraines. Often, when I reach orgasm, my head throbs. So while in Thailand, I would get an Asian . . ." I paused. "Masseuse . . ."— I drew it out—". . . to *relax* me."

"Go on."

I went into the lurid imaginary details. Of how the young, toned Thai masseuse would take off my shirt. Of how she would put oil on my body and start rubbing me, beginning at my shoulders. Of how she would move her way down.

"Without her clothes on?" he interrupted.

I hadn't thought of that detail. "Yes, sir, it's shameful. They always begin the session by removing their clothes. First her top. Then her panties. When she is totally naked, she rubs her body with herbal oil. It smells so good."

"Like what?"

"It's hard to explain. You'd have to be there in the room to understand it. The smell I like best reminds me of tropical forests in the morning after a long rainy night. You can just forget all your problems by inhaling the fresh air." Rosewater was hooked. He wasn't saying a word. I have to admit, I was enjoying my made-up story as well. "Before she climbs on top of you to begin the massage, you can smell the herbs. The smell relaxes you right away."

Rosewater sighed quietly. I knew that with my story, I was torturing this miserable man, who spent all his time in dark cells beating and torturing innocent people. That gave me such pleasure.

CHAPTER SIXTEEN

"What do you think of my performance, Mazi?" Rosewater asked a few days later. From the sound of his voice I could sense that he was sitting in front of me. He had done this only a handful of times, and always when he had questions that contained at least a trace of truth. I guessed that he wanted to study my reactions in order to find out whether or not I was lying.

"I'm sorry sir, I don't understand. What do you mean by 'performance'?"

"I mean, do you think I'm a good interrogator?"

You're a bloody psychopath, I thought. "Well, you certainly have made me confess things that I have never confessed to anyone in my life," I answered.

"Example?"

"My shameful acts in Thailand, which I had to explain the other day."

"But there are many things that you haven't confessed, Mazi."

"Sir, if I haven't confessed things, it means that I didn't want to lie to you," I said. "I think your beatings extract the truth from me. The beatings hurt, but I feel better because of them. They are like a hard, long exercise session or, rather, like chemotherapy. Making me honest with myself has made me feel much better." Somehow, he took me at my word, though I'd never confessed to anything during a beating.

"I didn't want to tell you this, Maziar," he said, "but my father was a political prisoner in the shah's time. He was so severely tortured by SAVAK"—the shah's secret police—"that he has a difficult time walking now. They pulled out his toenails and damaged his feet so badly that even now, thirty years later, he has to use a cane to walk. I never did that to you, did I?"

I was surprised to hear this. How could a man whose father had endured such torture now administer torture himself? What a senseless, absurd cycle of violence this was. "Why was your father in prison?" I asked.

"He was a follower of Imam Khomeini. In fact, he was willing to sacrifice his life for the imam." By this point, I'd spent enough time with Rosewater under the darkness of my blindfold to be able to understand the meaning behind every noise he made, and now I could hear the tears in his voice. He walked closer to me—I could see his black slippers beneath the crease in the blindfold—and put his hand gently on my shoulder. "I asked you a question, Maziar. Answer me," Rosewater said quietly. "Have I ever tortured you?"

I didn't know how to answer. I was the prisoner of a manic-depressive man, someone with a huge ego and yet highly insecure, constantly seeking other people's approval. A wrong answer could lead to more punching and slapping, and, frankly, I was tired of that. And the more I thought about Paola's efforts to get me released, which I trusted were ongoing, given the small hints my mother was able to make on the phone, and the attention my case may have been getting around the world, the more powerful I was coming to feel in his presence.

I heard my father's voice: "Go with it, Mazi. He's losing strength. You can manipulate him. You may even come to control him."

I paused for a few seconds, then said, "I think you have

shown me your strength." I paused again, melodramatically. "I think you had to carry out your duty by exerting maximum pressure on me to find the truth."

Rosewater inhaled heavily and chuckled, but his voice remained distant. "It's not been maximum pressure, Mazi. You still don't know what I'm capable of."

"What's interesting is that you are sometimes soft and kind like a brother, and sometimes as harsh as a disciplinarian father," I said. "I think that is an amazing achievement."

Rosewater laughed. "It's my art," he said, with obvious pride. "Your art is making films and writing. My art is being a proficient interrogator. The only difference is that I use my art to help our holy system and you use it against God and the supreme leader." I sensed him settling into the chair. He went on for a while in this vein, and when he finished speaking, he instructed me to get up, turn my chair to the wall, and remove my blindfold. I sensed that he was preparing to beat me again.

"I know that on a personal level, I have a lot of shortcomings," I said. "I know about the weaknesses and faults in my character and behavior."

"Example?" He couldn't hide the anticipation in his voice, and we both knew where this was going. He was dying to hear more about Thai women and oil massages. He was hooked. I spoke without interruption for hours about how shameless it was of me to receive massages by naked Thai women. How depraved I believed myself to be when I felt a pair of perfumed, perfectly shaped breasts on my back.

Of course, I'd never actually had a sexual Thai massage. My improvised monologues were based, instead, on years of watching pornography on illegally imported Betamax and VHS tapes in the 1980s and reading and rereading Persian translations of *Lady Chatterley's Lover, La Ronde, Madame Bovary,* and dozens of other romantic and erotic novels as a teenager. In that school chair in an Evin interrogation room, I felt that I was back in school telling my classmates intertwined stories of Arthur Schnitzler's *La Ronde* in order to make myself popular. I remembered making the turn-of-the-twentieth-century story even more lecherous to pique my friends' interest. Like those secondary school students, Rosewater remained mostly quiet, except for a few questions here and there, to clarify the images in his big, horny head.

The next day, he had more questions for me. "Mazi, is it true that one can go to the Champs-Élysées street in Paris, grab a woman's hand, and have sex with her anytime he wants?"

"Sir, you'll be arrested within a few seconds and charged with rape," I explained. "I'm sure no one does that."

"Why not?"

"In the West, a woman can call the police even if you touch her hand," I said.

"But wait a second," Rosewater objected. "One of our lecturers at the university who'd spent so many years in the West and received his PhD degree from a Western university told us that people behave like animals in the West. That you can live with a woman without being married to her."

"Sir, there's a difference between living with someone you're not married to and jumping on anyone you desire on the street, like an animal," I said as respectfully as I could. "Marriage is a symbolic gesture for many people in the West and also legally entitles you to certain things, but I know people who've been together for decades and are not married. Yet in terms of being faithful, they're more dedicated to each other than any married couple."

"I can't believe it," Rosewater said. "So why did you marry your wife?" Once again, I felt extremely grateful that Rosewater believed I was married. If he knew that I lived with Paola and, worse, that she was pregnant and we were not married, I could be accused of having an illegal affair.

"Because both her family and my family are very traditional," I lied. "Neither of us could even think about living together without first being married."

"It must be liberating not to be bound by traditions," Rosewater said. I wasn't sure if he was testing me or was genuinely distilling his frustrations.

"Well, we are always trapped by our traditions wherever we go," I answered. "It is like a virtual cage we take around with us."

"It is not a cage, Maziar," Rosewater chuckled. "But I often wonder how people live without any religious values. You may feel free and happy in this world, but what about the hereafter? How would you be able to answer God about all the sins you have committed in this world?

"Every time I think about life in the West, my whole body trembles," he went on. "How would I be able to control my desires, how would I control my relationship with my wife? It must be hell to live in such a decadent environment."

I had often wondered why Rosewater had chosen to be an interrogator. Maybe, I thought, the answer lay in the fact that in his head, freedom was synonymous with sin and punishment. Could it be that he felt safe only in a restricted, claustrophobic environment?

* * *

One day, after many hours of asking about different aspects of life in the West, Rosewater returned to a subject he'd only briefly mentioned earlier in the interrogation.

"Have you spent much time in New Jersey?" he asked anxiously.

"Not really," I said. "Maybe a few days."

"Why is New Jersey so famous?" he asked.

Is it? I wondered. "I'm not sure it is famous," I said.

"Really?" He sounded embarrassed about his lack of New Jersey knowledge. "People who go to America are always saying, 'New Jersey this, New Jersey that.'"

"I really don't know, sir," I said, in my best it's-okay-not-to-know-about-New-Jersey tone of voice. "It's a state like any other state in the U.S. It has nice places and not-so-nice places. Many people who work in New York live in New Jersey."

"Is it because it's nicer?" Rosewater asked.

"It's more affordable," I said, thinking that making a scathing comment about New Jersey could lead him to beat me. "But New Jersey is full of nice places. It is even called the Garden State."

"And the health system?" he asked. "Is it better than other places in the U.S.?"

"I'm really not sure, sir," I answered apologetically. "I really haven't spent much time there."

"And Jews?"

Where did that come from? I wondered. "What about the Jews?"

"Are there any Jews in New Jersey?"

I knew that by saying that there were thousands of Jews living in New Jersey I might be subjected to more beatings, but the prospect of bursting his Jew-free bubble was very tempting. "Sir, there are Jews living all over the United States. They are American citizens. There are thousands if not millions of Jews living in New York and its surrounding areas, including New Jersey. So I think there must be a lot of Jews who live in New Jersey."

Rosewater paced the room. "*Ajab, ajab,*" he said, almost as if speaking to himself. "I wonder why."

I couldn't understand why he was fascinated with New Jersey, and later in my cell, as I designed my crossword puzzles, I thought there were two possibilities. The first was simply that certain foreign names sound exotic to Iranian ears. As a child,

I'd been enthralled by two places: Massachusetts and Connecticut. I'd never understood why, but they'd always sounded like fascinating places to me, and I'd made sure to visit them during my first visit to the United States, in 1988. The second involved an absurd U.S. law that bans Iranian diplomats working at the United Nations from traveling more than twenty-five miles from their offices on Third Avenue. Many diplomats live in New Jersey, and maybe Rosewater had had a conversation with an Iranian envoy. This, among so many other things about Rosewater, would forever remain a mystery to me.

* * *

Sunday, September 13, 2009, was a hot day. The air-conditioning, though hardly cooling my cell, was making more noise than usual. I hadn't been beaten for a few days, so I was feeling well, and walked briskly during the morning's *hava khori*. Around the time of noon prayers, after I'd done more than fifty push-ups and was on to my sit-ups, Brown Sandals interrupted me.

"Mr. Hillary Clinton, get ready for your specialist after the prayers," he said before passing my blindfold through the slot.

I sprang up from the floor, toward the door. "What? Hillary Clinton?!" I yelled, struggling to make myself heard over the clatter of the air-conditioning.

"Yeah, she's been talking about you a lot lately," Brown Sandals said knowingly. "Does she know you personally? Huh? You *sheytoon*, naughty boy?"

I didn't answer. I sat back down on the floor and continued my sit-ups. I had grown so sure that I'd never hear good news again, and I wanted to kiss Brown Sandals for giving me the best piece of news I'd had since I'd arrived. *There must be a massive campaign going on for me,* I thought. *Otherwise, why would the American secretary of state mention an Iranian-Canadian?* "Mr. Hillary Clinton!" I said aloud as I counted the number of sit-ups. *One hundred and twelve, one hundred and thirteen, one hundred and fourteen.* "Mr. Maziar Hillary Bahari Clinton!" *Two hundred and eighty-three, two hundred and eighty-four, two hundred and eighty-five.* The possibility that Hillary Clinton was speaking publicly about me gave me an energy unlike anything I'd ever felt. *Four hundred and thirty-eight, four hundred and thirty-nine, four hundred and forty.*

"I'm not alone!" I shouted in my head. I continued my sit-ups and continued to count: *Six hundred and eighteen, six hundred and nineteen, six hundred and twenty!* I'd never done as many sit-ups in my life before being called Mr. Hillary Clinton. I suddenly felt a sharp pain in my groin. I lay back and raised my hands as if I'd won the marathon in the Olympics.

*   *   *

After the noon prayers, instead of having lunch, I was taken to the interrogation room. Rosewater didn't sound happy. I was desperate with hope that he, too, would mention Hillary Clinton to me. He started slapping my head even before he sat me down.

"Where did you meet your wife?" he asked. I'd already told him several times that Paola and I had met at a lecture in London, but he wasn't interested in my answer. "I'm sure an intelligence agency introduced you two to each other. Otherwise, why would an English woman marry an Iranian man? Also, you should know that she's making very derogatory comments about Iran and Iranians in her interviews with the media."

I felt my heart skip a beat. "She's doing interviews with the media?" I blurted, willing myself not to break out into the relieved, nearly maniacal laughter I felt building up inside me.

"Yes, it's despicable. She talks too much," Rosewater said.

What incredible news. Combined with Brown Sandals' Mr. Hillary Clinton comment, I finally allowed myself to believe what I'd been praying for since the day I'd been brought to Evin: Paola was successfully advocating for me. She and I had frequently talked about the possibility of my arrest. I had even joked about it with her, although she would frown whenever I did. "Seriously, Mazi," she'd say, "if you are ever arrested, I will make such a fuss that they will have to release you."

"She's insulting our nation, our people," Rosewater yelled. "If you have any dignity as an Iranian, you will tell your wife to stop talking about you."

Before I could respond, Rosewater had grabbed my arm and was dragging me down a hallway lit by fluorescent bulbs. Standing me before a gray pay phone attached to the wall, he lifted my blindfold and told me that it was time for me to call Paola and tell her to stop talking. I wanted nothing more than to speak to Paola—to hear her voice, to listen to her breathe. But at the same time, I didn't want the call to happen like this—out of the blue. Paola is a very emotional person, and I feared that being pregnant might have made her even more sensitive. What if the shock of hearing from me harmed her or the baby? I had not been able to protect her or our baby since I'd been taken away, but this was my chance. I randomly dialed a wrong number.

"She's not answering, sir," I told Rosewater.

"Hmmmmm," he said from behind me. "That's not good."

"No, but perhaps you might allow me to call my brother-in-law so he can ask my wife to wait for my call tomorrow."

Rosewater agreed, and after I made a very brief call to Mohammad, he took me back to the interrogation room. He went over what I had to tell Paola the next day, not knowing how much hope he was giving me. He particularly didn't like the fact that Paola had written to the Italian government—her mother is from Italy—asking Prime Minister Silvio Berlusconi to intervene on my behalf. I was so proud of Paola at that moment. "She's asking that bald bastard to help you," Rosewater said with derision. "What can that baldy, that member of the Mafia, do for you? Tell her that we're a sovereign nation. We have a lawful country. The Roman Empire is dead," he continued, marking each sentence with a slap. "The British Empire is finished. And the American Empire is dying. I want you to make her understand that her comments only make your life more complicated."

Back in my cell that day, I felt Paola's presence right next to me. My love for her grew deeper than ever as I sat in the corner of the cell, applying pressure to my temples with my index fingers—trying to stave off the migraine I felt creeping up the back of my neck. I couldn't get Rosewater's words out of my head: Paola was talking too much. She was getting attention for my cause. And as Brown Sandals had suggested, Hillary Clinton was aware of me.

Maybe I was going to survive.

* * *

It's difficult to say why you fall in love with someone, but I knew that one of the main reasons I loved Paola was her staunchness: her no-nonsense attitude, her strong principles, and her deep commitment to her family. When it comes to family matters, she just gets things done. When we were first together, my priorities had been all over the place, which had occasionally led to a battle of wills. Paola's mother is hot-tempered, and Paola inherited much of her fiery Italian nature. During some of those arguments, we could be quite nasty to each other.

As I dialed Paola's number the next morning, I remembered her tears after one of our silly fights. I felt homesick and guilty. I couldn't forgive myself for having been cruel to her. It was crucial to me that she sense that I was healthy—strong, even— and unscathed by the isolation and terror of almost three months of imprisonment.

"Hi, Mazi, hi, hi," Paola said when she picked up, as if wondering what her first words should be. Despite my best intentions, the moment I heard her voice, I could no longer control myself, and tears rolled down my cheeks. Rosewater hit me on the back of my head. "*Mard baash!*" he said. "Be a man!" He then pressed his head against mine to eavesdrop on what Paola was saying, even though we were speaking English and he couldn't understand us. I wanted to beat his big head to a pulp with the receiver, but I didn't dare move even the slightest bit, fearing that he would stop my conversation. I had so much to say to Paola, only I couldn't find the words. "I love you," I uttered between bursts of tears.

Paola was calm and strong. "The whole world is thinking about you, Mazi," she said. "Everybody cares about you." Her words were as reassuring and calming as my mother's. It was almost as if she, too, had experienced decades of arrests and imprisonments in her own family. "We will get you out of prison, Mazi," she told me.

"Tell her about Berlusconi and not giving interviews," Rosewater said, shoving a note into my hand and pushing my blindfold up so I could read it.

Again Paola knew exactly how to avoid answering my question about her letter to Berlusconi. "Let me think, let me think," she said innocently. "I don't think I've written any letter to him. I'm fine. I've been to the doctor a few times and everything's fine. I swim and walk every day."

When Maryam died, Paola and I had agreed to name the baby Marianna Maryam if it was a girl, to reflect Paola's Italian ancestry and my sister's name, but we hadn't decided on a boy's name. Since the Leonard Cohen dream, I had decided that I wanted to call the baby Leo if it was a boy.

"Is it a boy or a girl?" I asked Paola.

"I haven't found out yet. You'll be home soon." She paused,

and I thought I detected tears in her voice. "I'm waiting for us to find out together."

"But I have to know, darling," I told Paola. "I had a dream and want to call the baby Leo if it's a boy."

Rosewater was getting impatient. "Have you told her that you've made mistakes?" he wrote on another slip of paper.

"You haven't done anything wrong, Mazi," Paola reassured me. "I know that the call is monitored, but no one thinks you've done anything wrong and everybody's supporting you. Everybody!"

Hearing this news, I felt the weight lift from my chest, and for the first time in weeks, I could breathe normally again. A prisoner's worst nightmare is thinking that he's been forgotten, and Paola's words reassured me that this idea—which had plagued me for weeks—was false.

"Please find out if it's a boy or a girl," I said to Paola as Rosewater reached toward the phone to end the call.

I tried to say "I love you" one more time, but the line had already gone dead.

"I love you!" he mocked as he handed me back to the prison guards.

But his words didn't touch me the way they had over the last several weeks. That night, as I rolled one blanket into a pillow and lay down in the darkness and silence, I envisioned the day when I would finally get to see Paola again. I had so often entertained this thought while alone in my cell, or during interrogations, but doing so had always been painful. The experience had been very much like the weeks and months after Maryam died, when I would fall asleep praying for it all to be different—for the chance just to see her again.

But that night, as I pictured holding Paola's hand, and kissing her pregnant belly, the thoughts felt different: they no longer felt like a hopeless fantasy.

"I'll get home to you," I whispered into the darkness. "I

will." I wrapped the second blanket tightly around my body, and for the first time in weeks, I slept through the night.

*   *   *

Ramadan ended on September 19, and the weather in Tehran turned cooler. Rosewater no longer had to fast, and he wasn't suffering from the sweltering summer heat. He started to leave the window of the interrogation room open to let the breeze in, and I often tried to bring my chair as close as I could to the window, where I could breathe in the cool mountain air. Rosewater would sometimes join me near the window, where he'd stop asking questions and begin to sing—always religious songs in praise of the family of the Prophet Mohammad. That always put him in a better mood.

Over the next few weeks, my father and Maryam stayed with me during the interrogations, and gave me the confidence to push aside my fears and try to steer our discussions away from me. Instead of talking about my alleged spying, we talked about aspects of life in the West that I knew Rosewater wanted to explore—sex, of course, but also the welfare system, mortgages, and even the price of a secondhand car. With each day, I felt him becoming more and more relaxed with me, which meant far less frequent beatings.

I began to think that he was willing to allow me to direct the discussions because he simply had no other questions left to ask me. By now, I was sure, he knew that I was not guilty of the crimes he'd so badly wanted to believe I'd committed when I'd first arrived at Evin. I hoped the reason his questions about my alleged illegal activities had subsided was that I was closer to being released. Now, it seemed, his time spent with me was a bit of a reprieve for him—he was even beginning to enjoy my company, and taking a break from beating and insulting other prisoners.

"Mazi, what would you write about me if you had the chance?" he asked one morning.

"I would love to do an interview with you, if that's possible," I answered. I really meant it.

"You're so diplomatic, but this isn't an interrogation," he said. "I want to know what questions you would ask me."

I, of course, couldn't tell him the truth: What makes a man choose a job that includes beating other men, making threats to end their lives, and playing mind games with them? Especially a man whose father endured all of this. "I think it's important for young people to know your opinion about different issues so they don't end up like me, being interrogated by you."

"Who do you think this interview will help?" Rosewater asked. "It can only help the enemy, the Americans and Zionists, to know our secrets."

"Well, it may help the enemy, but it can also help people to gain a better understanding of what the government thinks." I hesitated, then continued: "I had all the necessary accreditations and took all the recommended precautions, but you still arrested me and put me through interrogations. I don't want that to happen to other people."

"Mazi, don't think that just because I'm not asking you about the crimes you've committed means we're ready to let you off the hook," he said unconvincingly. "We have our think tanks, and they are conducting research about you."

He then walked away from me and remained silent for a few minutes, deeply inhaling the fresh morning air. There was a light breeze that reminded me of London.

"Look at this," Rosewater said. I had been sitting facing the wall, without my blindfold, and I turned toward him. He suddenly, and perhaps out of habit, slapped me hard across one cheek. "Don't turn your face, I said."

"But you said, 'Look at this.'"

"Haven't you learned that you shouldn't turn your head even if I make a mistake?" he demanded, before calming down. "I'm just saying, look at these people who come to work at this time. It's eight-twenty and they're supposed to be here by seven-thirty. I can't understand how some people can be so unprincipled. No one has forced them to take this job. They've chosen it."

My face was stinging with pain. Rosewater seemed to be genuinely upset about other torturers slacking off at work. "We have a tough job, Mazi. We have to work long hours, as you know. We have to travel around the country, and sometimes we sleep in the office for only a couple of hours before going back to work. So many wives of my colleagues have asked for a divorce because they couldn't take it anymore."

Rosewater pulled up a chair and sat behind me. I could sense a trace of regret in his tone. He told me that his wife was different from the wives of other interrogators; that she understood that he had dedicated himself to Islam and the return of Imam Mahdi and therefore she didn't object to his long working hours, which kept him away from home.

"I kiss her hands and her feet because she's so good to me," Rosewater told me. "From the moment we went to her house and she served me and my family tea and sweets, I knew that she was right for me." In arranged marriages in Iran, it is customary that after the family of the boy asks the family of the girl for her hand, they go to her house to discuss the arrangements with her parents. The girl shows her face only once, when she serves tea and sweets to the guests. "The moment I took the tea from the tray and our eyes met, I knew that she would be a faithful wife," Rosewater whispered.

He took a Kleenex and blew his nose quietly. "I have a surprise for you," he told me. "I'm going to let you talk to your wife one more time."

He didn't say anything as he held my arm and led me to the phone, but I could hear him inhale heavily as he repeated the words "*La elaha ella Allah*": There's no God but Allah.

I managed to get through to Paola at once, but the international calling card Rosewater was using had credit for only two minutes of conversation. I quickly asked Paola if she had found out the sex of the baby.

"Yes!" she giggled. "What do you think?"

"Darling, we only have two minutes—a boy or a girl?"

"It's a girl. I wish you could see the pictures from the scan. It's a beautiful healthy girl."

"Marianna Maryam Bahari," I told Paola. "I can't wait to be with you and Marianna." I couldn't control my emotions when I mentioned Marianna's name.

"You'll be home soon, Mazi," Paola said, trying to calm me down. "I'm sure you'll be home soon."

CHAPTER SEVENTEEN

On the morning of October 6, I was lying on my back in my cell and cycling with my legs in the air. I was pretending to ride my bike. I had taken a detour through Hampstead Heath and High-gate, and was just coming down through Belsize Park toward Primrose Hill. I was full of energy.

I hadn't seen Rosewater for a few days. Typically, a few days without human contact had left me feeling anxious and desper-ate, but this day, remembering the sound of Paola's voice, and the work I now knew she was doing on my behalf, I practiced feeling better. The day before, for the first time since my arrest, I had been allowed a newspaper. Reading something besides my interrogation notes had given me energy, even though it was *Kayhan* ("The Universe"), the hard-liners' mouthpiece. I de-voured every single word in the paper. But most importantly, after months of designing my own crossword puzzles, I finally had access to a professional one. I studied it for hours, trying to learn from it. That morning, as I cycled toward Primrose Hill, thinking of the post-ride coffee that awaited me and designing a new crossword puzzle in my head, there was a commotion in the hallway. I stood up to listen, and heard prison guards telling some of the prisoners to pack up and clean their rooms. Blue-Eyed Seyyed opened my door and gave me a blindfold.

"*Ostad Bahari*"—Maestro Bahari—"we're gonna miss you," he said.

"What do you mean? Are they going to release me?"

"*Na baba, hol nasho.* You wish. You're going to the communal cell."

I had heard that when they transferred someone to a communal cell, it typically meant that his case had moved from one stage to another. I was still under investigation, and, as far as I knew, there'd been no change in my status. Blue-Eyed Seyyed led me through Evin's labyrinthine complex, to a small alleyway with a building at the end of it. I had my blindfold on, but by then I'd learned how to raise my head and look through the gap beneath it without being caught. The guard opened a large blue gate and closed the door behind me.

"Can I take my blindfold off?" I asked.

"Of course you can," said a man standing in front of me. I removed it and saw that it was Mohammad Atrianfar, the former deputy minister of interior who had praised Khamenei's greatness in the press conference after the show trial. The fifty-six-year-old Atrianfar had been a revolutionary since his student days in the early 1970s. After the revolution, he became part of the Islamic government's security and military apparatus. I had interviewed Atrianfar several times and had always enjoyed his stories about traveling to Libya and Syria to buy contraband arms during the Iran-Iraq War, when Iran was embargoed by most of the world. He kissed me on both cheeks. "Welcome, Maziar. Isn't this great? Coming here has got to be a good omen. I think we'll be freed soon." He stroked his thick gray beard. "You have to make sure that you feed the rat," he told me.

I assumed "feeding the rat" meant something like bribing the guards or being nice to them. "Feed the rat?" I asked.

"Yeah," he said with a big smile. "We have a big rat that comes to the courtyard, and we take turns feeding it."

I looked around my new environment. The cell was surrounded by high walls and had two large windows and a glass door—all of which were covered by metal grates. It also had its own small courtyard, kitchen, bathroom, and shower—even a television set. This shared cell was definitely an improvement over solitary confinement, but it was also obvious that we'd be more scrutinized here: two security cameras, mounted in the courtyard, pointed at the cell, and I noticed several microphones placed throughout the room as well.

There were five individual beds in the cell, with proper mattresses, clean sheets, and blankets. For the first time in more than three months, I even had a real pillow. The walls were made of three-inch bricks, and the courtyard was covered with polished gray cement. I later learned that the cell was part of the block that belonged to the internal affairs unit of the Revolutionary Guards. It was here that they kept high-ranking commanders who had been arrested on various charges.

Atrianfar told me that he had been moved to the communal cell two days earlier, and in the meantime, he had transformed it into a cozy studio apartment, anticipating the arrival of his new cellmates. He had tea and sweets waiting; he had prepared them himself. We could give the guards a shopping list for fruits and vegetables twice a week, he explained; the money was then deducted from the cash they'd taken away from us on the day of our arrest.

I later learned that since a couple of days before Ramadan, I'd been considered one of twelve VIP prisoners. Not long after I arrived in the new cell, Saeed Shariati, the spokesman for the Islamic Iran Participation Front, the main reformist party, which had supported Mousavi during the presidential election, walked in. I'd met him on several previous occasions, and it was nice to see another friendly face. But after hugging Shariati hello, I noticed how broken and distressed he looked. During his imprisonment, he had apologized publicly to Khamenei and had stated that the reformists had pursued the wrong policies prior to the election. I could see the apologetic, dejected expression in his eyes, and wondered if others detected the same look in my own.

The next prisoner to join us that day was another reformist politician, Feizollah Arabsorkhi, a handsome man with a kind face and big eyes. Arabsorkhi was a leader of the Mojahedin of the Islamic Revolution Organization (MIRO), a semiclandestine reformist party whose heads had been among the founding members of the Revolutionary Guards. As some of the most extremist and radical activists at the beginning of the revolution, the founders of the MIRO were close to Khomeini.

That evening, my cellmates and I sat on the floor of our new home, sharing tea. As we talked, I detected regret in the eyes of both Arabsorkhi and Atrianfar. Both of them were now sorry for the part they'd played in creating a regime that was a far cry from their youthful ideals. They had believed that anyone and anything could be sacrificed on the path to establishing an Islamic state, but with time, they had become witnesses to the transformation of that state into a corrupt, tyrannical regime. They were victims of their own making.

Unlike Atrianfar, Shariati, and me, Arabsorkhi had refused to apologize and appear on television. He said that because of this, his interrogators had practically abandoned him, and had left him in limbo for weeks. He wasn't sure what charges were going to be brought against him. But though he was the only one of us who had refused to work with his captors, he still believed that the Islamic regime could be reformed. Atrianfar and Shariati, on the other hand, had each pledged their allegiance to the regime in their televised confessions, seeming to know that the system was rotten to the core and that it wasn't worth their lives to try to reform it. They were no longer risking their lives for their ideals—they just wanted to get out of prison.

We were all caught in that uncomfortable zone between trying to save our lives and betraying ourselves.

Mohsen Safaei Farahani was our fifth cellmate. Farahani had been a member of parliament, deputy minister, and the head of Iran's football federation. When Safaei entered the room later that night, he gave me a sad smile. We had met on a few previous occasions, and he had also known my father. In fact, he was the revolutionary who'd replaced him as CEO of Mana Construction Company after the revolution. "How are you, Mr. Bahari?" Safaei asked. "I'm so sorry I didn't call you after your father passed away."

Safaei had got to know my father well after taking over his job. I remember him calling our house seeking my father's help in managing the company's ten thousand employees. Even though my father was bitter about getting kicked out of his job for no good reason, he still felt responsible for the company he had built from scratch. My father spent hours explaining the company's operations and personnel.

Unlike other new revolutionary leaders, Safaei wanted to learn from the experience of others, and this impressed my father. But he was still surprised by the naïveté of Safaei and many of his generation, how they thought they could change the world within a few years.

"It's going to take a few decades for them to learn," my father would say after each call with Safaei.

In 2000, when Safaei was elected as a reformist member of the parliament and spoke out against the hard-liners in the government, my father said with a sad smile and even sadder cynicism, "It took the reformists two decades to learn from their mistakes, but I'm sure they will be forced out of the government and will be replaced by a new group of idiots." My father's prophecy came true in 2005, when Ahmadinejad came to power and stripped Safaei and other reformists of all official positions.

I sat next to Safaei on the carpeted floor. He held my hand in his as he asked about my father, and I could sense his regret for dedicating his life to a government that had paid him back by putting him behind bars.

I asked him if he knew why we had all been transferred to a communal cell and, more importantly, why I had been put in the same cell with four politicians.

"They had a scenario that didn't work," Safaei said as he stretched his back. "We were all arrested according to a plan, a scenario. But their plan was too complicated for the Revolutionary Guards to execute, and it didn't work."

Over the next several hours, happy and relieved to have others to speak with, we talked incessantly about the circumstances behind our arrests. We eventually came to the shared conclusion that the Guards had been planning the arrests months in advance and the postelection turmoil had provided a perfect excuse to execute them. Trusting in Khamenei's words to the very letter, the Guards leadership truly believed that the green movement was led by a few dozen reformists who were aided by the West. By arresting those reformists and those who connected them with the West, the Guards' higher-ups thought, they could finish people's demands for reforms and put a stop to the greens.

As we spoke, I came to understand that among the VIP prisoners, Safaei and I had suffered more physical abuse than the others. Some of my new cellmates had heard Rosewater's screams and insults while he was interrogating me, and had wondered what was going on. Safaei's physical torture was an anomaly among my cellmates; none of them had been beaten. They were all religious people, and their "religious" torturers had known how to put psychological pressure on them. They had threatened to harm the prisoners' loved ones and friends and had even fabricated lies about the private lives of reformist leaders. Some interrogators had gone further and forced a number of women into making false confessions, swearing that they'd had illicit sexual relations with the prisoners, a crime punishable by death.

*   *   *

One of the real luxuries of the communal cell was the small television which showed the six main state channels. On the second day in the new cell, I was watching football when Rosewater summoned me to the interrogation room. I wished I could ask him to wait. It was the first time in months—since even before my arrest—that I had had a chance to watch a game. This one was a repeat showing of my favorite team, Liverpool, playing against Chelsea, but I didn't know the final score, so it felt as if I were watching it live.

Unfortunately, I had no choice in the matter. In the interrogation room, Rosewater sat me in the chair, opened the window, and asked, "Digestive or orange flavor?" Without waiting for my answer, he placed a cup of tea, a few sugar cubes, and a saucer holding some biscuits on the writing arm of my chair.

"To start with," he said in his most baritone voice, "I'd like to apologize for everything that's happened so far."

Apologize? I didn't know what to say. I nodded politely.

"You know interrogation is a difficult process. This is the beginning of a new phase." From beneath my blindfold I saw Rosewater take a biscuit from my plate. "May I?" he asked.

"Sure," I said, my voice revealing the anticipation I felt that this nightmare might finally be coming to an end.

"Our think tanks and several of our colleagues have been investigating your case, and I'm glad to say that we now know you're not a spy. And the holy Islamic system is going to treat you with kindness."

I had thought that I'd feel elated when I finally heard these words; instead, all I felt was furious. *So, it's all water under the bridge?* I thought. *You bloody bastard. All the beatings? All the insults?* I remained quiet.

"I hope you aren't resentful, Mazi," Rosewater said in a pseudoconcerned tone, as if he were talking to a child whose candies had been taken away from him. "In the past few months I've had the privilege of sharing your company. I learned a lot from you."

I hope you rot in hell, I thought. "You're very kind, sir."

"It was me who recommended a quick investigation into your case. As you know, this could have taken several more months, even years, otherwise. You know that, don't you, Mazi?"

"Yes, sir, thank you very much," I mumbled, knowing that he'd had nothing to do with it. This had to be because of Paola's work, and the efforts of others.

"No problem. What I wanted to talk to you about today can determine whether you will be released or not." He pulled a chair close to me and sat down. He took another biscuit from my plate. "Even though we know that you're not a spy in the classical sense of the word, you're a media spy."

"What is a media spy?" I asked faintly.

"Well, Mazi, we haven't found a clear definition for it," Rosewater said as he moved his head closer to me. "That's the beauty of it. We're giving you a chance to work with us to find a definition for it, and help us defeat media espionage."

I was utterly confused. "Sorry, sir—am I being charged with something that you don't have a definition for?"

"Well, 'charged' may be too strong a word for it." Rosewater had obviously been briefed about media espionage but hadn't had time to familiarize himself with the idea. I heard him going through some notes.

"Maziar, what is a spy?"

"A person who passes secret information related to the national security of a country to another country."

"What is a journalist?"

My patience was running thin, but I had to humor him to see

where this would ultimately lead. "Someone who reports about events for print media, TV, or radio or Internet sites or blogs," I said as calculatingly as I could. "The difference between a spy and a journalist is that a spy works secretly against the national security of a country for another government, but a journalist works openly—even if he uses secret sources—to inform the public. With all due respect, I really don't understand what a media spy is, sir."

"Slow down, Mazi. Don't get ahead of yourself," Rosewater said curtly. "So both journalists and spies deal with information. Isn't that right?"

"Different kinds of information."

"Information, nonetheless." He was getting annoyed with my noncompliance. "What if a journalist's reports are used against the national security of a country? For example, you filmed the demonstrations after the election despite the government's orders that you should not report anything. The enemies have used your footage and writing against our holy Islamic Republic. Should we just revoke your press card or should we charge you with something more?"

Just cancel my press card and let me go, you motherfucker! "Just cancel my press card, sir."

"Of course you'd say that. But we think that what you've done is an example of media espionage. Even if we still can't offer a cohesive definition of media espionage." He stood up and began to pace the room. "As I told you in the beginning, no one can make a decision about your fate except for us, the Revolutionary Guards Corps." This was the first time he'd mentioned that he was part of the Guards. "Mazi, you're very lucky that we would like you to be freed and to help the Islamic system."

This was not the first time I'd been promised release in exchange for my cooperation, and I was reluctant to allow the hope I was beginning to feel to truly take hold. "I'm willing to help any way I can," I said. "I'm a filmmaker and a journalist, and I can offer you my services when I'm out of prison."

"Of course you can," Rosewater said. "But the gentleman who's going to be here in a few minutes will tell you how else you can help us. He's my boss, so be very careful when you talk to him."

Rosewater had left the room to get more tea and biscuits when his boss walked in. The Boss sounded like an old man, and his strong and distinct accent betrayed that he was from the city of Isfahan. The Boss pulled a chair up next to mine and began to gently rub my back. "I hope you've had a pleasant time, Mr. Bahari."

"Well, sir," I said, "because of its nature, prison is a very difficult place to be."

"Soon you'll be out of here," the Boss reassured me. I closed my eyes under the blindfold, trying to absorb his words. "But there are certain formalities that we have to go through before releasing you. I'm sure you know what I mean?"

"Not really, sir," I said apologetically.

"Well, do you know why we're releasing you?" the Boss asked.

"Because I've repented?"

"Yes, but what will the manifestations of this repentance be?"

"I'll make films for you and write articles in defense of the Islamic Republic," I offered.

"That's very good, but we need you to cooperate with us in other ways." The Boss got up from his chair and moved even closer to me. He had polished brown shoes and creased brown trousers. Rosewater walked in and put a fresh cup of tea and digestive biscuits on the arm of my chair.

"Would you like me to stay, sir?" Rosewater asked the Boss.

"Maybe it's better if I have a private talk with Mr. Bahari," the Boss answered. I heard Rosewater leave the room.

"He is a very devout soldier," the Boss said about Rosewater. "He's tough and a firm believer but you and I . . . we are intellectuals. I think we can work this out between ourselves. If not, I can just leave and ask your interrogator to carry on his duty."

I was too afraid to say anything. I wanted to hear him tell me again that I would be released. Keeping my eyes closed, I quietly sipped my tea.

"I was really impressed with your first TV interview, and even then I thought, *Here's a man we can work with,*" the Boss said as he tapped my shoulder. "You have many contacts in the West who are among the opposition to our holy regime. You also know the Western media inside out. So, Mr. Bahari, all we're asking from you is to help us identify how the Americans and Zionists are using the media to wage a war against our government. And in doing so, Mr. Bahari, you will help us to defeat our enemies."

He placed a list on my chair: dozens of names of journalists and opposition activists working inside and outside Iran, including many of my friends, as well as some people I'd never met.

"This is a partial list of people we would like you to monitor," the Boss said. He then laid out his plan for me: after my release, I would provide them with a weekly report about anti-Iranian activities in the West. To accomplish this, I was to approach different journalists and politicians, become friends with them, and then report their activities to the Revolutionary Guards.

I accepted immediately and without hesitation. The Boss lifted my blindfold, and I reached for the pen he handed me and signed the letter of commitment on my desk:

I, Maziar Bahari, will be working with the brothers in the Revolutionary Guards Corps, and I will report to them every week about my activities and the activities of the anti-revolutionary elements I will be in contact with. I accept that I will be responsible for the consequences of my failure to act upon my promises and my failure will result in punishment.

As I saw it, I was not being asked to admit to any guilt. I was simply being forced to make a promise that I had no intention of keeping. This was a useless piece of paper—of course I would sign it. I was elated. There was a real possibility that I would be released in time to be with Paola for the birth of our baby daughter.

Rosewater reentered the room.

"Congratulations, sir," the Boss said to Rosewater. "Because of your endeavor, Mr. Bahari seems to have learned about the might of our forces, sir. It's an important achievement."

"With your permission, sir," Rosewater said, "I would like to remind Mazi—this is the term of endearment I use for Mr. Bahari, sir—that when he steps out of Evin Prison, he should not feel that he's safe. The Revolutionary Guards Corps has allies all over the world. If Mr. Bahari ever decides to abuse our trust and act against us, we can always bring him back in a bag."

"Mr. Bahari is a wise and intelligent man," the Boss said. "He knows that we are his friends. Don't you, Mr. Bahari?"

"Of course. When will I be released, sir?" I asked. "My wife is going to give birth in twenty days, on October twenty-sixth. Will I be able to see the birth of my child?"

"I think so," said the Boss vaguely. "This letter of commitment means that you've trusted the Islamic system, and in return we'll make sure that you don't have to go through the bitter experience of the last three months for much longer."

The thought of being with Paola for Marianna's birth made me happy, but I also knew that I could never trust these people.

Over the next several days, I spent most of my time in the interrogation room, reviewing the different lists of names Rosewater or the Boss had been preparing for me. The lists included a variety of people, from former secretary of state Henry Kissinger to friends of mine who worked as junior producers for the BBC. As in my Thai massage stories, I let my imagination roam freely, making up details about how I would approach each person and spy on them.

"I've met Kissinger. He's a German Jew and he really liked my film about the Holocaust," I lied to the Boss one day. (I'd never met Kissinger in my life.) "He is the man behind all the decisions in America regarding Iran and the Middle East. I can go to Kissinger's office, pretend that I want to do an interview with him, find out about his plans for Iran, and report back to you."

I also told them that I'd be willing to spy on my friends for the Revolutionary Guards.

"You're friends with Masoud Behnoud, aren't you, Mazi?" Rosewater asked, referring to a well-known Iranian journalist who lives in exile in London. "If we give you an eavesdropping device, will you be able to plant it in his house?"

"No problem," I answered. In speaking with Rosewater, I described how Masoud lived in a grand luxury house in central London, though, in fact, he lived in a modest, two-bedroom flat in a suburb. They thought that Masoud was spying for MI6 and that he was a wealthy man, and I happily went along with their narrative. "I can put the device under his desk, and I might even be able to download his computer files," I said.

"*Ahsant!* Bravo!" said Rosewater.

To secure my release, Rosewater explained, I would have to post bail in the amount of three billion rials (£200,000). I didn't have that much cash, of course, but told him that I could register my mother's apartment as the deposit.

"If you ever make the mistake of not returning to Iran," Rosewater warned me, "the first thing we'll do is kick your mother out of that apartment and throw all your tapes and books into the street."

It was another attempt to manipulate and scare me, but it wasn't going to work. I knew my mother would rather get kicked out of her home than have me endure even one more day in prison, and even if she were evicted, I would be free, and able to enlist the help of our friends and relatives in finding her a new place; plus, it sounded like an empty threat. From their constant emphasis on the bail, I knew that they didn't believe that I was going to spy for them. I guessed it was just protocol that in order to be released, prisoners had to sign a letter saying that they were going to spy for the regime; it was a way for the Revolutionary Guards to save face. I had no way of knowing if my guess was correct, but I didn't care. All I wanted was to be released.

*   *   *

As I prepared for my release—never knowing the exact date when it would occur—I was allowed to call my mother every day. She told me that she and Mohammad had started the legal procedure to register the deed to my mother's house to be used for my bail. She also told me that Paola had been admitted to the hospital three times. She had been diagnosed with placenta previa, a condition in which the placenta attaches to the uterus so low down that it borders on or covers the cervix. It had resulted in heavy bleeding, which was dangerous for Paola and the baby. My mother and Mohammad reassured me that the hospitalizations were only a preventive measure, but the news still devastated me.

As my cellmates chatted and shared stories, I tried to keep myself busy by exercising. But I was consumed with worry for Paola. I began to imagine the worst, to the extent that, at times,

I actually longed to be back in solitary confinement, where I could cry freely without bothering anyone.

Though being in Evin had been a very emotional experience, I generally don't like to show my emotions. My stoicism bothered Rosewater to the last day. My conversations with my family were recorded, and Rosewater didn't try to hide the fact that he'd been listening to them.

"How's Paola?" he asked. It was Friday, October 16. By then all the legal steps regarding my bail had been completed, and I was ready to be released. "I hope she and the baby will survive this."

I knew he wanted to purposely raise doubts in my mind about Paola's health. Using a man's wife and child to put pressure on him was pushing the moral boundaries to the limit, even for an interrogator working for the Islamic Republic. But nothing about Rosewater surprised me anymore.

"I'm sure they'll survive, sir," I said quietly.

"You're so cold, Maziar," he remarked. "We're talking about your wife's and your baby's lives here."

"They'll be fine," I said firmly, while burning inside. "I'm not worried about them."

"But what your family is telling you about the bleeding and everything isn't very reassuring."

"They'll be fine, sir."

Rosewater took away the plate of digestive biscuits and the cup of tea he'd put on the arm of my chair. "Listen." He tapped my shoulder as hard as he could. "Don't forget who you are. When you step out of here, I need you to report every single thing you do. I want to know about every person you meet and every thought you have. You'll be fine when I say you're fine. Your family will be fine when I say they're fine. And when you're out, always remember the bag. We can always bring you back in a bag." He grabbed my ear for the first time in weeks and squeezed it as hard as he could. "Understood?"

I didn't want to reply, but then I considered that it wasn't defiance that had got me to this point.

"Understood?" he repeated, squeezing harder.

Let him hear what he wants to hear, I thought. *You'll be jogging in Regent's Park with Paola and the baby soon.*

"Yes," I said. "Understood."

Part III

SURVIVAL

CHAPTER EIGHTEEN

On the morning of October 17, I was taken to Judge Mohammadzadeh's office. If the number of files on his desk was any
indication, the Islamic Republic had managed to make many
more enemies for itself in the months since my arrest. I wondered how many innocent lives were in the hands of this vicious, hypocritical judge.

Unlike the first time I'd met him, when he'd made rude, sexual gestures, today his manner was businesslike and efficient.
He quickly read aloud the thirteen charges against me, which
included everything from the still undefined "media espionage"
to taking part in illegal demonstrations and undermining the
security of the state. When he finished reading, I spoke up.

"When will I be freed?"

"*Inshallah*, within a couple of hours," answered Mohammadzadeh. I'd come to hate the expression *inshallah*—"God
willing"—which may be the most overused and least meaning-
ful phrase spoken by Muslims. It allows individuals to pretend
that they care, while doing nothing.

"*Possibly* within a couple of hours? Or within a couple of
hours for sure?" I asked.

My question clearly angered Mohammadzadeh. "What did
you say, you little spy?" he barked. "Do you want me to tear up
your release order and let you rot here for the rest of your life?"

"I just wanted to know, sir," I said quietly.

"If it was up to me, I would execute you and everyone like you. You're lucky that our Islamic regime has been kind enough to let you join your family temporarily. But don't worry: I will make sure that you receive the harshest sentence possible." He closed my file. His next words hit me harder than any of Rosewater's punches.

"Actually, I'm going to call the court to ask them to annul your bail order," he said. "Now put the blindfold on and get out of my office before I kick the life out of you."

Was he serious? I thought of my mother and Paola, who must've heard the news of my imminent release and would now have their hopes dashed. My knees felt so weak that I could hardly walk.

I went back to my cell at nine thirty-seven A.M. I lay down and waited to see what decision the judge—in all of his "Islamic kindness"—was going to make about my case. As I shut my eyes, trying to think of nothing, I could feel the excruciating pain of each passing second. Each one felt like a day. I couldn't think of anything except for my hatred of the Islamic Republic, its potentate, and his servants.

Trying to pass the time, I reviewed all the things I would have to do as soon as I got out of prison. I would buy a ticket for the first available flight to London. I wondered if my travel agent had heard about my ordeal. How about my other friends and acquaintances? I went through their faces and names one by one. I would contact my friends on Rosewater's list, and check on them to make sure they had not been imprisoned.

But among the long list of things I needed to do, one particular task weighed most heavily: I had to find a way to tell the world of the atrocities I had witnessed during the demonstrations and what I'd experienced at Evin. I knew that in hundreds of other cells lining the dusty hallways of this prison, innocent people were undergoing the same experience I had—people who did not have the benefit of a powerful magazine and a very stubborn, outspoken wife behind them. I had an opportunity to be the voice of my imprisoned friends and colleagues. It was only the thought of exposing the regime that tempered the excruciating pain of those endless moments while I waited to learn my fate.

*   *   *

I was brought to see Rosewater a few minutes before eleven A.M. He told me that my brother-in-law, Mohammad, was waiting outside Evin with the deed to my mother's apartment.

"Call him and say that you may not be released today," Rosewater ordered.

"But why?" I asked weakly. "What's happened?"

"Nothing. We just need a signature, and we're not sure when we can get it from that official."

My heart sank. In Iran, many lives were spared and others were ended because of a final signature of an official. I wasn't sure whether Rosewater was telling me the truth or if Mohammadzadeh had annulled my release out of spite.

"*Inshallah,* the official will be found today," I told Rosewater.

"*Inshallah,*" Rosewater answered, as he handed me the phone to call Mohammad.

Mohammad said that he wasn't going anywhere until I was freed. "I told Moloojoon that I'd come home with you, and she's waiting for both of us," he said. Mohammad, who'd gone through a much longer and harsher incarceration than I, knew how heartbreaking it would be for my mother to hear that I had to stay in prison even for one more day. As usual, his words were reassuring. "Don't worry about anything," he told me. "I'm sure you'll be released today."

"It's a free country," Rosewater said sarcastically. He'd been listening in on the call. "He can wait outside as long as he wants."

I went back to my cell. After lunch, Rosewater called me to the interrogation room twice. Again he went through the list of names of people I was expected to spy on in London. Both times, I felt that there was someone else in the room, and at one point, I thought I heard the buzz of a camera recording our conversation. I'd used video cameras enough in my life to recognize the sound. The fact that I was being filmed gave me hope. I thought, *They're recording me for the last time before they release me, so they can prove that I've been cooperating with them.*

Rosewater had told me that I shouldn't talk about my release with my cellmates, but after I was called to the interrogation room for the second time that afternoon, they began to wonder what was going on.

"I don't know what he wants from me," I told them. "He keeps on asking me the same questions over and over again." I wasn't sure if they believed me or not, and at that point, I didn't care. The only thing I was thinking about was my freedom, and joining Paola in London to witness the birth of our baby in nine days.

*   *   *

"Mr. Bahari," a guard called to me about two hours later. "Collect your stuff. You're moving to another cell."

"But why?" I asked. The guard didn't answer. He led me out of the building, and after a long walk through Evin's labyrinthine courtyards, we entered an office I'd never been to.

"Here's your Mr. Bahari, sir," the guard said. I recognized Rosewater's slippers.

"Take your blindfold off," ordered Rosewater. I didn't understand. He was sitting right in front of me, the lights were on, and he was asking me to remove my blindfold. "We obtained the necessary signature," Rosewater said. "Now take the blindfold off and sit down on the sofa."

It was the first time I'd seen his face clearly since the day he'd arrested me. I'd mentally reviewed the details of his face during the many sessions when he'd beaten and humiliated me. When he'd slapped me on the back of my head, I had wondered about the size of his hands. When he'd screamed and insulted me and spit on my face, I had tried to remember the shape of his mouth. And in his moments of silence, I'd wondered about his gaze.

Now he was sitting right in front of me on a white plastic chair, one of many that were scattered around the courtyards of Evin, with his legs crossed. His light brown suit looked even tighter than it had on the day I'd been arrested. What was the point of the blindfold, if I was allowed to see his face on the first day and the last day? I guessed it was so he didn't have to look into my eyes while making false accusations and insulting and beating me, even though in his heart he knew that he was torturing an innocent man.

I looked down. I could feel that he was staring at me, but I didn't want to look into his eyes. There was an uncomfortable silence between us. Even on the brink of my freedom, he was silently trying to tell me that I was still his prisoner. And quietly, I refused to accept his suggestion. At that point, I hated him so much that I was afraid I might do or say something that could enrage him and make him reverse my release.

At his feet were six big plastic bags that contained my confiscated laptops, mobile phones, documents, CDs, and DVDs. "What time is it, sir?" I finally said. "I think my brother-in-law is waiting outside. It must be getting cold."

"Yes. And I'm sure you want to go home so you can eat your mother's cooking, don't you?" Rosewater asked.

I finally looked into his eyes. They were as hateful as I'd remembered. But he was much uglier than I'd thought. The expression on his face revealed an obscene mind. The way he squeezed his lips after each sentence betrayed an insecure bully. But there was also a childlike quality about him. He grinned after his own unfunny comments and blew into his cheeks when he talked about the strength of the regime. As he went through, for the umpteenth time, the list of people I'd promised to inform him about, he looked more relaxed than he had the day he'd arrested me. He didn't have to keep a stern face anymore.

When he finished giving me instructions, he leaned forward and handed me a bag of my clothes, but when I took it, he refused to let it go. "Remember our talk about the power of the Revolutionary Guards, Mazi," he said. He looked into my eyes, maybe searching for the fear he wanted to see. "You're never going to be safe."

*   *   *

After I got dressed, they put my blindfold back on and drove me out of Evin. As soon as I was permitted, I took off the blindfold. I looked at my watch. It was nine fifty-four P.M. on October 17, 2009. I'd been arrested exactly 118 days, 12 hours, and 54 minutes earlier. I knew that I was about to embark on yet another extraordinary journey, but I wasn't sure about anything. Was I really free? Or was it a joke, a cruel trick like Maryam's mock execution? Were they going to arrest me again? I was full of the doubts that Rosewater had worked so hard to instill in me.

Mohammad was waiting outside the prison gates, along with many other people waiting for their loved ones. I kissed both his cheeks. I wanted to hug him for a long time, but I also wanted to get away from Evin as soon as possible. Evin's main gate is off a busy street in north Tehran. We hailed a cab as soon as we saw one.

At home, my mother and Iran, Maryam and Mohammad's daughter, were waiting for me. I immediately took my mother in my arms and cried for several minutes—not only because I had missed her so much, but also because I knew that our greeting was just the beginning of what could be a very long good-bye.

Then I called Paola. She couldn't believe that I was finally out. She wanted to picture me in my home to help her believe that I really was not in Evin anymore. "Are you there with your mother?" she asked me. "What time did you get home?" She became more excited with every answer, as each one confirmed that I had been freed and I would be with her soon. Very soon. But our excitement was overshadowed by the fact that I was still in Iran. I kept my conversation with Paola to a minimum. I wasn't sure if the Guards had put me under surveillance and were tapping my phone calls. I had told them that I would be returning to Iran within a couple of months, so I avoided any conversation about how long I was going to be in London or any other important subject. Fortunately, Paola instinctively knew not to ask many questions.

Paola had been in the hospital for more than a week. My friends at Channel 4 News had paid for a private room for her, she told me. She had her own television set and computer there. My family had already told her about my release, but reporters from all around the world were also calling her to find out the news. Before saying good-bye, I told her that I didn't want to do any interviews and asked her not to talk to any reporters.

I took my laptop to the living room. As my mother, Mohammad, and Iran told me about the latest family news and political developments, I went through my emails. The Guards had deleted many of my messages. However, I still had hundreds of emails from friends and total strangers who'd written to wish me well, thinking that maybe—miraculously, perhaps—I had access to the Internet in prison. I was moved by the generosity of all those who had cared about me during my time in Evin. Seeing the attention I had received while in prison made me more determined than ever to help the hundreds of prisoners who were not as fortunate as me.

As I went through my emails, my niece told me about the details of *Newsweek*'s and Paola's campaign.

On Sunday, June 21, 2009, the day of my arrest, Paola, who was five months pregnant at the time, had been walking in Primrose Hill. It was a hot day, and Paola looked for a place in the shade where she could sit down and relax. Just as she found a bench, her mobile phone rang. It was my friend Malu. "Check your email," she told Paola. "Maziar's been arrested."

Paola rushed home and found Khaled's message waiting in her in-box. Khaled had heard the news of my arrest from my mother, who had called him as soon as I had been led away in handcuffs. From his student apartment in Adelaide, Australia, Khaled had sent a message to everyone on the list I had prepared of friends and colleagues in different media outlets around the world. I had often told Khaled that the Iranian government had never released any prisoner because his family and friends had remained quiet. If you wanted your loved ones freed in Iran, you had to make noise. In his email, Khaled made it clear that I needed as much publicity as possible.

A flurry of emails flew among the people on Khaled's list—my editors at *Newsweek* and Channel 4, and my other friends and colleagues. Paola recognized few of these parties. It occurred to her then that she would have to head the campaign for my freedom. There was never any question in her mind that this task would fall to anyone else. But my world was somehow unfamiliar to her. She was a financial lawyer. My world was the world of the media, and Paola didn't know many of my friends and colleagues. Indeed, in those early days in prison, I'd often wondered whether people were going to be more surprised by my arrest or by the fact that Paola was pregnant. I'd been traveling so much in the months before the election that I had not had the opportunity to tell my close friends in person about the pregnancy. I'd wanted to announce it properly after I came back from Iran. Many of my friends and certainly my colleagues at

Newsweek didn't even know that Paola and I had become engaged.

At home, Paola took a deep breath and concentrated on playing catch-up with the emails. Nisid Hajari, who had been my editor at *Newsweek* since 2006, seemed to have already taken control of the situation. He had decided on a strategy and had drafted a statement to be released to the press that same day. Ironically, Nisid had sent me an email the night before my arrest, asking what my plan was if the government were to start a crackdown on journalists; I'd never got the chance to reply.

Don Graham, the CEO of the Washington Post Company, which owned *Newsweek* at the time, and Jon Meacham, then the magazine's editor, told Nisid to do whatever he could, regardless of the time it took or the money it cost. When Paola called Nisid later that day, she felt an enormous sense of relief that strong and dependable Nisid was going to coordinate the campaign, to which she would give her heart and soul until I was free. There and then, she placed her full trust in Nisid, and never once would she doubt that she had made the right decision.

From that day onward, Nisid relinquished almost all of his day-to-day editing duties and committed himself to leading the effort to free me. On the other side of the Atlantic, Chris Dickey, *Newsweek*'s Paris bureau chief and Middle East editor, took the train to London to meet Paola and offer his support. Chris had brought me to *Newsweek*. He knew Iran as well as anybody and was able to offer Nisid sage advice on every decision. Their first task was to find out where I was and who had taken me. Information started to come in from different sources, many of whom had friends inside the Iranian government. However, when the Revolutionary Guards took over much of the government, the rules of the game changed. Many people inside the government itself did not know anything about my situation and were unknowingly misled into passing on false information.

From time to time, news of my whereabouts and imminent release would seep through from some seemingly dependable source to Nisid and Chris. At the beginning, they would call Paola and they'd all privately rejoice. But then days would pass with no further news. Chris and Nisid chided themselves for having been so credulous and, in particular, for having given Paola false hope.

Paola, meanwhile, hid from them her utter despair—a despair that seemed to emanate from the deepest part within her. She imagined the baby inside her to be at the epicenter of the turmoil, and as she watched her body shake uncontrollably, she was racked with guilt. She was grateful that her twin sister, Barbara, was there. Barbara always knew what to say and the right tone to take. This time she was firm and matter-of-fact: "Paola, be strong for the baby. That's what Maziar wants." And with those words, Paola's body stopped shaking. She picked herself up and got back to work.

From the beginning, *Newsweek* ensured that the news of my arrest would go viral. The arrest of an innocent journalist hit a nerve among thousands of people around the world. Paola was inundated with messages from people who knew me, even former school friends from many years ago. They started websites and Facebook pages and worked with Paola and *Newsweek* to disseminate petitions for my release across the world. Night after night, as I sat in that prison cell, designing crossword puzzles and playing miniature basketball and thinking that I'd perhaps been forgotten, my friends and colleagues were working tirelessly for my release.

On the diplomatic level, Nisid knew that he had to allow Canada to lead the governmental efforts to obtain my release, since I was a Canadian citizen. But the Canadian government, being the Canadian government, was not as aggressive and persistent in its approach as Nisid and the others would have liked.

When it comes to human-rights abuses, the Canadian government has always taken the lead in condemning the Iranian government, but its officials use bureaucratic tactics and follow very strict protocols.

The Iranian government, meanwhile, was caught off guard by the attention paid to my arrest. The Revolutionary Guards did not explain its reasons for arresting me to the other branches of the government, and made sure that the rest of the government understood that my arrest and the arrest of others taken by the Guards was no one else's business. Iranian diplomats felt powerless. Many of them were ashamed of their government, but they feared dismissal and arrest, and had to continue to work to make a living. Of course, they could not say that to *Newsweek,* so they pretended to be in the know about my situation. In this way, many encouraging but false pieces of information were passed on to *Newsweek* and Paola.

As the weeks passed with no solid information about my status, everybody grew increasingly worried, and very impatient. They waited and waited for good news, but none came. Meanwhile, in late July, Nisid learned from sources in Iran that officials from the Guards were saying that *Newsweek*'s quiet campaign on my behalf meant that *Newsweek* agreed that I was a spy. The war team's strategy had to change. My case had to have the maximum amount of publicity possible.

A few days later, Hillary Clinton appeared on Fareed Zakaria's show *GPS,* on CNN. Fareed was the editor of *Newsweek International.* He'd been mentioning me often on his show—in fact, every chance he could get—and he took the opportunity to ask Clinton what she thought of my arrest and the staged trials going on in Iran at the time. She replied, "Well, I am just appalled at the treatment that Mr. Bahari and others are receiving. It is a show trial. There is no doubt that it demonstrates, I think, better than any of us could ever say, that this

Iranian leadership is afraid of their own people, and afraid of the truth and the facts coming out. We've expressed our concern about Mr. Bahari's confinement, and now the trial."

Clinton spoke about me a few times after that as well, and her comments made diplomats around the world more aware of my ordeal. Nisid knew that they needed to continue the publicity in order to keep the story of my incarceration fresh. The only problem was that after the election, hundreds of people had been arrested. *Newsweek* had to find a creative way to convince people that my story was worthy of extra attention. Paola was the difference. Paola's efforts while visibly pregnant helped make my story interesting to the international media.

On September 8, Paola agreed to give an interview to Channel 4 News at our home in London. That morning, despite being over seven months pregnant, she had rushed around town to get some medical letters regarding her condition legalized and sent to the lawyer in Iran. As she walked to the notary's office, she regretted not having taken a taxi. The sun was streaming down and the baby had started to kick vigorously. Just as she felt about to faint, she arrived at the notary's and collapsed onto the black leather sofa. The receptionist, who knew her well by this point, rushed to her with a glass of water. "You have to take it easy. Can't someone else deal with all these medical letters?" she asked Paola. "Not really," Paola replied. Barbara had already taken a week off from her job to help her and had been made to feel irresponsible by her boss afterward. Paola's friends were at work, and the rest of her family abroad.

Paola took a taxi home. As she swept the floor and tidied all the papers to prepare the flat for the interview that evening, she resolved to slow down a little. Throughout the campaign, the baby had been the reason for her strength, but now she had to acknowledge that she felt physically drained. That evening the crew from Channel 4 News arrived. She helped them remodel the living room into a mini studio. Just as the last touches to the room were being made, the show's host, my friend Jon Snow, arrived. They sat down opposite each other, Paola relieved to finally be off her feet. "Do you have a message for the Iranian government?" he asked as the camera rolled. "Yes: Fuck you!" Paola laughed, knowing that Jon would edit that part out.

After Jon and the crew left the flat, Paola went into the bedroom to rest. As she lay back against the pillows, she took in a sharp breath: she could feel that she'd begun bleeding heavily. She rushed to the phone and called an ambulance. A couple of minutes later, as she ran out the front door, grabbing on the way the hospital bag she had prepared for emergencies, she saw Barbara walking up the front steps. "I'm bleeding," she said, with tears streaming down her face. "This time it's really serious. I think I'm going to lose the baby!"

At the hospital, the doctors told Paola that she should be prepared for an emergency cesarean. Thankfully, this was not necessary. They released her after a few days, with the warning that should she start to bleed again, they would keep her in the hospital until the baby's birth.

I was grateful to learn about the campaign, and I knew I could never thank everyone enough for what they had done for me. My family and I talked until three in the morning. During our conversation, I went to the kitchen several times and looked at the bottle of Johnnie Walker in the cabinet, but I didn't dare pour a drink. I couldn't help the paranoid thoughts that kept creeping into my mind, and I was worried that the Guards would raid the house and arrest me for drinking alcohol. During those 118 days, Rosewater had managed to instill in me such paralyzing paranoia that I couldn't even act freely in my own mother's house.

Before going to bed, I took a shower. I hadn't looked at my body in a mirror since the day I'd been arrested. I knew that I had lost a lot of weight, but I had seen only faint reflections of my naked form on the metal door of the shower cubicles in

Evin. Confronted with the mirror now, I drew back in shock. I didn't recognize myself. My rib cage protruded under my skin, and my shoulders looked like a clothes hanger.

When I saw my backside, I gasped. "I have no arse!" I said aloud. "They have left me no arse!" For some strange reason, the reality of what had happened to me in Evin fully hit me only in the familiar setting of my mother's bathroom, when I noticed that my buttocks had shrunk to one-third of their former size.

*   *   *

The next morning, I booked a ticket for the first direct flight from Tehran to London; I would leave Tehran in two days. I immediately started the countdown, but at the same time, I felt guilty for doing so. I didn't want to look forward to leaving my country. I didn't want to go into exile. I didn't want to leave Moloojoon. But I couldn't stay in Iran.

Dozens of relatives, friends, and colleagues came to see me during my short stay in Tehran. I tried to keep a calm face, but the fear that our house would be raided again was suffocating. It wasn't just a worry born out of more than one hundred days of interrogation and torture; there were numerous precedents for the Islamic government's security forces bursting into the homes of recently freed prisoners and arresting them and their guests. I was constantly on edge and avoided any real conversation by cracking jokes and answering questions with questions. When a friend asked me about life in prison, I smiled and told him that I'd lost thirty-three pounds. "The Evin diet is better than any other," I laughed. "Even better than Atkins!"

The subject I most wanted to avoid was my televised "confession." Many of my friends and relatives had spent time in prison. They recognized that I was uncomfortable talking about it and wanted to let me know that I hadn't done anything I should be ashamed of. "We're all proud of you, Maziar," they told me. But their words never gave me comfort. Sitting in the living room, I often stared at the chair where my father used to sit. I could feel my father's gaze on me until the moment when I left the house for the airport. He wanted to know what my plans for the future were. "What are you going to do now, Maziar?" he asked me. "Just sit on your hands and do nothing? Or will you speak out against the injustices committed against your people?"

Before I left, I held my mother in my arms for a long time. I felt her tears seeping through my shirt, and onto my skin. We both knew that I would not be back in Iran for a long time, if ever. I kissed her cheeks several times and told her repeatedly, "*Dorost misheh, dorost misheh*": It will be fine. But even as I held her, I was also talking to my father. I was promising him that I would not be silent—that I would make the world aware of the injustices suffered by the people of Iran. I would never forget my people, or my duty to help my friends and colleagues languishing behind bars. I would do my best to defeat Rosewater and his masters, in any way I could.

CHAPTER NINETEEN

The hours between five A.M., when I left the house, and eight A.M., when the British Midland flight took off, were the longest of my life. As I showed my passport and passed through the two security checkpoints, I fully expected to be prevented from boarding the plane. A few days earlier, three of my friends—fellow filmmakers—had had their passports confiscated just as they were about to board a plane, and a few months before that, another friend and his wife had been arrested and escorted off a plane.

Even after the plane took off, I still did not feel safe. In fact, I would not feel safe until we had crossed out of Iranian airspace. I switched on my TV screen and selected the funniest film I could find: *The Hangover*. I then leaned over to the empty seat next to mine and selected the channel displaying the route map. I tried to concentrate on the film—as the various characters stole Mike Tyson's tiger, married a lap dancer, and fathered a baby—but my attention kept straying to the other screen. It seemed as though the plane were edging forward tentatively. Every time I stole a glance at the map, the plane seemed to be standing still. When I saw that we were over Tabriz, in the western part of the country, I closed my eyes and waited for as long as I could. When I looked up, it had happened: we had crossed into Turkey.

I took a deep breath; it felt like the first breath I'd taken in months. I was a free man. The flight attendant appeared beside me.

"Is there anything you need?" she asked.

I knew the exact answer. "Yes," I said. "A whiskey."

Within a few minutes, seven or eight passengers—total strangers to me—were standing beside me congratulating me on my freedom and, to my surprise, on the impending birth of my child. Even though I had, by this time, learned about the efforts to release me, and read the reports of my ordeal that had appeared in media outlets around the world, it was only on the flight that I fully realized that my imprisonment had not been a private matter. I had become a public figure. I was surprised by how much people knew about me. I hadn't expected anything like this.

"How's your mother?" asked a middle-aged woman, who told me that she was living in Sweden, and like me, had lost her father.

"Is it a boy or a girl?" her husband asked, holding their son in his arms.

"Whatever it is, a child is a blessing," the woman said.

Many people also asked me about the conditions inside Evin and wanted to know the details of my experience. Before long, I realized how eager these people were to express themselves, especially about human-rights abuses in Iran. The questions went on. Did they beat you a lot? Who did you see inside? Were you in solitary confinement or a communal cell? Were you able to talk to your wife? Where is your wife from? As I answered their questions and sipped my whiskey, I hoped these well-wishing strangers would sense my unease and allow me some space to be alone. Because even though I smiled and chatted amiably with them, deep down, I still feared that at any moment the plane would reverse course and return me to Iran.

*   *   *

At Heathrow, Chris Dickey was waiting for me with a security officer. In order to avoid reporters and any unforeseen problems, *Newsweek* had organized my exit through a private corridor. Even though Chris knew that I had left Tehran, he still couldn't believe that I was free until he saw me with his own eyes. "There he is!" he said with a broad smile.

I was finally in London. I'd never thought that I would love so much the sight of yellow-suited maintenance workers strolling across the gray tarmac under a light drizzle and a dull London sky. *Soon I'll be on the M4, Euston Road, and with Paola at University College Hospital.* I was finally free to go where I pleased; to go to see Paola. There were so many things I wanted to tell Chris.

Barbara was waiting for us in the VIP lounge. Since I'd met Paola, in 2007, Barbara had become like my own sister. She was all smiles when she saw me. "Talk to Paola, talk to Paola, she's waiting," Barbara said, a mobile phone in her hand.

I took the phone and excitedly told Paola that I was going directly from the airport to the hospital to see her. In the car, Chris and Barbara peppered me with questions about what had happened and how I felt. My mind was elsewhere. I knew there was something I needed to do. I asked the driver to stop by our flat on the way to the hospital.

When I walked inside, I felt as if I had stepped into one of the drawings I'd left behind on the floor of my cell. Everything I had experienced since leaving Evin still didn't seem real. It felt more like the way I had imagined things when dreaming in my prison cell. I felt Rosewater's ghost following me everywhere. I needed to get rid of him.

I took my laptop to our bedroom and typed the email I had been composing in my mind for the last several hours:

"*Baa man tamas nagirid. Man ta beh hal barayeh hitch kas jasoosi nakardam va barayeh shoma ham nakhaham kard.*"

Don't contact me anymore. I've never spied for anyone and I'm not going to start by spying for you.

I couldn't stop myself from adding one more sentence: "*Gooreh pedaretoon!*" Fuck you!

I breathed a deep sigh of relief. At last, I was free. I turned off the light and walked downstairs, ready, finally, to see Paola, prepare for Marianna, and take back my life.

* * *

I was on the fourth floor of the hospital, outside Paola's room. I opened the door slowly. On hearing me, Paola, who had been lying down in bed, pulled herself up into a sitting position. As I walked into the room, my eyes immediately met hers. For a moment we stared at each other like shy strangers. Then tears overwhelmed us both. We smiled at each other weakly, with an unparalleled relief and a look that seemed to say, "We've both changed, haven't we?" She was shocked by how thin I was, and I, by how beautiful she was. I felt overwhelmed by sadness. I had missed most of Paola's pregnancy.

I crossed the room and sat down beside her. Taking her in my arms, I leaned over and kissed her belly for a long time. I put my head on her bump and talked to our daughter inside her belly: "Hello, honey bunny, hello, darling, Mummy and Daddy are waiting for you." I had been imagining this moment for months.

I could feel Paola's tears on the nape of my neck. I was assaulted by so many thoughts and emotions that I felt numb. I didn't want this moment to end. All I could do was tell Paola how much I'd missed her and ask her questions. The last thing I wanted to do was to speak of my experience.

As Paola ran her fingers through my hair, I was transported to the time before my ordeal. Her touch felt unnaturally normal. I held Paola's beautiful face in my palms and looked into her wide blue eyes. I almost felt normal. I had defeated my captors. I hadn't turned into what they wanted me to be.

* * *

I decided that I was not going to do any interviews for the time being. Instead, I spent almost all my time with Paola. We asked for an extra bed in the hospital room so that I could stay overnight with her. I also threw myself into the many practical tasks—rearranging the spare room for the baby, and buying clothes and other necessary items for the nursery—so that I didn't have much time to think of anything else. And thanks to the fact that *Newsweek* had continued to deposit my monthly retainer into Paola's account, I didn't have to worry about my finances.

But at night, as soon as I shut my eyes, I was back in Evin, back beside Rosewater. His face hovered in my dreams, turning them into nightmares. In a recurring nightmare, I was sitting in the school chair in the interrogation room while Rosewater walked around me, kicking and punching me intermittently.

In my waking hours, I forced the images of him—his stubble, his glasses, his stench—out of my head and strove to replace them with images of Marianna growing up. I would often think about the "Sisters of Mercy" dream I'd had in prison. When I played the Leonard Cohen song for Paola in the hospital room, she understood that I was still grieving over the death of my sister, Maryam. I knew that one of the sisters in my dream was Maryam, but I wondered who the other one was.

The next day I listened to the Cohen song over and over again. In the afternoon, Paola hummed the song in her hospital bed while reading a book. I watched her without saying anything. Knowing that I was sitting only a few feet from her, Paola looked peaceful and relaxed. I was fascinated with her belly and the angel resting inside it. At that moment I knew who the other woman in my "Sisters of Mercy" dream was: Marianna Maryam Bahari.

* * *

The night before Marianna's birth was the night Rosewater vanished from my dreams. I was sitting with Paola and Marianna—who was a beautiful precocious teenage girl, with long, curly brown hair—at my family dining room table in Tehran. Opposite were my mother, my father, and Maryam. I was telling my family about my prison experiences. My father was angry: "Those sisterfuckers who work for this regime are as stupid as those who worked for the shah." There was a large bottle of Johnnie Walker Black Label in front of him. As I poured him a glass of whiskey, my father gazed at me with a chastising expression. He seemed to still be mad at me for making the false confessions and apologizing to Khamenei. Marianna grabbed my father's hand and pointed toward the television. There I was, revealing what was happening in Iranian jails and campaigning for the release of other prisoners. Marianna leaned forward to my father and smiled at him. My father looked at me and nodded. His eyes were much softer.

The next morning, as I sat beside Paola, just hours before Marianna's birth, I slowly tried to absorb the idea that a difficult period of my life was over and a new, more gratifying period was about to start, but I couldn't stop worrying about what might happen. I slipped out of the room for a moment and called my mother.

"I hope Paola and the baby will be okay," I told her. "Paola's been through a lot."

My mother had no time for my unnecessary worries. She spoke to me with her usual strength and directness: "Mazi *jaan*, you shouldn't worry about Paola or the baby's health. They will be fine. All you have to worry about now is how well you can raise the baby. And I know you won't have any problem doing that. Now go back to Paola."

We were called to the operating room soon after. Given the

difficulties Paola had experienced, the doctors planned to deliver Marianna through cesarean surgery, and the room was filled with nurses and the doctors' assistants. Even though we'd been told that Marianna's birth had a higher than normal risk for complications, the mood in the room was jovial and Paola and I were full of excitement.

Within minutes, Marianna was born into the world, in even better health than we had dreamt of. A nurse placed Marianna in Paola's arms. We were both mesmerized by her beauty. We looked at each other but didn't say anything. As Marianna let out a tiny, perfect cry, I could have sworn I heard someone singing a familiar song:

> *They were waiting for me when I thought that I just can't go on.*
> *And they brought me their comfort and later they brought me this song.*

*   *   *

We were able to bring Marianna home within a few days. She slept like an angel. Paola soon recovered from her surgery. At night, as I watched Paola sleeping with the baby beside her, a voice inside me, perhaps my father's, urged me on: "Okay, that's done. What now? Are you going to rest on your laurels and let those bastards get away with murder?"

CHAPTER TWENTY

It didn't take very long for the Revolutionary Guards to contact me. "Mr. Bahari, we're waiting to see you," said Rosewater's boss in a message left on my mobile phone one day. "We're sure that we're going to see you very soon."

Many of my friends and colleagues who had spent time in prison in Iran had remained silent about what happened to them. They feared that their comments about their experiences in prison would incense the regime, and that their families would have to suffer the consequences. But their silence gnawed at them from inside. Like me, many of them had been forced to make confessions. They felt guilty and angry about what the regime had put them through, and their anguish swelled because of the fear they suffered, even in freedom.

I couldn't allow that to happen to me. Instead, I knew that I had a responsibility to campaign on behalf of the hundreds of people who remained in prison. But I had to consult with Paola and my mother first. My decisions would affect them more than anyone else.

"Throughout the ordeal, I was sure of one thing only," Paola told me when I explained to her what I felt I had to do. "It was that you knew what you were doing. I still believe that."

My mother was even stronger in her support. When I called to ask what she thought about me writing about my experiences, she didn't hesitate. "What've you been waiting for?" she said with her characteristic candor. "Of course you should talk about these *ashghals,* this rubbish. They've ruined the lives of people inside the country, and they think that they can get away with bullying people outside of the country as well."

A few weeks after my release, I wrote a cover story for *Newsweek* entitled "118 Days in Hell." It was one of the first accounts of postelection brutalities in Iran, but a few months after the article was published, many prisoners said that they'd gone through the same ordeal as I had. After the article, I did a series of television, radio, and print interviews in which I provided more information about my captivity. I was sure to make two points clear: (1) I had made my confessions under duress, and (2) hundreds of innocent prisoners remained inside Iranian jails, enduring the same brutal ordeal I had.

Back in London, with the help of a number of international organizations, I started a campaign calling for the release of my journalist friends and colleagues. More than one hundred journalists had been arrested after the June 2009 presidential election, and since then the Islamic regime has made journalists its prime target in its fight against what it calls "sedition." To kick off the campaign, I wrote an open letter to Khamenei that was published in the *International Herald Tribune* and subsequently translated by dozens of Persian websites. "The only accusation against many reporters who are languishing in Iranian jails is that they held a mirror to the actions of the Iranian government," I wrote. "They did not want to overthrow it. They never took up arms. All of them did their job as peacefully as journalists elsewhere in the world. Many a time my torturer told me that he kicked me to make you happy. He told me, 'Each time I slap you I can feel that the Master is smiling at me.' Ayatollah Khamenei, I think you are responsible for what happened to me."

The Guards reacted immediately. An article in *Javan,* a newspaper run by the Guards, called me "a natural born criminal who should never have been allowed out of jail," and Iranian television mocked my media appearances by calling my actions "courage in the comfort of the West." Rosewater's cohorts also tried to intimidate me by threatening my family. The Guards instructed my brother-in-law, Mohammad, on the phone, "Tell Maziar that he shouldn't think we can't reach him because he is not in Iran. The situation is getting really dangerous now. Anything can happen without advance notice." The Iranian government has assassinated dozens of dissidents outside Iran, and the threatening calls unsettled me. In the beginning, I thought it best to remain silent, believing that publicizing the threats would only make the situation worse for my mother and Mohammad. But the calls continued for months, so in April 2010, after a particularly menacing call to my family, I decided to break my silence and talk about the threats publicly.

In interviews after the threats, I asked those who made the threats a simple question: "I know that the mighty Revolutionary Guards have agents around the world and can get to me whenever they want. But then what? What do they want to do to me? If they want to kill me, then they're accepting that they're part of a terrorist regime, and if they want to kidnap me, then they are admitting that they are a hostage-taking government. I think the brothers in the Revolutionary Guards should be more transparent about their intentions."

Publicizing the threats made them less frequent. The Islamic regime was still worried about its image in the world, so, according to my sources, the smarter people within the Iranian government told the Guards to stop threatening me through my eighty-four-year-old mother. Yet the Guards were so infuriated with me that they decided to harass my family in a different way. To this day, they have been calling my mother periodically, telling her to be ready for an imminent confiscation of her house because I jumped bail. That confiscation has not yet taken place, but the threat of being forced out of her home hangs over my mother's head.

Moloojoon's reaction to the calls was classic, and it makes me so proud of her. After losing her husband, first-born son, and daughter within four years, she had in many ways lost the desire to live, but the calls gave her a reason to be strong once again and to fight. "Who are you?" my elderly mother demanded, challenging one anonymous caller. "Maziar is out of your hands, he is free, and you can't do anything to him anymore." She then simply hung up and phoned me to say that the *ashghals* have been calling her again.

It is very difficult for both of us that, for the foreseeable future, I cannot return to Iran to see her. However, my mother can travel outside of the country and has come to London to visit us three times since my release from prison. As much as I'd love for her to live closer to Paola, Marianna, and me, she has no desire to leave Iran permanently. "Your mother doesn't want to leave the country to the wolves," a family friend told me recently. "She's a proud Iranian who tries to keep the spirit of the country alive in her own way. Your father was also one such Iranian; so was Maryam." Although I chose a path toward building a more democratic Iran that was different from that of Maryam and my father, their memory still gives me hope and inspires me.

EPILOGUE

On May 9, 2010, I was tried in absentia by a revolutionary court, a type of court that deals primarily with political crimes. My sentence—thirteen and a half years' imprisonment plus seventy-four lashes—was one of the most severe imposed on any postelection prisoner. There was no court session, and my lawyer never heard the charges. Rosewater and the Revolutionary Guards' intelligence unit, which had arrested me, dictated the following sentence to the judge:

1. *Five years' imprisonment for unlawful assembly and conspiring against the security of the state.* This had to do with my reporting on, and taking part in, four days of peaceful demonstrations after the election, along with millions of other Iranians.
2. *Four years for collecting and keeping secret and classified documents.* In 2002, a septuagenarian leader of the opposition group Freedom Movement of Iran gave me a court document regarding a trial of certain members of his group. There was nothing secret in the document, all its contents had been announced by the judiciary, and the file is widely available on the Internet. During the interrogations I was asked only once about the document, which even Rosewater didn't think was sensitive.

3. *One year for propagandizing against the holy system of the Islamic Republic.* This was for all the articles I had written and the films I had made in Iran.

4. *One-year imprisonment and seventy-four lashes for disrupting the public order.* This referred to my *Newsweek* article and Channel 4 report on the attack against the Basij base after the first peaceful demonstration. Even though I had condemned the violence in my report, the revolutionary court agreed with Rosewater that I was a "peaceful terrorist."

5. *Two years for insulting the supreme leader, Ayatollah Ali Khamenei.* Nothing would be complete in Iran without mentioning the supreme leader. In an email I'd written to my *Newsweek* editors Nisid and Chris, which the Guards had found, I'd said that Khamenei had learned from the mistakes the shah had made when he was overthrown by the Islamic Revolution. I mentioned that Khamenei tries to nip any opposition in the bud by arresting its leaders and preventing people from taking to the streets. Rosewater had told me that by comparing Khamenei to the shah I had implied that the supreme leader was a tyrant, and therefore I had to be punished.

6. *Six months for implying that the president was a homosexual.* This was the real icing on the cake. I received this sentence for the picture of a young man kissing Ahmadinejad, which someone else had tagged on my Facebook wall.

My only reaction to the sentence was to laugh it off publicly and dismiss it as a bizarre judgment passed by an irrational government. I saw it as part of the regime's attempt to discourage other freed prisoners from speaking out. The explicit message was that anyone could be subjected to the same sentence if he or she dared to talk about the horrors of prison.

My sentence has made me more determined to speak out

against the injustices committed by the Islamic regime. I believe I have a duty to be the voice of the hundreds of journalists, students, civil rights activists, and even mullahs who oppose Khamenei's tyrannical rule and still languish in Iranian jails in the hands of Rosewater and his colleagues.

*　*　*

My motorcycle cabbie Davood called me a few days after my release, on the day I arrived in London. He told me that as soon as he had heard the news of my arrest, he'd changed his mobile phone number and moved back to his hometown of Tabriz, where he now works as a shop assistant and tries to keep his head down. Rosewater had lied. Davood was not arrested after me. However, in January 2010, Davood saw two Basij members arresting a young girl for wearing too much makeup, and he rammed into them with his motorcycle. The Basijis called for help, and Davood was caught and taken to the local prison, where he was badly beaten and spent a few days in a cell with a group of ten student activists. Their cell had been designed for solitary confinement, so they had to sleep in shifts and had no privacy when they used the toilet in the cell. Davood's cellmates begged him not to complain about the situation because the last time they'd complained, two of the young students were taken to another area of the prison, where drug smugglers and thieves were kept. That night, the two students were gagged by the thugs and raped repeatedly. The thugs even used bottles and screwdrivers to hurt the students further. The convicts had been promised by the police that "if they taught the students a lesson," their sentences would be commuted.

This was not the first time I'd heard such a story. Rape has become a form of punishment in the Islamic Republic. Many Iranian refugees in neighboring countries and around the world have had similar experiences, and I'm sure many young, proud Iranians are too ashamed to come forward to tell their stories.

Davood was released a month later. "What kind of regime does that to the educated people of their country?" Davood asked me on the phone. "It's become so difficult to live in this country, Mr. Maziar. People are getting poorer, and even the little freedom we used to have is almost gone." Davood sounded frustrated, and a bit tipsy. When I asked him if he was still drinking, he answered that getting drunk on homemade vodka with his friends was his only solace.

In an ironic twist of fate, his retired Revolutionary Guard father is helping Davood's younger brother leave the country so he will not have to serve in the military. "My father says this regime is not worth fighting for. I wasted two years in the military, so my father is trying to sell everything he has to send my brother abroad."

Like many people of his generation, Davood was disheartened by the violent suppression of the green movement in Iran. But, of course, the movement was later rejuvenated in January 2011 after the overthrow of Zine El Abidine Ben Ali, the Tunisian dictator, and, a month later, of the Egyptian despot Hosni Mubarak by pro-democracy young Arabs. These actions revived the protests in Iran, and thousands of young Iranians once again gathered on the streets of Iran, calling for the removal of Khamenei. Davood told me, "Our slogan was 'After Mubarak and Ben Ali, it is the turn of Seyyed Ali' "—that is, Ali Khamenei. "I was really depressed after I came out of prison, but what happened in Egypt sparked something in my heart, in all our hearts. We have realized that if we are united we can change this regime through peaceful means. We are really hopeful."

Davood still plans to travel, and possibly study, for a while outside of Iran. "I already have a gift for your daughter, Mr. Maziar," Davood told me affectionately. "I can't wait to give it to her myself."

*   *   *

Since Ahmadinejad's reelection, many of those who opposed him have turned their anger against Khamenei as the main culprit behind the fraudulent election and the atrocities committed in its aftermath. Whereas during the postelection protests people chanted, "Where is my vote?" and "Death to Ahmadinejad," these days one can rarely hear anti-Ahmadinejad slogans. People overwhelmingly blame Khamenei for the rapes, tortures, and murders. According to the people who know him, Khamenei recognizes that the gap between the people and his government is widening. But rather than looking for a long-term solution or listening to his people, he is trying to narrow that gap through brute force. The supreme leader is becoming ever more isolated and deluded about his own powers.

My friend Amir no longer uses honorifics when he talks about the supreme leader. "Khamenei thinks the current situation is temporary," Amir told me when I spoke with him on Skype soon after my release. "He thinks that by jailing a few people, he can put a stop to the green movement. He is incapable of understanding that many Iranians cannot accept a god-king and want to be in charge of their own destiny in the twenty-first century."

These days, Amir is a worried man. He is in what he likes to call "a contemplative period."

He has very little choice. Like those of many other reformists, Amir's actions are carefully watched by Khamenei's henchmen, just as, like many despots before him, Khamenei now seeks revenge against former friends and allies who have broken ranks with him.

Amir says that he has received several threatening messages by phone or through friends, warning him that he should watch his actions and words. Even so, he continued to visit Mousavi until February 2011, when the regime put Mousavi and his brave wife under house arrest. Since then, only Mousavi's two daughters can visit them. On March 31, 2011, Mousavi's 103-year-old father died. Mousavi's father was a distant cousin of Khamenei and had given him shelter before the 1979 revolution, when Khamenei was fighting against the shah. After hearing the news, I asked Amir on Skype if he was going to attend the funeral. "An intelligence officer called one of our friends only a few minutes ago and warned me against going there," Amir told me. "I don't think they're going to let the funeral proceed peacefully." Amir was right. With Khamenei's tacit approval, the funeral was disrupted and several people were arrested and imprisoned.

"Before the 2009 elections we thought we could persuade him to change, but we were wrong. Khamenei and his regime cannot be reformed. This regime is like an old car that can't be repaired anymore. You might be able to use it for spare parts, but the car itself should be scrapped."

Amir says he is "like a father whose son has become a drug addict and a thief."

In April 2011, I flew to Dubai for a few days to meet Amir. We sat in the lobby of a luxurious hotel, smoking Havana cigars, as the music of the Lebanese diva Fairouz played in the background. I asked him whether rising up in revolt against the shah's dictatorship under the guidance of Khomeini had been the right thing to do, and if he supported the idea of another violent revolution in Iran.

He couldn't have responded more quickly: "No and no."

He then paused for a few minutes as he quietly puffed his cigar. "To tell you the truth, Maziar, we were young and immature at the time of the revolution. The shah's government was no doubt a corrupt dictatorship, but we didn't even think once about what kind of government we wanted to replace it with. We kept on talking about an 'Islamic government,' but we had no idea what this government would look like. What were its economic policies? What were its foreign policies supposed to be? What about the police, army, et cetera? We didn't ask these questions, and that's why we're in the situation we are in now. Three decades after the revolution, we have not been able to achieve most of what we dreamt about."

Amir cleared the ashes from his suit and then gave me a stare. "There you have it," he told me curtly. "You've asked me about my regrets several times in the past, and I always avoided answering you. But I owe it to you now. I owe it to Maziar Bahari, who has suffered by the regime I helped bring to power. If you really want to know, my life is nothing but regrets these days. Nothing but regrets."

Amir got up and, uncharacteristically, went up to his room without saying good-bye.

Security agents stopped Amir at the airport when he returned to Iran. They took his passport and interrogated him for three days. He is still banned from leaving the country and awaits a trial.

*   *   *

These days, I spend at least an hour a day talking to my friends and sources in Iran. Our conversations about the latest outrage committed by the regime and what may happen next are what I call "Liza Minnelli dialogues": we cry, we laugh, we cry while laughing, and laugh again teary-eyed. And then, we all look really confused.

No one can be certain of what the future holds for Iran. Anyone who tells you what will happen next is either delusional or a scam artist, trying to make a buck through political clairvoyance.

The brutality of Khamenei and the Guards after the disputed election has created an uncertain situation. On the one hand, dissent is growing and people are becoming more disenchanted with the regime every day. On the other, three decades of revolution, war, and violence have made most Iranians mistrustful of any sudden violent changes.

It is too optimistic to think that the relatively peaceful changes in Egypt can be emulated in Iran. Egyptians rose up against a corrupt dictator with no legitimacy whatsoever. Khamenei is still regarded by his followers as Allah's representative on earth. Also unlike Mubarak, Khamenei has been very careful about his image, especially about financial corruption in his family, an issue that is very sensitive for Iranians. This has granted him an aura of sainthood that has created a cult around him. The majority of Iranians are unhappy with Khamenei's tyranny and the misery that has befallen them as a result of his despotic policies, but assassins around him are still willing to kill and die for their *agha* (master).

Iran's future depends on a host of domestic and foreign players: Khamenei, the Guards, the economy, the price of oil, the United States, Israel, Iraq, Afghanistan, and other countries in the region will all play important roles. Most critically, what will happen in Iran will depend on the zeitgeist of the Iranian people at a given point, and that has historically been very difficult to predict.

Extrapolating from my conversations with friends and sources inside Iran and a daily study of the country's politics, economy, and, most important of all, culture, I constantly shift between two future scenarios. The first is a depressing prospect in which violent clashes continue to erupt between the regime and those who oppose it, and Iran is simultaneously attacked by the United States and its allies. In the other, much more positive scenario, the people of Iran, with the help of the international community, somehow peacefully transform the current regime into a relatively democratic government.

The regime has managed to remain in power through violence. The opposition knows that Khamenei and his cronies are willing to go to any length to stay in power, and they have asked people not to resort to violence. Yet the regime itself resorts to more violence every day. The number of executions has multiplied since the 2009 presidential election, and many people have been thrown in jail for writing an article or giving an interview. The people, so far, have shown incredible self-discipline, but they are becoming more disenchanted with Khamenei's regime. The two big questions, for which no one yet has any answers, are: When are people going to reach a boiling point? And, once that happens, what will the people and the government do?

No one can answer these questions. But many officials in Iran have realized that the situation has become unsustainable, so they've implicitly tried to distance themselves from Khamenei. Even Ahmadinejad, who became president only because of Khamenei's support, is now trying ever so discreetly to dissociate himself from his master before it is too late. Since his reelection in 2009, Ahmadinejad and his gang, including some members of the Guards, have expanded their Mafia-like grip on power by replacing more moderate supporters of Khamenei with their own, while presenting themselves as an alternative to the clerical establishment.

The next phase of infighting in Iran will be a clash between conservative supporters of Khamenei and Ahmadinejad's hardline, Mafia-like supporters. The main difference between the two groups is their revolutionary backgrounds. The conservatives are generally people who either fought themselves during the revolution or belong to families that rose to prominence in the government or the Guards. The hard-liners are low-ranking members of the Guards or junior officials from those years. The main point of contention between the two groups is less ideological and has simply to do with their desire to be in power, and in charge of spending the nation's significant oil revenue. Many Iranians dismiss the differences by saying that "conservatives ruined the country for three decades and now it is the

hard-liners' turn to finish the job!" Both groups despise the reformists and have their own supporters within the Guards.

The number of Guards supporting different factions is not
clear, but the general understanding is that many Guards commanders look at Ahmadinejad's policies and actions with suspi-
cion, and in case of any possible future clash between Ahmadinejad and Khamenei, they will support their master, Khamenei.

Ahmadinejad and his people know this and have been very
careful not to voice any explicit criticism of Khamenei. But they
have been developing a long-term plan that involves undermining Khamenei and the clerical establishment by manipulating
Iranians' nationalist sentiments, which has traditionally been
the best way to stay in power. They challenge the regime's policy of emphasizing Iranians' Shia identity by putting forward
new theories about "Iranian Islam." They glorify ancient Iranian traditions, claiming that Islam as a religion has benefited
from Iranian culture. The hard-liners refer to conservatives as
reactionaries, calling them out of touch with the modern world.
If this new brand of nationalism were presented by a group of
scholars, it would be worthy of an academic debate, but as presented by a group of thugs with little knowledge of the religion
who have shown very little respect for the people of Iran, these
revisionist theories can only be seen as a political ploy to remain
in power.

The infighting within his regime has put Khamenei in a difficult position. He has chastised individual members of Ahmadinejad's cabal, while continuing to tolerate them and support
Ahmadinejad's presidency, if only to take every opportunity to
maintain an image of a unity among his people. Khamenei
should look at his supporters' infighting with worry. Before the
fall, every dictator's supporters bicker with one another first,
then eventually turn against their master.

In order to prolong his reign, Khamenei is bestowing more
power to the Guards and transforming the Islamic Republic

into a military dictatorship. Recently, retired Revolutionary Guards have been filling many official posts and entering the parliament, and they are taking over Iranian industry as much as they can. Almost every day we hear that the Guards have won a lucrative contract to build a road, pipeline, or refinery by pushing aside the competition. Many Iranian businessmen and industrialists have told me that sometimes even if the Guards are not in charge of a project, they still demand a commission to let the construction go ahead.

Iranians are becoming more suppressed and poorer at the same time. Facing an ideological and industrial military monster, many young Iranians have come to believe that violence is the only language the regime can understand.

But using violence to defy the regime will not result in progress. This military Islamic regime is prepared to defend itself by force, and even if a group can manage to topple it through violent means, that future government will just be another tyranny in the history of tyrannies in Iran. I often remind young Iranians of the betrayed ideals of the 1979 Islamic Revolution and tell them that nothing good can be achieved through violence. Nothing.

Alongside the horrifying specter of mayhem inside the country, there is also the danger of a military confrontation between Iran and the United States or Iran and Israel, prompted by Iran's nuclear ambitions. Khamenei has repeatedly declared that Iran doesn't want to build a nuclear bomb, and he has even asserted that doing so would be against Islamic principles. But he lies. Khamenei may not want to develop a nuclear weapon, but he does want to be one turn of a screw away from a bomb. He needs nuclear capability to threaten the West and the countries in the region and prevent them from helping the opposition inside the country. To Khamenei, giving up the nuclear program equals surrendering to the will of foreigners, and to a tyrant nothing is more important than his power.

Khamenei knows that he can always rely on the mistakes of his enemies, especially the United States, to expand his power. The American misadventures in Afghanistan and Iraq led to the toppling of two of Iran's biggest regional enemies, the Taliban and Saddam Hussein. Their demise has helped make Iran a regional superpower. Through proxies in Iraq, Lebanon, and the Palestinian territories, Iran can always challenge the United States and Israel outside of its borders. As Rosewater said, Hamas, in Gaza, and Hezbollah, in Lebanon, are in a sense two branches of the Revolutionary Guards.

Yet Khamenei's plans, devised in the isolation of his house under the protection of thousands of guardsmen, can backfire, with disastrous consequences for both Iran and his regime. Israel will never tolerate a nuclear Iran. Ahmadinejad denies the Jewish Holocaust and promises to wipe the Jewish state off the map. Furthermore, Israel feels an existential threat from any country in the region, friend or foe, that has a stronger military capability than it does. Israel objected to Iran's nuclear program even when the shah—a friend to Israel—was in power in the 1970s. The Israelis, hitherto, have been patient and have backed negotiations and sanctions to stop Iran's nuclear program, but they may soon change their tactics.

Of course, Israel will not take action without the blessing of its major ally, the United States, which has so much to lose if Iran becomes a nuclear state. There are thousands of American troops stationed in the region, and many American allies feel threatened by Iran's rogue behavior. Countries such as Saudi Arabia, Kuwait, and Bahrain buy arms and other products and services from the United States and, in turn, provide it with crude oil and/or military bases. The unpopular authoritarian regimes in these countries are rattled by Ahmadinejad's and Khamenei's extremist rhetoric, and the prospect of a nuclear Iran instills fear in them. As secret U.S. diplomatic cables released by Wikileaks revealed, many American allies in the Mid-

dle East have repeatedly asked the United States to attack Iran
in order to stop its nuclear program. The American government
has so far adopted a diplomatic approach to handling Iran. But
the situation is untenable. These countries are important allies
in America's war against terrorism, and protecting them from
Iran is integral to the United States as a military and economic
superpower.

So far, the United States has been trying to stop Iran's nuclear
program through financial and economic sanctions. But Iranians
have lived with sanctions since the beginning of the revolution,
and shrewd Iranian officials know quite well how to use legal
and financial loopholes in the international system to their own
advantage. Opening front companies and bank accounts and
laundering money to acquire arms—in other words, employing
the same methods used by international criminal cartels—has
become second nature to them. Iran has also managed to divide
the international community by making strategic alliances with
America's main rivals, Russia and China, as well as such emerg-
ing powers as Turkey and Brazil. But even those countries'
patience has a limit, and they too are becoming increasingly
frustrated with Iran's intransigence. They also understand that
eventually they will have to choose between supporting Iran and
doing business with the United States. It is not a difficult choice,
and more countries have started to support American policies
against Iran.

The idea of an American or Israeli attack against Iran is, at
the moment, a nightmare, but it could quickly turn into reality,
with disastrous results for both Iran and the rest of the world. I
can understand other countries' frustration with the lack of development in nuclear negotiations with Iran. After all, many
Iranian diplomats and officials are erratic thugs like Rosewater
(incidentally, some Iranian diplomats are former interrogators
and torturers). I also know that many American politicians seek
reelection by displays of saber rattling with Iran. But a military

attack against Iran will militarize the regime further, and will encourage even nationalist pro-Western Iranians to side with the government against a foreign enemy.

My nightmare scenario of a violent crushing of all remnants of the democratic movement in Iran and a foreign military attack would also mean jeopardizing Western interests in the region for the foreseeable future.

On my more optimistic days, I think of a positive scenario: one in which Iran can change peacefully with the help of the rest of the world. As the democratic changes in the rest of the Middle East have shown, pro-Western tyranny and Islamic fundamentalism are not the only choices for Iranians. The West, especially the United States, should respect Iran's independence and the nationalist sentiments of Iranians. A democratic, independent government in Iran that respects the people's religious and cultural traditions will most likely have serious disagreements with the West, but those issues can be negotiated in a civilized manner without recourse to violence by either side.

Change toward a more democratic Iran cannot, and should not, happen overnight. I am proud of the maturity and the restraint shown by a generation of educated young Iranians who refuse to become the mirror image of the brutes who rule them. The current despotic system is based on ignorance and backwardness, and given enough time and support by the international community, young Iranians can move their country toward democracy. I am not sure how long it will take, but I often remind myself that it took the Soviet Union more than seventy years to collapse.

My optimism is not a foolish hopefulness. It is based on facts. The Islamic regime has two main weak spots: information and the economy. The West can help Iranians by manipulating these weaknesses over a period of time to bring about a peaceful change in the country. With Iran's history of tyranny and monarchy, many people are used to being the subjects of a despot; democracy is a foreign concept to them. But the number of extremist religious Iranians who want a monarch to rule them is rapidly shrinking. More young Iranians are becoming better educated every year, with greater access to the outside world through satellite TV and the Internet. These enlightened Iranians are the West's most important allies in the region. The international community should continue targeted sanctions against Iran's nuclear program and Iranian human-rights violators while lifting some of the current sanctions that hurt ordinary Iranians, such as sanctions on medical facilities and airplane spare parts. Through investing in satellite television channels and the Internet, the West can help these young Iranians learn even more about the outside world and question the legitimacy of their government.

I am often asked if the green movement is dead. My answer is no. People may not be able to demonstrate their anger at the government, but the movement is getting stronger every day. The protests I witnessed in the streets of Tehran in June 2009 were part of a civil rights movement, through which people peacefully demanded their rights as citizens of the country. Those who expected the green movement to topple Khamenei's government and bring a Western-style democracy to power were wrong.

The green movement is a collective cry among Iranians for a normal life. In fact, for the first time in the history of Iran, this political movement is based on a fundamental respect for life, rather than an ideological notion that people must sacrifice themselves for a cause. My parents' and even Maryam's generation believed that there was nothing more sacred than martyrdom, but the new generation of young Iranians do not believe that any idea or cause is worth dying for; they want to remain alive and celebrate life.

* * *

Soon after my release, many of my friends and more than a few strangers with connections inside the government started to contact me to tell me the details that had eventually led to my arrest and the arrest of hundreds of other people. Fearing the government's reprisal, they contacted me by email and Skype using pseudonyms, or called me from temporary mobile phone numbers so that their identities could not be tracked. In some cases, they risked losing their jobs or being incarcerated to tell me what they knew; they did it, they said, because they felt that what happened to me was wrong.

According to these accounts, the Revolutionary Guards came up with a plan to incriminate the reformists a year before the election, and received Khamenei's blessing to carry it out. The Guards' plan was to crack down on the reformists by connecting them with Western powers. The Guards knew that many Iranians resented Western interference in Iran and the Middle East region, and they shrewdly wanted to take advantage of it.

By getting rid of reformists through a smear campaign, the Guards hoped to guarantee the survival of Khamenei's regime for the foreseeable future. "In fact, many of the Guards did not think they were concocting a plot," a government insider told me. "They genuinely believed that the reformists received money and guidance from the West, and that under sufficient pressure they would spill the beans."

This information, which was told to me off the record, was later corroborated by certain courageous, anonymous Iranian journalists and regime insiders, who exposed the Guards' secret plan on the Internet.

According to the Guards' scenario, three people would act as interlocutors with the West: Hossein Rassam, a political analyst with the British embassy, was supposed to be the diplomatic contact with the West; Kian Tajbakhsh, the Open Society Institute's representative in Iran, was given the role of nongovernmental go-between; and I was the connection between the evil Western media and the reformists.

The half-baked script didn't work, because there was no such connection between the reformists and the West, and most Iranians simply did not believe the regime's propaganda. Within a few months of our arrests, therefore, the Guards gave up the plan and had to release all three of us. Rassam and Tajbakhsh are still prohibited from leaving Iran. "You were lucky your wife was pregnant," a friend told me. The Guards were worried that Paola could die because of the stress of my incarceration. "The last thing the Guards wanted was to have a dead British mother or baby on their hands. That's why they let you leave the country."

Since my release I have been trying to find out why I was let go, beyond the government worrying about Paola's situation. According to a story corroborated by multiple sources, the Islamic government finally decided to release me after Ahmadinejad's visit to the United Nations in September 2009. During that trip, Ahmadinejad and the Iranian foreign minister at the time, Manouchehr Mottaki, were bombarded with questions about me. *Newsweek* made sure that journalists asked about me in their interviews with Ahmadinejad, as did diplomats from all around the world and in every level of government. After Ahmadinejad returned to Iran, my name and questions regarding my fate were mentioned in his reports to Khamenei.

Khamenei had heard my name several times before and had asked his office to look into my case; he wanted to know if there was any advantage in holding me. By September, the Guards had realized that I was not going to be much help to the regime and would never name names. The answer to Khamenei's office was that I was an espionage suspect, but that my case would be coming to a close very soon. That answer was not good enough for Khamenei's people.

A few days later, Iranian diplomats asked Guards personnel

to make a decision about me as soon as they could. "We're hearing Bahari's name everywhere," one envoy said. "This Bahari has become more of a liability than an asset. Isn't it about time to let him go?"

At the time, Khamenei had put Hossein Taeb, the commander of the Basij during the postelection crackdown, in charge of the Guards' intelligence unit, the unit that had arrested me. Once the Guards' plan to incriminate the reformists through me had failed, Rosewater and his team could not convince Taeb that there was any point in keeping me.

Rosewater and the Boss had to let me go, but they had to find a graceful way to do so. As I'd suspected at the time, my commitment to spy for them upon release was a face-saving measure. That way, Rosewater's team could claim that they had transformed me during my time in Evin and that my reporting on the opposition was going to benefit the regime.

According to several sources, Rosewater argued against my release until an hour before I was let go. He allegedly tried to convince his superiors that if they allowed him to exert more pressure on me, I would sing like a canary and admit that I was a spy. "I'm not sure what you did to him," a government source told me, "but he really wanted to hold on to you." I'm not sure either, and I'm glad that I never found out. But I imagine one of his reasons was to learn more about New Jersey or Thailand!

*   *   *

Rosewater's organizational name is Javadi. He was born in 1978 and joined the Guards in 1996. A colonel in the Guards, he comes from a traditional religious family originally from the city of Isfahan; his parents moved to Tehran before he was born. Javadi's father was, as he told me, a Khomeini follower, and had been imprisoned during the shah's time. Javadi's uncle and older brothers are also Guards members. He was among the first generation of Guards to go through the Basirat, or Wisdom, indoctrination courses. Javadi received a master's degree in political science from Tehran University and had taken several anti-espionage courses. He is usually referred to as Gondeheh, the Big Guy, because of his size, or Char Cheshmi, the Four-Eyed One, because of his thick glasses.

Throughout my interrogation, Javadi told his bosses that he was making good progress with me. Having forced many student activists since 2000 to make false confessions, he has gained a reputation as one of the Guards' toughest interrogators. Because of this, his bosses trusted him and left him alone with me for long periods of time.

I also learned that Javadi had personally chosen me as the individual who could connect the reformists to the foreign media. According to a Guards member, they first thought of arresting my friend Nazila Fathi, a *New York Times* reporter, but Rosewater convinced them to arrest me. I was a filmmaker and a journalist, and I worked both in Iran and outside it, so by arresting me they could intimidate different groups of people. "He told everyone that he had caught a real spy after the first interrogation sessions. In his book, only a spy could travel as much as you did and have as many friends as you have," the guardsman told me. "After the media campaign for you started, he became certain that you were a spy."

According to another anonymous guardsman, "The Big Guy still thinks you are a spy and follows your every move. He never fails to remind his bosses that you shouldn't have been released."

What seems to be particularly incensing to the Guards is my invitation to nonviolence and peaceful resistance against Khamenei's regime. In almost all the interviews I've done since my release, I've emphasized that the most successful achievement of the regime would be transforming the opposition into a mirror image of the regime itself: a vicious, bigoted thug. "The Guards understand violence," an Iranian diplomat told me. "But your insistence on nonviolence is difficult for them to fathom, and because of that they are cursing themselves for letting you go." The man who woke me up on that morning in June 2009 and put me through a nightmare for 118 days lives a nightmare every day. He is the one who spends his time in Evin, in a small, dark room, beating and humiliating innocent people. He is just another employee of a bad system, a by-product of ignorance and religious zealotry. One of these days I'll send him a package, addressed care of Evin Prison, Tehran, Iran. The package will include a plane ticket to New Jersey, a collection of Chekhov plays, and a Leonard Cohen CD. And, before I forget, a new perfume.

Javadi may still hold a personal grudge against me, but I can honestly say that I feel no animosity toward him. In the first few weeks after my release, I was practically allergic to the smell of rosewater—one whiff would make me nauseous—and I dreamt of him almost every night. But soon after Marianna's birth, those nightmares were interrupted by her cries. When I held Marianna in my arms, I did not think of anything except for how much I love her and how much I want to share with her in the future. These days I rarely have nightmares about Rosewater; even the scent of rosewater doesn't bother me anymore. Moloojoon, Paola, and Marianna are my world. Marianna is learning Persian, and I will try to keep her aware of her roots. She will be part of a generation who will make a better Iran, and a better world. I only wish Maryam and Baba Akbar were here to see her growing up. I'm sure they would be proud of her.

ACKNOWLEDGMENTS

This acknowledgment can't do justice to those who have done nothing less than save my life. I am indebted to anyone whose thoughts, words, and actions saved me from languishing in Evin Prison.

Nisid Hajari, Christopher Dickey, Fareed Zakaria, Jon Meacham, Mark Miller, Daniel Klaidman, Lally Weymouth, Frank De Maria, and all my former colleagues at *Newsweek* launched the most amazing campaign for my release. While doing so, they had the full support of Don Graham and Ann McDaniel of the Washington Post Company.

Newsweek, The Washington Post, and their lawyer Robert Kimmitt successfully rallied international diplomats and dignitaries to support me in private and public meetings with Iranian officials. I especially have to thank American secretary of state Hillary Clinton; former secretary of state Madeleine Albright; Bishop Desmond Tutu (thanks, Susan, John, and everyone at Search for Common Ground); Canadian foreign minister Lawrence Cannon; Canadian prime minister Stephen Harper; as well as Canadian consular and diplomatic officers in Tehran, London, and Ottawa. Canadian opposition leaders Michael Ignatieff of the Liberal Party and Jack Layton of the New Democratic Party (thanks, Amy Marcus) also did their utmost to bring public attention to my case. Dozens of diplomats from all around the world do not want their names mentioned, but I appreciate their efforts and thank them all.

The help of my friends at Channel 4 News—Deborah Rayner (as well as R and MG), Jim Grey, Ben De Pear, Jonathan Miller, Lindsey Hillsum, Jon Snow, Sarah Corp, Dorothy Byrne, and others—was integral to the campaign, as was the support given by my friends at the BBC, especially Adrienne van Heteren, Jane Corbin, and Sandy Smith.

Iranian journalists and filmmakers bravely objected to my arrest in several letters to the authorities. They showed the Iranian government that my arrest would not intimidate and scare them (*Chakereh hamegi!*). My lawyer in Iran, Saleh Nikbakht, continues to show exemplary valor by defending the rights of prisoners of conscience in the country despite constant harassment by the government (*Mokhlesim!*).

My friends and colleagues at the International Documentary Film Festival Amsterdam, the Committee to Protect Journalists, Index on Censorship, Canadian Journalists for Free Expression, PEN, Reporters Sans Frontières, the International Bar Association, and many other groups brought together an outstanding collection of individuals to sign petitions for my release and lobbied the Iranian government. People in the Iranian government tell me that the regime paid attention to every single petition. I am indebted to every person who signed the petitions.

Please continue supporting the efforts of organizations that champion human rights and freedom of expression, wherever you live. Remember that dozens of Iranian prisoners of conscience are going through the same ordeal I did. Silent diplomacy usually does not work. Speak out loudly in support of human rights!

Thank you to the people behind Facebook, Twitter, and YouTube, for making the lives of authoritarian regimes more difficult. Bravo David Piaia, who organized the Facebook campaign, and David Shem-tov, who set up the www.freemaziar bahari.org website.

Countless friends and family members supported Paola during the ordeal and have continued to support us since my release, especially Barbara, who supported Paola during her pregnancy and the launch of the campaign. I owe so much to our friends at Latham & Watkins, as well as Malu, David, Chus, Lizzy, Masoud, Siavush, Jo, Fariba (and the family), Simon, Kirsten, Fred, Cynthia, Jacki, and Greg, who all put their thoughts together and staged the most remarkable campaign.

YOU don't want your name to be mentioned, but I really don't know how I can ever pay back YOUR kindness. You are my brothers. *Taa aakhareh omr madyoon SHOMAA hastam.*

Rosewater's memorable, albeit idiotic, narrow-minded, and terrifying, lines were difficult to forget. I started to write down my memories of Evin as soon as I left Iran. I had also sent long emails to my *Newsweek* editors and kept notes of my reporting of the pre-election period. This book has been based on those notes.

Rosewater and his cohorts shouldn't look for Amir. He is a composite character based on a few different high-ranking former members of the Iranian government. They were revolutionaries in 1979 but now hate the current Khamenei regime. *Hamashoon az gozashtashoon pashimoonand. Shomaa ham yek rooz pashimoon mishid.*

The readers can understand that I had to create the composite character of Amir in order to show the differences of opinion within the Islamic Republic establishment. I also had to change the name of my motorcycle cabbie at his request.

This book would not be possible without the support of the best people in the publishing world. Amanda Urban at ICM has been the guardian angel of the book. My co-writer, Aimee Molloy, put my scattered thoughts together and helped me get over my fear of writing my first book and the trauma of remembering the ordeal. The suggestions made by my editors, Kate Medina and Lindsey Schwoeri, took the book to another level. The book benefited a lot from comments by Barbara, John, Karim, Farideh, Jon, Naghmeh, Siavush, David, and Chris, who were kind enough to read the first draft.

Thank you, Maryam Dilmaghani, Ahmad Karimi Hakkak, and Mahvash Shahegh, who kindly gave me permission to use their translations of Persian poetry of Farrokhzad, Shamlu, and Akhavan Sales, respectively, in the book.

The main joy of writing this book was feeling Baba Akbar's and Maryam's presence next to me. *Khayli delam baraatoon tang shodeh.* The support that Mohammad, Khaled, and Iran give to me every day means so much to me. Moloojoon's detailed memory surprises me; many of the historical details about my family came out of long interviews with Moloojoon. Each conversation made me love her even more for her patience, perseverance, and strength. *Khayli khayli doostetoon daaram.*

Paola and I were finally married in June 2010, more than a year after our lives were rudely interrupted. I had never expected that I'd be holding my baby at my wedding, but on that day I was so happy that Marianna was there to witness Paola and me celebrating the end of a dark chapter of our lives together.

Paola's campaign was, of course, the main reason that I was released, but her sharp criticism and attention to details were also integral in giving the book its current shape. I'm so sorry for my knee-jerk reactions to your criticisms. I love you very much, Mrs. Bahari!

WHO'S WHO

Mohammad Ali Abtahi (b. 1958): reformist cleric and former vice president of Iran; adviser to presidential candidate Mehdi Karroubi during the 2009 election.

Mahmoud Ahmadinejad (b. 1956): current president of Iran; former mayor of Tehran (2004–05) and former governor of Ardabil Province (1993–97).

Feizollah Arabsorkhi (b. 1952): reformist politician; a founding member of the reformist party Mojahedin of the Islamic Revolution Organization (MIRO).

Mohammad Atrianfar (b. 1953): newspaper publisher and reformist politician; former intelligence official.

Mehdi Karroubi (b. 1937): a leader of the opposition and the head of the National Trust Party; former speaker of parliament (1989–92 and 2000–04).

Ali Hosseini Khamenei (b. 1939): current supreme leader of Iran; former president (1981–89). One of the leaders of the 1979 Islamic Revolution and an adviser to Ruhollah Khomeini.

Mohammad Khatami (b. 1943): one of the main opposition leaders; former president of Iran (1997–2005).

Ruhollah Khomeini (1902–1989): leader of the 1979 Islamic Revolution.

Sadegh Mahsouli (b. 1959): current minister of welfare and social security; minister of interior during the 2009 presidential election; former Revolutionary Guards commander and one of the wealthiest men in Iran.

Hossein Ali Montazeri (1922–2009): the highest-ranking critic of the Islamic regime among Iran's Shia clerics; an acolyte of Ruhollah Khomeini and his heir apparent (1979–88).

Judge Saeed Mortazavi (b. 1967): general prosecutor of Tehran (2003–09). As a judge (1997–2003), he was responsible for sentencing scores of jour-

334 WHO'S WHO

nalists and human-rights activists and shutting down dozens of newspapers.

Mir Hossein Mousavi (b. 1942): an opposition leader and the main reformist presidential candidate during the 2009 election; former prime minister of Iran (1981–89).

Behzad Nabavi (b. 1941): reformist politician; a founding member of the reformist party Mojahedin of the Islamic Revolution Organization (MIRO); former deputy speaker of parliament (2000–04) and minister of industries (1985–89).

Mohammad Reza Pahlavi (1919–1980): the last shah of Iran (1941–79).

Akbar Hashemi Rafsanjani (b. 1934): former president of Iran (1989–97); former speaker of the Majlis (1980–89). One of the leaders of the 1979 Islamic Revolution and an adviser to Ruhollah Khomeini.

Mehdi Hashemi Rafsanjani (b. 1969): the fourth child of Akbar Hashemi Rafsanjani. Mehdi was part of a reformists' committee to prevent fraud in the 2009 elections and bankrolled at least one anti-Ahmadinejad website before the election.

Massoud Rajavi (b. 1948): the leader of the Mujahideen Khalq Organization (MKO) since the 1970s.

Mohsen Rezaei (b. 1954): current secretary of the Expediency Council; a presidential candidate during the 2009 election; former chief commander of the Islamic Revolutionary Guards Corps (1981–97).

Reza Shah (1878–1944): father of Mohammad Reza Pahlavi and shah of Iran (1925–41).

Mohsen Safaei Farahani (b. 1946): reformist politician; founding member of the Islamic Iran Participation Front. A former high-ranking official of the Islamic Republic (1979–2005).

Youssef Sanei (b. 1937): one of the highest-ranking critics of the regime among Shia clerics; former chair of the Council of Guardians (1980–88).

Saeed Shariati (b. 1973): a reformist activist and spokesman for the Islamic Iran Participation Front (2003–09).

Hossein Taeb (b. 1943): head of the Revolutionary Guards' intelligence unit and a member of the Revolutionary Guards since 1981; commander of the Basij (2007–09).

Kian Tajbakhsh (b. 1962): an Iranian-American scholar. He worked as a consultant for a number of international organizations and is the author of two books and numerous articles on Iranian state institutions and the policy-making process in Iran.

TIME LINE

This time line is not meant to be a history of Iran. Rather, it is designed to provide background information on some of the events in the book while highlighting Iranians' ongoing struggle for self-determination since 1906.

Iran

The home of one of the most ancient civilizations in the world has been called Iran by the natives since A.D. 200. The country was known to the West as Persia until 1935.

1906: Persian constitutional revolution

Persia is ruled by the corrupt, religious, and reactionary kings of the Qajar dynasty, who came to power in the late eighteenth century. Persia in the time of the Qajars is a collection of fiefdoms run by local strongmen and princes. Meanwhile in the capital, Tehran, the shahs, or kings, support their lavish lifestyles by acting as puppets to the British and Russian Empires, which bribe the shahs and treat Iran as part of their territories.

After centuries of tyrannical rule under the shahs and foreign interference in their country, Persian merchants, clerics, and secular intellectuals rebel and, in the first revolution of its kind in Asia, force the shah to accept the establishment of the Majlis, or parliament, and the passage of a constitution. The king at the time, Mozaffaredin Shah, reluctantly signs a decree, according to which the crown becomes "a divine gift given to the shah by the people." This is the first time that a monarch in Asia accepts the idea that his actions should be supervised by representatives of the people.

A year later, the new king, Mohammad Ali Shah, attacks the parliament building with cannons and tries to abolish the Majlis. For many years, the country is engulfed in chaos. Persians look for a government to provide them with security and rule of law, as well as the freedom promised to them in the Constitution.

1908: Discovery of oil

Under the supervision of British engineers and scientists, oil is discovered in the southwestern province of Khuzestan. A British entrepreneur named William Knox D'Arcy had already obtained exclusive rights to pump oil in many parts of the country. The company that inherits D'Arcy's rights is called the Anglo-Persian Oil Company, later known as BP, British Petroleum. Even though Iran has not been a British colony, the British Empire has treated it as one for many years. After the discovery of oil, the situation becomes worse. Corrupt and weak central and local officials are bribed or coerced into helping the British exploit Persian oil freely. The taxes paid by the oil company to the British government are more than the percentage paid to Iran for the oil itself.

1921: The Reign of Reza Shah

Reza Khan, a commander of the Persian army, and several other disgruntled prominent Iranians stage a coup to rid Iran of corruption and insecurity and establish a strong central government. Reza Khan, who eventually becomes the head of the army, wants to abolish the monarchy in Iran and establish a republic. But the mullahs, or Shia clerics, object to this decision. The mullahs believe that Persia needs a strong king who can protect Islam in the country.

Reza Khan becomes the new king in 1925, and is subsequently known as Reza Shah. He changes the country's international name to Iran in 1935. Reza Shah tries to resurrect the glory of the Persian kings while modernizing Iran by using Western models. New industries, roads, and railroads are built, universities are established, and hundreds of young Iranians are sent to Europe to be educated. A generation of the Persian elite learns Western technical know-how, and at the same time becomes familiarized with such modern concepts as democracy, rule of law, and freedom of expression. Despite his fascination with the West, Reza Shah, a ruthless despot, has little patience for civil liberties. He jails, tortures, and kills his critics and bans opposition political parties. Reza Shah also thinks of the mullahs, who helped him come to power, as obstacles to his modernizing of Iran. He bans the wearing of the Islamic veil for women and forces men and women to wear Western clothes.

1941: The fall of Reza Shah, foreign occupation, a new shah

Toward the end of his reign, Reza Shah tries to put an end to British and Russian interference in Iranian affairs by allying with Nazi Germany. During the Second World War, the Allied powers—Britain, the United States, and the Soviet Union—invade and occupy Iran for use as a route to strengthen the eastern front against Hitler. The Allies remove Reza Shah from power and replace him with his twenty-two-year-old son, Mohammad Reza Pahlavi, who becomes known as the shah.

Occupation means more chaos and insecurity in Iran, as well as, for ordinary Iranians, the humiliation of living under foreign occupation. But the end of Reza Shah's tyranny also brings a certain level of freedom to the country, and different political parties are established. The most influential of these is the communist Tudeh Party, which receives organizational and financial help from the Soviet Union. The Tudeh attracts many educated and working-class Iranians who are tired of centuries of corrupt autocratic rule in their country. The Tudeh also acts as the Soviet Union's fifth column and works against British and American influence in Iran.

At the end of the Second World War, the Soviet Union refuses to pull its troops from Iran's province of Azerbaijan, in the northwest of the country. The Soviets help Iranian communists establish the People's Republic of Azerbaijan. The American president, Harry S. Truman, warns Joseph Stalin of the negative consequences of occupying Iran, and, according to some sources, threatens Stalin with a nuclear bomb. In a meeting in Moscow, Iranian prime minister Ahmad Qavam negotiates a deal in which Stalin will withdraw from the province in exchange for certain rights in Iran; Qavam later makes sure that these never materialize. After the Soviet troops withdraw, in December 1946, the shah's army and Iranian nationalists massacre thousands of communists. In 1949, an unsuccessful assassination attempt against the shah, allegedly by a member of the Tudeh Party, gives the shah the perfect excuse to declare the Tudeh Party illegal and jail many of its leaders.

1951: Nationalization of oil

Mohammad Mossadegh, a popular nationalist politician, is chosen by the shah and the Majlis as the new prime minister; in less than a month he nationalizes Iranian oil, which had been controlled by the British for half a century. Mossadegh also tries to restrict the powers of the shah and turn him into a titular head of state. The British government embargoes Iran, lands troops in the Persian Gulf, and starts a secret campaign against Mossadegh with the help of the shah and his supporters. The British also warn the United

States that Mossadegh's government will lead to a Soviet annexation of Iran.

Mossadegh tries to garner American help in his battle to put an end to British interference in Iran. He tells the Americans that his failure will lead to a communist takeover of his country. Communists call Mossadegh an American stooge and try to undermine him through riots and by getting their members in trade unions and an underground military network to conspire against his government. President Truman remains sympathetic to Mossadegh until the last day of his presidency, in January 1953. Republicans in the U.S. Congress, led by Senator Joseph McCarthy, criticize Truman for not taking a tough stance against Soviet influence around the world.

1953: CIA-backed coup

After two years of embargo, Iranians are poorer, less secure, and disenchanted with Mossadegh's government. Meanwhile, the communists are becoming more vocal and increasing their activities. The British secretly convince the new American administration of Dwight D. Eisenhower, which comes to power in January 1953, to help remove Mossadegh. On August 19, 1953, a coup plotted by the Central Intelligence Agency and a British spy network in Iran is executed by Iranian army officers. Mossadegh is put on trial, and within the next few years dozens of Iranian communists are incarcerated and executed.

1963: Khomeini's first uprising

After the 1953 coup, the shah, with American help, expands his authority; like his father, he eventually becomes a tyrant. He continues to industrialize Iran, and has the same contempt for his critics and the mullahs. He calls himself the Shadow of God and tries to change the country through a series of decrees. In 1961, the shah grants women the right to vote and distributes large tracts of land among the farmers. These changes, among others intended to modernize Iran, later become known as the White Revolution.

The large landowners have been the main benefactors of the clerical establishment, and the majority of mullahs regard women as second-class citizens. In October 1962, in a letter to the shah, Ayatollah Ruhollah Khomeini, a high-ranking seminarian at the time, expresses his concern about the shah's reforms and calls them un-Islamic.

The shah refers to his religious critics as "black reactionaries," and he claims they are working with the communists to undermine Iran and take it back to the Dark Ages. In June 1963, after Khomeini is arrested, his followers rebel against the shah, and the shah's army kills dozens of people in clashes all over the country.

In November 1964, after months under house arrest and in prison, Khomeini is sent into exile. He eventually settles in the Iraqi holy city of Najaf, the bastion of Shia Islam. In exile, Khomeini communicates with his followers inside Iran through letters, leaflets, and, eventually, audiocassettes.

In Najaf, Khomeini publishes his theory of *velayat-e faqih,* or the governance of the jurisprudent, a collection of his teachings about the necessity of establishing a system of government in which a high-ranking cleric is in charge of the affairs of the state until the reappearance of Imam Mahdi, the twelfth saint of Shias. The book is a theological text with many references to the teachings of traditional Shia theologians and interpretations of the Koran. Many nonreligious opponents of the shah, among them socialists, nationalists, and communists, support Khomeini's anti-shah struggle but don't read his book on governance. They dismiss it as a complicated, esoteric text like thousands of books on Shia theology before it. Years later, they regret following Khomeini's path without having understood his philosophy.

1970s: The sharp rise and fall of the shah

The 1973 oil crisis, triggered by many factors, including an embargo of the West by the Organization of the Petroleum Exporting Countries (OPEC) and an earlier stock market crash, benefits Iran immensely. The increasing oil prices mean that the shah has more money with which to buy arms and new technology from the West. Consequently, he becomes even more ambitious—some claim that he is delusional—in his plans to modernize Iran. He believes that by the end of the twentieth century, Iran can be among the five most advanced nations in the world. In the early 1970s, the shah is diagnosed with cancer, but for many years he keeps his illness secret from most people, including his wife. Many observers contend that the shah's insistence on the fast pace of change stems from his feeling that he is fighting against time.

Much of the progress in Iran happens in its major cities, and many villagers from traditional religious communities move to the big cities in hope of finding a better life. As OPEC members again start selling oil to the West, the price of oil decreases and the shah has a hard time financing his ambitious projects. Most of the villagers who have migrated to the cities do not benefit from his changes. They live mainly on the outskirts and feel alienated by the fast pace of Westernization.

Contrary to public opinion, the shah is not a stooge of the West. In fact, toward the end of his reign, he becomes quite resentful of Western attitudes toward Iran. In interviews, the shah reprimands the West for allowing too much freedom and for the decline of its economies and cultures. In 1976,

Jimmy Carter becomes president of the United States. Because one of Carter's campaign promises entailed pressuring American allies, such as Iran, to have more respect for human rights, Carter's election convinces the shah's opponents that they have an ally in the White House. They become more vocal in their opposition to the shah. The shah, whose illness has worsened in the past few years, becomes paranoid about the change in American attitude, but he refuses to make any compromises with the opposition.

1978: The anti-Khomeini article and the second uprising

In January 1978, the shah orders the biggest Iranian daily newspaper, *Etela'at,* to publish an article against Khomeini. The article calls the ayatollah "a non-Iranian of Indian origin and a reactionary agent of the British who rose against the shah in protest against advancement of the country, including the progress of women." The publication of the article leads to a series of demonstrations in the cities of Qom and Tabriz, where the shah's army kills many protestors. According to Shia tradition, people gather to mourn for the dead forty days after their death. The suppression of each gathering on the fortieth day results in yet another protest, and increasing numbers of murdered protestors every forty days.

In this period Khomeini's supporters start calling him Imam Khomeini for the first time, even though "imam" is a title reserved by Shias for saints. On September 8, 1978, the shah announces martial law in Tehran and eleven other cities. Many Khomeini followers take to the streets. The army opens fire on them in central Tehran. The reported number of dead varies from forty to eighty, but in the absence of any accurate report, and as anti-shah sentiments heighten in the country, there are rumors that four thousand people were martyred by the shah's henchmen. The rumors intensify the public's resentment of the shah.

A few weeks after the massacre, the shah forces the government of Iraq to deport Khomeini to another country. The shah hopes that Khomeini's influence will subside once he is outside Iraq, but Khomeini moves to Paris, where he gains access to international media and can easily communicate with his followers inside Iran. Over the next four months he grants hundreds of interviews in which he promises greater liberties and prosperity for Iranians. There is not a single mention of governance of the jurisprudent; in many interviews, he offers freedom of expression, equality between men and women, and a better economic situation for every Iranian.

Khomeini recognizes the weakening of the shah's regime and asks his followers not to resort to violence. Despite the martial law, people continue to demonstrate against the shah. In early November 1978, millions of Iranians in Tehran and cities around the country peacefully demonstrate on the holy days of Tasu'a and Ashura, during which Shias commemorate the martyrdom of Hossein, their third imam.

The shah is surprised by the public's hatred of him. He becomes erratic and unable to make firm decisions. He frees hundreds of political prisoners, who will join the revolution, and orders the arrest of his top officials. In November, he appears on television and says that he has heard the voice of the people's revolution and he will reform his system. But most Iranians believe that the shah's time is over. He leaves Iran two months later. The shah spends the rest of his life in exile, in Morocco, the United States, Panama, Mexico, and Egypt, where he dies on July 27, 1980.

Early 1979: The Iranian revolution

Khomeini returns to Tehran on February 1, 1979. Exactly ten days later, a group of commanders of the Royal Iranian Army reach an agreement with Khomeini to put down their guns and accept a new revolutionary government, assigned by Khomeini. The Iranian revolution is victorious. Twenty-five hundred years of monarchy in Iran come to an end.

Less than two months later, in a referendum, 98.2 percent of Iranians vote for the establishment of an Islamic republic. Later in the year, an assembly writes the Islamic Republic of Iran's Constitution, according to which Khomeini's concept of governance of the jurisprudent effectively becomes Iran's form of government.

Late 1979: Hostage taking, suppression of dissent

On November 4, 1979, a group of radical students, with Khomeini's blessing, raids the American embassy in Iran and takes sixty-six Americans hostage. On the surface, the hostage taking is a protest against the American government's support of the shah's dictatorship, but in reality, it is a way for Khomeini to fully consolidate his authority by suppressing the moderates in his government, who criticize the takeover. The hostages are freed after 444 days, but the crisis brings formal Iran-U.S. relations to an end and ignites a series of American-imposed sanctions that are still in place more than three decades later.

Khomeini is the new Iranian tyrant. He accepts no criticism of his absolute rule, and members of opposition groups, even the nonviolent ones, are thrown into jail, tortured, and executed. In turn, violent groups take arms against the regime. Within a few years, terrorist groups assassinate a president, a prime minister, a head of the judiciary, and dozens of top officials, as well as ordinary sympathizers of Khomeini's regime. The main opposition group is the Marxist-Islamist MKO (Mujahideen Khalq Organization).

Two close confidants of Khomeini's, Akbar Hashemi Rafsanjani and Ali Khamenei, survive separate assassination attempts. Ali Khamenei's right hand is paralyzed.

1980: The Iran-Iraq war

A few months after the Iranian revolution, Saddam Hussein—who has been Iraq's strongman for almost a decade—becomes the country's president. In 1975, Saddam was forced by the shah to reluctantly accept a border settlement with Iran.

After gaining power, Khomeini promises to export the revolution and asks Muslims around the world to rise against the despots who rule them. Khomeini is surrounded by exiled Iraqis who oppose Saddam Hussein and makes a number of critical remarks about the treatment of Shias in Iraq. As the Islamic government antagonizes the West, and becomes increasingly opposed by various political groups, Saddam Hussein thinks it is an opportune time to both revisit the border dispute and end Khomeini's rule.

Iraqi forces invade Iran in September 1980. Saddam Hussein is surprised by the solidarity of Iranians from different backgrounds in defending their country and withdraws from most of the occupied territories in less than two years. But the war gives Khomeini the perfect opportunity to tighten his grip on power and suppress the opposition. Iranian forces invade Iraqi territories, and a war of attrition continues for eight years.

1981–89: President Ali Khamenei, Prime Minister Mir Hossein Mousavi

After the impeachment of one president and the killing of another, Ali Khamenei becomes president in October 1981. A junior cleric with conservative ideas, Khamenei has been a follower of Khomeini's since the early 1960s. In the government, he is regarded as one of the closest people to Khomeini and a member of the more moderate faction of the Islamic regime. Yet Khomeini feels closer to the more radical faction and orders Ali Khamenei to appoint Mir Hossein Mousavi, a radical young architect, as prime minister. Mousavi remains Khamenei's prime minister for the rest of his tenure as president, until 1989. The relationship between the two men is contentious, and they can't see eye to eye on many important issues.

Khamenei represents the right, the conservative branch of revolutionaries who support private ownership and a more moderate rhetoric. Mousavi is regarded as a member of the left, the more radical group within the Islamic establishment, which advocates a more socialist economy and supports more government interference in people's lives. Khomeini never fully supports one group against the others, but there are more leftists surrounding Khomeini than members of the right. Khomeini often has to mediate between Khamenei and Mousavi, and usually takes Mousavi's side in decisions. Mousavi becomes known as "the imam's prime minister." Ali Khamenei's strongest ally in the government is the head of the Majlis, Akbar Hashemi Rafsanjani, the closest person to Khomeini.

1988: The end of the Iran-Iraq war, crimes against humanity

After eight years of atrocities committed by both sides, the morale of the Iranian troops is weakened and international pressure on Iran to end the war mounts. Khomeini accepts the cease-fire in August 1988. He compares this to drinking "a chalice of poison." The war ends with one million people wounded or killed, mostly Iranian. There is no tangible gain for either nation, except for a more tyrannical rule in both countries.

Before the end of the war, in 1986, the MKO terrorist group moves its headquarters to Iraq. After killing thousands of ordinary Iranians and top officials of the regime, and the imprisonment, torture, and execution of thousands of its own members, the MKO becomes part of Saddam Hussein's army at the height of the Iran-Iraq War. Toward the end of the war, the leader of the group, Massoud Rajavi, tells his people that a weakened Khomeini regime is vulnerable and that the MKO can take over Tehran in less than a week. Almost seven thousand MKO members enter Iranian territory and are swiftly defeated by the Iranian army and the Revolutionary Guards. The number of casualties from both sides is somewhere between four and ten thousand killed or wounded.

The attack gives Khomeini the perfect excuse to reaffirm his waning authority at the end of the war by ordering the massacre of members of the MKO and other opposition groups. In less than six months, almost five thousand people, many of them prisoners and former prisoners, are summarily executed. The massacre is the most organized killing of opposition members in modern Iranian history. More than twenty years later, many of the people involved in the massacre are still in power in Iran or have become members of the opposition inside the country.

None of the high-ranking members of the regime dares to object to Khomeini's actions, except for Ayatollah Hossein Ali Montazeri, who has been regarded as his natural successor since the beginning of the revolution. Montazeri has been Khomeini's acolyte since the 1940s, but his objection to the

killing of thousands of young men and women leads to his dismissal by Khomeini, after which he is forced to spend the remainder of his life under virtual
house arrest.

1989: Ruhollah Khomeini dies; Ali Khamenei becomes Supreme Leader

On June 3, 1989, Khomeini dies after eleven days of hospitalization for internal bleeding. His funeral is the largest public gathering in Iran's history.

After Khomeini's death, the Assembly of Experts, which chooses the supreme leader and supervises his actions, gathers to select a successor. In the
assembly, Rafsanjani lobbies for Ali Khamenei to succeed Khomeini. Many
suspect that Rafsanjani supports Khamenei because he sees him as a weak
character, a supreme leader he'll be able to control. Rafsanjani becomes president, the post of prime minister is abolished, and Mir Hossein Mousavi re-
signs from politics. Mousavi continues to work as an artist and architect and
eventually becomes the head of Iran's Academy of Arts.

1989–97: Akbar Hashemi Rafsanjani's presidency

Rafsanjani calls his tenure the "era of reconstruction" and proceeds with
repairing the damage of the Iran-Iraq War, allowing the private sector to be
more involved in industries and the economy, and improving Iran's relations
with the West. Rafsanjani becomes known as "Akbar Shah" because his
presidential style resembles that of the shah and the shah's father; he has the
same interest in the industrialization of Iran and a similar disdain for criticism and freedom of expression. He creates hundreds of new industries and
builds thousands of miles of roads, but at the same time scores of student
activists and opposition figures are jailed and dozens of intellectuals are mys-
teriously murdered.

Through unofficial channels, Rafsanjani presents himself as someone the
West can work with. His government starts a strategy of rapprochement with
the West and Iran's former enemies in the region, especially Saudi Arabia.
Rafsanjani tries to reverse Khomeini's xenophobic and socialist economic
policies by opening Iran's markets to the rest of the world and encouraging
foreign investment. Yet the privatization and free market benefit only a limited number of people, those referred to as Iran's economic mafia. One of the
most important achievements of Rafsanjani was helping to establish, and
later expand, the Free University in 1982. This semiprivate university has
educated millions of young Iranians who want to continue their education
but cannot pass the extremely difficult entrance exams of the national univer-

sities. This has helped to create a generation of politically aware, educated Iranians who will demand their rights as citizens in post-2009 elections.

Rafsanjani's reconstruction also means the return of consumerism to Iran after ten years of revolutionary idealism. While some technocrats and retired Revolutionary Guards who are hired by the government or have started their own businesses become enormously wealthy, many war veterans find themselves dispossessed. In order to gain more power, Khamenei taps into the nostalgic anguish of this war generation and builds a powerful base that will become increasingly strong in the next two decades.

1997: Mohammad Khatami, the reformist president

Radical supporters of Khomeini's, including many of the students who took over the American embassy, are removed from positions of power during Rafsanjani's presidency. Ostracized from the government, they study and criticize their past actions and create the Iranian reformist movement. During the 1997 presidential elections, they support Mohammad Khatami in a contest against Khamenei's preferred candidate, Ali Akbar Nateq Nouri. Khatami wins by a landslide. The majority of Iranians hope that the more honest, anti-establishment Khatami will bring an end to eight years of Rafsanjani's corrupt rule.

Khatami promises to establish a civil society in which debates are tolerated and people with different viewpoints and from different backgrounds can express themselves. Almost three years later, Khatami's supporters take over the Majlis. With the help of the Majlis, Khatami attempts to expand the responsibilities of the president and curb the power of the supreme leader. But by the time of Khatami's election, Khamenei has already developed a broad base of support among ideological religious Iranians, who regard him not only as their leader but as Allah's representative on earth. He also has the courts and the armed forces under his control. While Khatami's government tries to make Iran a more open society, Khamenei's judges and security forces work to suppress any voice of dissent. Dozens of newspapers are shut down, and many reformists are imprisoned on fabricated charges.

When, in the summer of 1999, a group of students protest against the closure of a newspaper, they are brutally beaten by pro-Khamenei vigilantes. Many students are disappointed that President Khatami remains quiet while atrocities are committed against his supporters and that he prefers to use a back channel to reach an agreement with Khamenei.

Khatami's tenure coincides with the decreasing price of oil in the international markets, which hits the Iranian economy hard. Iranians become poorer, and hard-liners blame the government's inefficiency for people's suffering and the economic crisis.

During Khatami's presidency, the United States and its allies invade Afghanistan and Iraq. Khatami advocates a dialogue among civilizations, but his attempts to improve Iran's relations with the United States are sabotaged by Khamenei's supporters. Iranian hard-liners think that resuming relations with the States will undermine their positions; at the same time, American neoconservatives promote a regime change in Iran. They believe that after what they see as their successes in Afghanistan and Iraq, Iran can be contained or even dominated militarily by the United States. In his State of the Union speech in January 2002, President George W. Bush calls Iran part of an "axis of evil," along with North Korea and Iraq.

A combination of diplomatic ineffectiveness, the poor economy, and the failure to realize a civil society leads to the demise of the reformist movement. Yet the eight years of Khatami's relatively democratic and open-minded style of governance and cultural policies change Iran forever and make ordinary Iranians more aware of their rights as citizens.

Khatami's tenure also makes the hard-liners more determined to do their utmost to stop reformists from ever again coming to power.

2005: Ahmadinejad's election

In June 2005, former president Rafsanjani; former speaker of the Majlis Mehdi Karroubi; a former Revolutionary Guards commander, Mohammad Bagher Ghalibaf; Tehran's mayor, Mahmoud Ahmadinejad; and three other candidates compete in a tight race for the presidency of the Islamic Republic.

The continuation of the reformist movement in Iran means a more accountable government, which will limit Khamenei's reign. In the sixteen years since he has become the supreme leader, Khamenei has not been able to establish an absolute rule because of Rafsanjani's prominence for the first eight years and Khatami's pro-reform policies for the next two terms. Khamenei needs a subservient president who will listen to him, and Khamenei's followers need one of their own in office to guarantee their survival.

Prior to the June 2005 election, the main question is: Who will Khamenei support during the campaign? Karroubi, a tribal leader from the western province of Lorestan, has been a maverick in the parliament and is too close to the reformists. The repeat of Rafsanjani's presidency would mean that Khamenei has to work with a president whose revolutionary background and political prominence equal or even exceed his own. Khamenei's first choice is Ghalibaf, who has been a Khamenei devotee for years and who, during the 1999 student demonstrations, signed a letter, along with twenty-three other Guards commanders, accusing Mohammad Khatami of throwing the Islamic

Republic into anarchy. But during his campaign, Ghalibaf avoids using pro-Khamenei ideological rhetoric. He dons a fashionable white suit instead of a military uniform and portrays himself as a modern independent leader. He famously says that he wants to be "an Islamic Reza Khan."

In the meantime, the fringe candidate Ahmadinejad chastises others for forgetting the ideals of the revolution and being corrupted by money and power. A former Revolutionary Guard, Ahmadinejad promises to clean Iran of corruption and make Iranians more prosperous. Unlike other candidates who spend lavishly on their campaigns and make well-produced films, Ahmadinejad opts for face-to-face campaigning and produces a low-budget documentary about his simple life and achievements. A month before the election, it is obvious that Ahmadinejad has the support of the majority of poor and disenfranchised Khamenei supporters.

A few weeks before the election, many members of the Basij (pro-government volunteers) and the Guards are told by their commanders that Ahmadinejad is the leader's choice for president. No candidate wins the clear majority in the first round of votes. The top two candidates are Rafsanjani, with 21.13 percent of the votes, and Ahmadinejad, with 19.43 percent.

In a letter to Khamenei, Mehdi Karroubi, who is third, with 17.24 percent, accuses Khamenei's son, the Guards, and the Basij of manipulating the votes in Ahmadinejad's favor. His objections are dismissed and newspapers are banned from publishing Karroubi's letter. In the second round, Rafsanjani gets only 35 percent of the votes. Ahmadinejad, with 61 percent, becomes president.

2005–09: Ahmadinejad's presidency

Blessed by the rising price of oil, Ahmadinejad runs the country as if it's a charity. During his monthly trips around Iran, he distributes the oil money as he sees fit. The failures of the United States and its allies in the two ongoing wars in Afghanistan and Iraq allow Ahmadinejad to adopt more combative international policies. Supported by Khamenei, Ahmadinejad rapidly develops Iran's nuclear program and increases Iran's help to such regional proxies as Hezbollah, in Lebanon, and Hamas, in Gaza.

During Ahmadinejad's tenure, the suppression of internal dissent continues, activists and students are jailed, newspapers are shut down, and hard-liners are put in charge of cultural organizations. Ahmadinejad assigns retired Revolutionary Guards to key positions, and many lucrative industrial contracts are given to the Guards' engineering companies. The Khamenei-Guards-Ahmadinejad alliance tightens its grip on all aspects of life in Iran. Most reformist officials are either dismissed, retired, or demoted to junior positions. Khamenei's power becomes near absolute. Even though many people close to him object to Ahmadinejad's erratic policies, Khamenei repeatedly expresses his satisfaction with the government and privately forbids other hard-liners from running against Ahmadinejad.

In order to return to power, prominent reformists decide to agree on a single candidate to defeat Ahmadinejad. In February 2009, Mohammad Khatami announces his intention to run for president again. Khamenei sends Khatami a private message to step down; Khatami is also threatened privately and publicly. A month later, on March 16, 2009, he steps down in favor of former prime minister Mir Hossein Mousavi, who has been away from politics for two decades.

Many young Iranians do not remember Mousavi, and it takes him two months to introduce his programs to the public. Karroubi announces his candidacy around the same time, but because of his impulsive behavior and lack of sophistication, many people do not take him seriously. Mousavi, the main reformist candidate, promises to repair the damage done to the country during the four years of Ahmadinejad's rule. He declares that he wants Iran to be a friend to the rest of the world, and pledges more freedom of expression and respect for human rights. Millions of educated young Iranians campaign for Mousavi all around the country. A secret poll by the Ministry of Intelligence, conducted in major cities around the country three weeks before the election, shows that Mousavi is well ahead of Ahmadinejad.

GLOSSARY OF TERMS

Ashura: The anniversary of the martyrdom of Hossein, the third imam of Shias and son of Ali, in a battle against the Sunni caliph in A.D. 680. *Ashura* means the tenth day of the month; Hossein's battle against Yazid took place on the tenth day of the month of Moharram. Like Catholicism, Shiism is a religion of icons and rituals. Ceremonies held on Ashura and on the previous day, Tasu'a, including self-flagellation and passion plays, symbolize the oppressive conditions Shias have endured throughout history and the necessity to fight for justice. Many Ashuras throughout Iran's history have provided Iranians with an opportunity to demonstrate against the atrocities of the regime.

ayatollah: A high-ranking Shia cleric. "Grand ayatollah" refers to the highest-ranking Shia clerics, who can interpret religious teachings for their followers.

Basij: Short for Niruyeh Moghavemat Basij (the Resistance Mobilization Force). The Basij was established at the beginning of the revolution to allow pro-government volunteers to dedicate part of their time to protecting the revolution. Each government office, educational institution, and neighborhood mosque has its own Basij office. The members of the Basij, called Basijis, receive their directives from the Islamic Revolutionary Guards Corps (IRGC). Even though Basijis are volunteers and most of them do not receive a salary, being a Basiji has its perks. Basijis have priority for places at universities and can receive bank loans more easily than ordinary citizens. Many Basij members have permits to carry a gun and are put in charge of the security of their neighborhoods or of other areas when the IRGC feels a threat. Basij members were instrumental in crushing postelection protests around Iran and were financially rewarded by the government accordingly.

chador: A traditional cloak worn by many Muslim women to conceal their bodies. Women from different social, economic, and cultural backgrounds choose different material for their chadors (for example, thick, thin, plain, floral, or with other patterns) and wear them in different styles (tight, loose, with a scarf underneath or without one).

Islamic Revolutionary Guards Corps (IRGC): The most powerful and influential branch of the Iranian army. The IRGC, commonly called the Revolutionary Guards, was set up after the 1979 Islamic Revolution when dozens of Royal Iranian Army officers were executed by the new government, which did not trust them. Throughout the years, the Revolutionary Guards has grown to become a mighty armed force, as well as an industrial conglomerate. There are no statistics about the number of Guards, but it is estimated to be about 200,000 military personnel, including navy, ground, and air forces. Guards commanders hold different political opinions, but all of them firmly believe in the Islamic Republic and are dedicated to the supreme leader, Ayatollah Khamenei, who personally appoints them. It is widely believed that the force is divided between the old guard, those who are less ideological and pragmatic, and the new guard, those more ideological and extremist. The current commander of the Guards, Mohammad Ali Jafari, is part of the new guard.

Mahdi, Imam: The twelfth imam of Shias, he was born in A.D. 869 and at the age of five went into hiding when his father, Hassan al Askari, the eleventh imam, was martyred. Shias believe that Imam Mahdi is not dead and will reappear before Judgment Day for a period of time, and will bring justice, equality, and happiness to people around the world.

manteau: A knee-length tunic that is preferred to the chador by many Iranian women, mostly in urban areas, and women working, studying, or from less traditional or less religious families. Manteaus vary widely in terms of color, pattern, and shape—they can be knee-length, waist-length, tight, baggy, straight, light, dark, and so on.

marja: Shias believe that during the absence of Imam Mahdi, *marjas* (objects of emulation) can lead Muslim communities. The *marjas* have to be grand ayatollahs (but not all grand ayatollahs are *marjas*). Shias are free to choose their *marjas,* and *marjas,* depending on their religious and political viewpoints, can be relatively liberal or conservative.

Ministry of Intelligence of the Islamic Republic of Iran: Iran's equivalent of MI5 and MI6. It was established in 1984 to gather information on internal and external threats to the legacy of the 1979 Islamic Revolution and the Islamic Republic. Since the concept of threat has been open to interpretation, the Ministry of Intelligence has gone beyond its mandate since its inception. In the 1980s and 1990s (during the Khamenei and Rafsanjani presidencies) the ministry became involved in economic activities, and many of its high officials became rich by driving out the competition in the name of national security. During the same period, the ministry was also involved in assassinating Iranian opposition members in Europe. From 1994 to 1999, as many as eighty intellectuals, authors, and ordinary Iranians were killed, allegedly by rogue members of the ministry. The uncovering of the perpetrators of the killings in 1999 (during Khatami's presidency) by reformist members and retired employees of the ministry resulted in a massive overhaul of the ministry, which put a stop to its economic activities and drove out several corrupt officials. Around the same time, with Khamenei's blessing, a parallel intelligence organization was formed. It was primarily made up of the cleansed former agents and members of the Revolutionary Guards' intelligence unit. During the postelection protests, the supporters of Khamenei and Ahmadinejad accused the ministry of working with the opposition, and on Khamenei's orders the parallel intelligence organization and the Guards' intelligence unit took over the intelligence apparatus. Soon, dozens of high-ranking officials of the ministry were forced to retire and the ministry agents were effectively put under the Guards' command.

mullah: A cleric; someone who studies or has studied religion. The word is not negative, but it has been used in negative contexts—for example, the mullahs' regime in Iran.

Shia Islam (also **Shiism**): The second-largest denomination in Islam. Unlike the majority of Muslims (Sunnis), who believe that the first four leaders of Muslims (the caliphs) were selected by the people, Shias (also called Shiites) believe that Ali, the cousin and son-in-law of the Prophet Mohammad, was his immediate and divinely chosen successor. Shias regard Ali and eleven of his descendants as their imams. The imams are infallible leaders who lead Muslim communities in all mundane and spiritual aspects during their lifetimes, and after their death, their words and legacies guide Shias.

The origins of Shia Islam can be traced to political differences among the followers of the Prophet Mohammad within different Muslim communities in the seventh century and later. As a minority, Shias have always regarded themselves as an oppressed and distinct group within Islam, and have developed a series of rituals and ceremonies that highlight tragedies in Shia history.

Shiism in Iran has not only been a religious belief; it has also been part of national culture and identity since the Safavid dynasty made Shia Islam Iran's official religion in the sixteenth century, in order to give the country a separate identity and stop the influence of the neighboring Sunni Ottoman Empire.

supreme leader: The spiritual leader of the Islamic Republic of Iran and the man who has the final say in all affairs of the state; the position is currently filled by Ayatollah Ali Khamenei. "Supreme leader" derives from the Persian term *valie faqih,* which literally means "jurisprudent guardian." The concept was developed by Ayatollah Khomeini in the 1960s; according to it, during the absence of the twelfth imam, a high-ranking cleric (not necessarily a *marja*) should be in charge of all affairs of the country. The majority of Shia theologians do not believe in *velayat-e faqih* (guardianship of the jurisprudent); rather, they believe that the *marjas'* guardianship should be limited to the most vulnerable members of society, such as orphans and widows. According to Article 109 of Iran's Constitution, the supreme leader should be a scholar in various fields, just, pious, have the right combination of political and social acuity, and be prudent and courageous. As no single man (the leader cannot be a woman) can have all these qualities, in Iran today, *velayat-e faqih* governance is essentially religious dictatorship.

Tudeh Party of Iran: Iran's communist party, established in 1941. In the beginning, the Tudeh claimed that it was a party of the oppressed and fought for the prosperity of all Iranians, and many educated Iranians, even some religious people, joined it. But eventually, after a series of factions separated from the party, it became a purely communist party. The Tudeh was banned in 1949, and many of its members were executed and tortured in the 1950s through the 1970s. Yet the majority of party leaders migrated to the Eastern bloc, under Soviet protection. After the 1979 Islamic Revolution, they returned to Iran and rejuvenated the party; it once again became one of the most influential parties in Iran. The Tudeh supported Ayatollah Khomeini's anti-American policies and even defended some of the atrocities committed by the regime in the name of revolutionary justice. In 1983, the Islamic government announced that the Tudeh was secretly trying to overthrow it. Khomeini ordered the arrest of Tudeh leaders, including some in the military. Most of them were executed between 1983 and 1987; many others spent over a decade in prison. Currently, the Tudeh has almost no activities inside Iran and survives in name only, with few supporters.

FURTHER READING, LISTENING, AND WATCHING

Nonfiction books

Tortured Confessions by Ervand Abrahamian (University of California Press, 1999)

The Pivot of the Universe by Abbas Amanat (I. B. Tauris, 2008)

The Quest for Democracy in Iran by Fakhreddin Azimi (Harvard University Press, 2010)

Mohammad Mosaddeq and the 1953 Coup in Iran, edited by Mark J. Gasiorowski and Malcolm Byrne (Syracuse University Press, 2004)

Transit Tehran, edited by Malu Halasa and Maziar Bahari (Garnet, 2008)

State and Society in Iran by Homa Katouzian (I. B. Tauris, 2006)

The Persian Sphinx by Abbas Milani (Mage, 2009)

The Mantle of the Prophet by Roy Mottahedeh (Oneworld, 2008)

Treacherous Alliance by Trita Parsi (Yale University Press, 2008)

The Iran Primer, edited by Robin Wright (United States Institute of Peace Press, 2010)

Fiction and poetry books

The poetry of Rumi, translated by Coleman Barks (HarperOne, different years)

Rubáiyát of Omar Khayyám, translated by Edward Fitzgerald (Oxford University Press, 2009)

The poetry of Hafiz, translated by Daniel Ladinsky (Penguin, different years)

Strange Times, My Dear, edited by Nahid Mozaffari and Ahmad Karimi Hakkak (Arcade Publishing, 2005)

My Uncle Napoleon by Iraj Pezeshkzad, translated by Dick Davis (Modern Library, 2006)

You will also enjoy listening to the classic Persian music of Hossein Alizadeh, Kayhan Kalhor, Shahram Nazeri, and Mohammad Reza Shajarian and the modern Iranian music of Hitchkas, Kiosk, and Mohsen Namjoo.

Those interested in Iran should also watch the following films:

Fiction films

Rakhshan Bani Etemad: *Nargess* and *Under the Skin of the City*
Asghar Farhadi: *Fireworks Wednesday* and *About Elly*
Bahman Ghobadi: *A Time for Drunken Horses*
Manijeh Hekmat: *Women's Prison*
Abbas Kiarostami: *The Traveler, Close-Up,* and *Ten*
Majid Majidi: *Baran* and *The Color of Paradise*
Dariush Mehrjui: *The Cow* and *The Tenants*
Jafar Panahi: *The Circle* and *Offside*
Kambuzia Partovi: *Border Café*

Documentary films

Mahnaz Afzali: *The Red Card*
Maziar Bahari: *And Along Came a Spider* and *An Iranian Odyssey*
Rakshan Bani Etemad: *Our Times*
Forough Farrokhzad: *The House Is Black*
Albert Lamorisse: *The Lovers' Wind*
Kim Longinotto and Ziba Mir-Hosseini: *Divorce, Iranian Style*
Mohsen Makhmalbaf: *Salaam Cinema*
Ebrahim Mokhtari: *The Tenancy* and *Zinat*
Mehrdad Oskouei: *Nose, Iranian Style* and *The Other Side of Burka*
Norma Percy: *Iran and the West*
Hamid Rahmanian: *The Glass House*
Kamran Shirdel: *The Night It Rained*